STUDIES IN MAJOR LITERARY AUTHORS

Edited by

William E. Cain
Professor of English
Wellesley College

A ROUTLEDGE SERIES

Studies in Major Literary Authors

William E. Cain, *General Editor*

EDITH WHARTON'S "EVOLUTIONARY CONCEPTION"

Darwinian Allegory in Her Major Novels

Paul J. Ohler

Routledge
New York & London

Published in 2006 by
Routledge
Taylor & Francis Group
270 Madison Avenue
New York, NY 10016

Published in Great Britain by
Routledge
Taylor & Francis Group
2 Park Square
Milton Park, Abingdon
Oxon OX14 4RN

Transferred to Digital Printing 2010

International Standard Book Number-10: 0-415-97719-3 (Hardcover)
International Standard Book Number-13: 978-0978-0-415-97719-7 (Hardcover)

ISBN10: 0-415-97719-3 (hbk)
ISBN10: 0-415-88006-8 (pbk)

ISBN13: 978-0-415-97719-7 (hbk)
ISBN13: 978-0-415-88006-0 (pbk)

Taylor & Francis Group
is the Academic Division of Informa plc.

Visit the Taylor & Francis Web site at
http://www.taylorandfrancis.com

and the Routledge Web site at
http://www.routledge-ny.com

For Patricia and Sophia

Contents

List of Abbreviations

Descent   Charles Darwin, *The Descent of Man, and Selection in Relation to Sex.* (1871). Princeton: Princeton UP, 1981.

Letters   R. W. B. Lewis and Nancy Lewis, eds., *The Letters of Edith Wharton.* New York: Collier Books, 1988.

Lewis   R. W. B. Lewis, *Edith Wharton: A Biography.* (1975). New York: Fromm, 1985.

Origin   Charles Darwin, *The Origin of Species by Means of Natural Selection or the Preservation of Favoured Races in the Struggle for Life.* (1859). Ed. John Burrow. New York: Penguin, 1968.

Reviews   James Tuttleton, Kristin O. Lauer, and Margaret P. Murray, eds. *Edith Wharton: The Contemporary Reviews.* New York: Cambridge UP, 1992.

Page references to Wharton's published works are indicated in the text using the following abbreviations, which refer to the listed editions.

AI   *The Age of Innocence* (1920) (New York: Collier, 1993)

BG   *A Backward Glance* (New York: Appleton-Century, 1934)

CC   *The Custom of the Country* (1913) (New York: Simon, 1997)

DH   *The Decoration of Houses* (1897) (with Ogden Codman, Jr.) (New York: Norton, 1997)

DM   "The Descent of Man" (*The Collected Short Stories of Edith Wharton, Vol. 1.* Ed. R. W. B. Lewis. New York: Scribner's 1968)

FT	*The Fruit of the Tree* (New York: Scribner's, 1907)
FW	*French Ways and Their Meaning* (New York: Appleton, 1919)
HM	*The House of Mirth* (1905) (New York: Penguin, 1985)
IB	*Italian Backgrounds* (1905) (London: Cape, 1928)
IM	*In Morocco* (New York: Scribner's, 1920)
WF	*The Writing of Fiction* (New York: Scribner's, 1925)

Acknowledgments

I am pleased to acknowledge those people who have helped to shape this book. At the University of British Columbia, Michael Zeitlin directed the dissertation from which this project emerged; he was a model of professionalism and enthusiastic support. I was fortunate to have worked also with Ross Labrie. He introduced me to works of biology and sociology that gave me insight into Edith Wharton's scientific frame of reference. Ira Nadel gave generously of his time and expertise, helping me to frame key issues. I would also like to thank Claire Preston. Her rigorous reading of the dissertation served as a blueprint for its development. I owe a special thanks to Mary Chapman, who read the manuscript at a later stage, providing invaluable suggestions and encouragement.

I am grateful to the staff of the Beinecke Library at Yale University for their assistance in microfilming documents in the Wharton collection when I could not travel. I also acknowledge the support of Kwantlen University College, which provided course release for work on revisions. At Routledge, Max Novick has kindly responded to my questions and concerns. Dania Sheldon expertly copy edited and indexed. Finally, I wish to extend my deepest gratitude to my family and to recognize the constant and heartening support of my friends. All quotations from Edith Wharton's published and unpublished writings are reprinted by permission of the Estate of Edith Wharton and the Watkins/Loomis Agency.

Preface

In a letter of 1908, Edith Wharton wrote of perceiving a human dimension in the scientific study that had become one of her central interests. She admitted that "[m]y biological reading is always embarrassed by the fact that I can't help seeing all these funny creatures with faces and gestures" (*Letters* 151). R. W. B. Lewis draws attention to

> her [. . .] reading in studies of ancient forms of life, evolution, and Mendel's theories of heredity. She confesses to being dumbfounded by some of the phenomena described—the biophors and determinants (units of germ plasm that convey heredity, and units made up of these); but she gains control by converting them into cartoon figures: 'the biophors . . . small and anxious to please, the determinants loud and domineering, with eyeglasses.' More awesome to her inventive imagination is 'that monstrous animal the heterozygote,' a hybrid form she had encountered in a text on Mendelism. (*Letters* 13)

Wharton, it seems, was "passionately addicted to scientific study" (Lewis 108), and the main objective of this book is to position *The House of Mirth* (1905), *The Custom of the Country* (1913), and *The Age of Innocence* (1920) within her scientific perspective. I attempt to analyze Wharton's effort to recognize and explore determining traces of evolution and biology in her society. Not only did "biophors" have human "faces and gestures," gestures, which Wharton conceived of as manners, had biological antecedents.

In the works I discuss in the following chapters, Wharton renders the social practices of New York's hereditary gentry, and a rising socioeconomic elite, from a perspective informed by the central concerns of Darwinism. I want to suggest that Wharton foresees commonalities between laws governing gradual change in the natural world described by Charles Darwin, T. H.

Huxley, and Herbert Spencer, and shifts in ideology, or the "general process of intellectual, spiritual, and aesthetic development" (Williams 90), of the privileged social groupings which were often her subject. Huxley and Spencer, it should be said at the outset, adumbrated certain of Darwin's ideas, a fact that Wharton recognized and responded to in her writing. The novels that result from Wharton's insights represent the effects on New York's traditional elite of a new and powerful class whose rise she attributes to social evolution; such change, the novels find, is conditioned by phenomena theorized in Darwin's work which were commonly thought to apply only in nature, not human culture. Hence, this study investigates the social transformation Wharton represents, and relates it to her scientific sources, illustrating the political dimension of her literary sociobiology.

In her book *The Critical Reception of Edith Wharton* (2001), Helen Killoran asserts that scholars "have yet to recognize the full dimensions of Edith Wharton's greatness because they have not yet recognized the knowledge, aesthetics, and magnificent technical innovations at the root of her creative philosophy" (xi). Only in the past decade has Wharton's scientific knowledge been considered relevant to the aesthetics and politics of her major novels. This study contends that Darwinism offered Wharton a context within which to fictionally analyze the indwellers of established New York society as organisms whose mores had a biological basis. These habitual moral practices were under great pressure from "the cultural upheaval marked by unprecedented technological, demographic, and political changes that were taking place between 1875 and 1920" (Nowlin 226) and a new elite foreign to the old ways. What emerges from this broad argument are two other key issues: that Wharton beheld fiction as a medium that could reveal the relation of the individual to unacknowledged life conditions such as the effects of evolutionary forces, and that she used whatever formal means she could—often hybridizing popular genres such as scientific works and the sentimental novel—to enter the literary marketplace with novels that would sell.

Supporting my claims for Wharton's programmatic use of evolutionary thought are close readings of her fiction, and of the scientific texts to which her writing frequently alludes and openly references. I apply Joseph Carroll's critical approach in *Literary Darwinism* (2004) to Wharton's work to frame her implicitly materialist understanding of human psychology. Carroll invokes

> the central principle of evolutionary epistemology, the idea that all human knowledge derives from a process of interaction between man as a physical entity, an active, perceiving subject, and the realities of an equally physical external world, the object of man's perception. (161)

Carroll, furthermore, finds literature to be "only a special case of cognitive activity aimed at orienting the organism to its environment" (161), sharing, in one respect, Wharton's vision of literature as an art form able to illustrate insufficiently understood truths such as the role of biology in culture. His description of "evolutionary epistemology" outlines one locus of Wharton's use of Darwinism in her narratives, for she imagines human psychology primarily to be a function of material reality often at odds with social training. This is true of Lily Bart in *The House of Mirth,* in which the "flesh and blood loveliness" (134) of Lily, fused to nature in the famous *tableaux vivants* scene through the "foliage" of her setting, defies the mannered "[. . .] trivialities of her little world" (135). Dale Bauer has argued that "dismissing Wharton as an antimodernist, a label suggesting uninterest in politics, wrongly erases Wharton's profound concern for changing her culture" (4); downplaying her politics also obscures Wharton's fictional challenges to social Darwinism— which advances the idea that "[. . .] it is 'natural' for the strong to vanquish the weak, and for the rich to exploit the poor" (Dennett 461)—and obfuscates her efforts to orient the readerly "organism" to the true complexities of its environment.

Between Wharton's fiction and the scientific works that texture it there exist shared themes, shared figurative language, and a common interest in proffering a non-metaphysical basis for the human intellectual endowments out of which arises what she called "that impalpable dust of ideas which is the real culture" ("The Great American Novel" 156). My analysis of the entwined discourses of literature and science in the fiction I examine is indebted to the interdisciplinary work of Wharton scholars who have investigated the formal and thematic elements of her writing in the context of sociology and anthropology. I carry forward their research by juxtaposing Wharton's writing with the Darwinian doctrines that figure in her fiction, and by extending Claire Preston's indispensable presentation of Wharton, in the context of the novelist's memoir *A Backward Glance* (1934), as a writer who "recognized her reading of Darwin at the age of twenty-two as the most important intellectual experience of her life. It was a 'new vision' which replaced any religious belief she had held. 'The world was more wonderful, the problem more interesting, the moral obligation more stern and ennobling'" (55). This book illustrates the complex relation of natural law to social tradition Wharton envisions. Within the chapters on the three major novels I investigate are considerations of other stories and novels that present the politically charged vision of "the poetic value of the evolutionary conception" ("George Eliot" 72) Wharton formulates in her criticism, letters, life writing, and fiction.

Chapter One establishes that the forms and themes of Wharton's major novels during the period 1905–1920 often rely upon her scientific knowledge for their depiction of connections between biology and human culture. By briefly considering the criticism of Wharton's study of evolutionary theory, sociology, and anthropology, I outline the current state of thought on Wharton's objective attitude and the ramifications for my analysis of this work. Associating class conflict between the gentry and the socioeconomic elite with the theory of natural selection, which Darwin describes as the "preservation of favorable variations and the rejection of injurious variations" (*Origin* 131), Wharton exhibits an interest evidently shared with Thorstein Veblen, who wrote of a "natural selection of institutions" (147). Veblen was another opponent of social Darwinism's assent to a diminished idea of human agency that saw environmental determinism in the human social context as natural. Wharton counted class as an "institution" subject to Darwinian forces, and she demonstrates her articulation of the challenges to achieving social equality posed by "primitive" (CC 470) and "instinctive" (CC 355) energies expressed by her characters. By pursuing this idea in her fiction, Wharton expresses her concern with the randomness of evolutionary change and the pressure it exerts on social collectives that would attempt to manage transformation. I argue that by using scientific language and concepts in the context of fictional social analysis, Wharton crafts biological allegories of social relations that conjoin nature and culture.

Chapter Two considers *The House of Mirth* for its allegorical depiction of Lily Bart as an "organism" (HM 301) destroyed by an altered social environment to which she is not suited. The depiction of Lily and her world imbricates the social and natural elements of her surroundings. This chapter finds that the novel portrays New York society from a perspective informed by the theory of natural selection presented in Charles Darwin's *The Origin of Species* (1859), and *The Descent of Man*'s (1871) biological view of social relations. In the final paragraph of *The Descent of Man*, Darwin wrote that

> Man may be excused for feeling some pride at having risen, though not through his own exertions, to the very summit of the organic scale [. . .]. With his god-like intellect which has penetrated into the movements and constitution of the solar system—with all these exalted powers—Man still bears in his bodily frame the indelible stamp of his lowly origin. (460)

Vigorously infused with allusions to this Darwinian principle, the novel assaults the idea that intense competitions for resources, and the extermination of the unfit, are aspects of social relations permissible because humankind's "lowly origins" cannot be assuaged.

Chapter Three considers *The Custom of the Country*'s portrait of its anti-heroine, Undine Spragg, who typifies a destructive and individualistic agency during a time of "social disintegration" (CC 77). This novel is unremitting in its application of scientific language and ideas to a half-blind elite whose decayed foundations—made porous through intermarriage between aristocrats characterized by Ralph Marvell as "Aborigines" and members of the "invading race" (77)—won't be repaired by his clever socio-logical analogy, or his passivity in matters of political action. In its argument with social Darwinism's misinterpretation of evolutionary theory, which would allow the withering of Marvell's class, Wharton demonstrates that illustration and analysis of problematic social trends precedes remedy, but only when mated to a willingness to act; Wharton thereby elevates her method to a culturally transformative activity in which writing is social praxis—as long as one's works are read, making her popularity part of her politics. Moreover, the novel reveals that members of the gentry are anxious about the rise of mass culture because of a loss of moral authority to "the Sunday papers" (CC 44) and ephemeral gossip sheets like *Town Talk* and the *Radiator* to which the populace turns for entertainment and guidance. Wharton positions her own writing between popular and elite forms. She analyzes the former while being caught up in the logic of the marketplace she criticizes as damaging to public dialogue on matters such as divorce, and wealth without responsibility. In *The Custom of the Country,* "Wharton's per-ception of the conflict between the gentry and the socioeconomic elite crys-tallized" (Bratton 211), and because of this, the novel is a good test case for my claim that Wharton depicts the vulnerability of the gentry to the "Invaders," already "modified by contact with the indigenous" elite (82). The invaders adopt "the speech of the conquered race" (82), emulate "the 'look' which signified social consecration" (57), and finally replace gentry values with their own.

Chapter Four examines *The Age of Innocence,* particularly the novel's focus on the hazards of a superficial scientific perspective, which Wharton analyzes less explicitly in the earlier novels critical of social Darwinism. *The Age of Innocence* arrays images and vocabulary drawn from anthropology and ethnography with the language and concepts of evolutionary biology present in the earlier novels. Here, classes are "tribes" (32), and stories regarding genealogy are passed down orally from one generation to the next. Yet, the ideology that might bind members of the hereditary elite and gentry to their values is weakening in the changing world of the 1870s; a new species of capitalist has evolved to thrive in an altered social environment. The omniscient voice expertly uses anthropological images and phrases, while the protagonist, Newland Archer, casually studies the discipline. But evolution and biology are not obscured by the presence of other discourses; Archer's attraction to the American-born and European-bred Ellen Olenska betrays an instinctive sexual response that causes his heart to beat "suffocatingly" (287).

The Age of Innocence maintains a critical stance toward the distancing of Archer's instinct by his intellect, drawing on social science and scientific discourses to frame its subjects: coercive tradition, and exclusionary policing of class membership, to name just two. Additionally, the novel judges Archer's quasi-scientific viewpoint. He derives his perspective from his scientific knowledge, which brings him into contact with the view that human culture grows from a biological foundation; but he is a "dilettante" (4), and thus unable to absorb this fact, which might free him from the constraints of his caste by demonstrating—the narrative's larger point—that instinct and culture are part of a continuum, and not separate spheres. Wharton's portrait of Archer finds him to be the kind of reader Wharton's fiction can seem designed to confront—"the mechanical reader [. . .] [who] by his passion for 'popular' renderings of abstruse and difficult subjects, by confounding the hastiest réchauffé of scientific truisms with the slowly-matured conceptions of the original thinker, [. . .] retards [the] true culture" ("The Vice of Reading" 104).

Chapter One

Metaphors of "Instinct and Tradition"

I. "THE POETIC VALUE OF THE EVOLUTIONARY CONCEPTION"

In *A Backward Glance* (1934) Edith Wharton acknowledged the role in her intellectual development of scientific works introduced to her by her friend Egerton Winthrop:

> He it was who gave me Wallace's 'Darwin and Darwinism,' and 'The Origin of Species,' and made known to me Huxley, Herbert Spencer, Romanes, Haeckel, Westermarck, and the various popular exponents of the great evolutionary movement. But it is idle to prolong the list, and hopeless to convey to a younger generation the first overwhelming sense of cosmic vastness which such 'magic casements' let into our little geocentric universe. (94)

Much earlier in her life, she had mentioned in a letter her reading of neo-Darwinist[1] works such as R. H. Lock's *Variation, Heredity and Evolution* (1906) and Vernon Kellog's *Darwinism Today* (1907). The French writer Paul Bourget, who met Wharton in 1893 and was thought by her to be "brilliant and stimulating" (BG 103), described her as deeply involved in scientific reading: "there is not a book of Darwin, Huxley, Spencer, Renan, Taine, which she has not studied" (qtd. in Lewis 69). Her engagement with the "evolutionary movement" was not unusual, for Wharton avidly consumed scientific texts during a period in which an "overwhelming interest in scientific developments and the new rationalism" took hold in the United States (Hofstadter 24).

While Wharton participated in the trend of keeping up with scientific developments, she recognized in her reading of Darwin, the neo-Darwinists, and biologists such as Ernst Haeckel (1834–1919) the applicability to human behavior and culture of theories that describe non-human animal behavior and change in nature. The contemporary contention "that it is not right to separate the Darwinian debate from broader cultural, ideological, political, and economic issues" (Young "Darwin and the Genre of Biography" 19) is one that Wharton's novels during the period 1905–1920 predict by insisting that morality, and the dialectics of ideology, are related to the evolutionary heritage of humankind. This issue resonates with contemporary research in sociobiology. The evolutionary biologist Steven Pinker reflects that "[a]gency, personal responsibility and so on can all be tied to brain function [. . .]. It's a fallacy to think that hunger and thirst and sex drive are biological but that reasoning and decision making and learning are something else, something non-biological" (qtd. in Rakoff 27). That Wharton perceived something like Pinker's contention is the topic of part one of this chapter. Part two considers the critical response to Wharton's explorations of science in order to delineate the current state of knowledge on the subject. The final part of this chapter describes Wharton's formal expression of evolutionary concepts as operant features within the social domain she details, and juxtaposes this feature of her fiction with her opinions on literary realism and naturalism.

*   *   *

One way Wharton summons the glittering surfaces of New York's social whirl into the range of Darwin's hypotheses lies in her depiction of male protagonists who are insensible to the possibility that cooperation among members of a class "tribe" (AI 32) might, if acknowledged and addressed, moderate the incinerating competition from the socioeconomic elite that predicts the end of gentry privilege. One statement of cooperation exists in *The Descent of Man,* in which Darwin writes that "an advancement in the standard of morality [. . .] will certainly give an immense advantage to one tribe over another" (185), delicately knitting the moral dimension of human behavior to the chancy processes of natural selection. Darwinism evidently offered Wharton a middle way between "the Spencerian notion of an accord between moral fitness and the ability to survive" (Beer *Darwin's Plots* 64), which is known as social Darwinism, and, for her, the insupportable idea that culture possesses complete autonomy from nature. In *The Fruit of the Tree* (1907), her multi-themed novel about labor, social reform, and euthanasia, she posits ethics as "the universal consensus—the result of the world's accumulated experience" (418), and it is arguable that ethics, a product of evolutionary processes in Darwin's *The Descent of Man,* is a result of "accumulated experience" that is not exclusively the result of "reasoning." For the group of novels addressed here, ethics is an aspect of the human experience that owes its existence to a combination of inherited biological predispositions and cultural history.

Wharton writes that "Milton's allusion to Galileo's 'optic glass' shows how early the poetic mind was ready to seize on any illustration furnished by the investigations of science" ("George Eliot" 72), and she summons an effective authorizing example for the disciplinary syncretism she practised. Relating to both formal and thematic issues, a set of questions arises from Wharton's own seizing of scientific language to illustrate her subjects: To what purpose is the hybridization of social analysis and evolutionary and biological science put in the novels? What is at stake for Wharton, politically, in the premise that cultural forms such as class hierarchies, courtship and marriage rituals, rites of exclusion, and the concept of equality itself, might arise from an evolutionary foundation? To what extent is Wharton's biological interpretation of culture an aesthetic conceit that capitalizes on a popular passion for things scientific, and to what degree does Wharton's fiction assert that biological laws function as agents of social change? In what ways, from novel to novel, does she alter her interjection in the debate about the meaning of Darwin's arguments, and in particular, what forms do her responses take to social Darwinist discourse regarding the idea that the "survival of the fittest" not only does obtain in human culture but should? As I address these questions, I also evaluate the success of the narrative strategies Wharton used to present these ideas in the literary marketplace, for her desire to rigorously analyze in fiction the social strata she depicted was matched by a need to persuade a wide audience of her conclusions.

The force of manners in distancing sexuality in the novels suggests ideology is a factor in the sublimation of desire some characters exhibit. A lack of awareness of ideological power displayed by many of Wharton's weak men is an aspect of ideology's depicted operation. A more substantial claim for Wharton's representation of ideology,[2] though, exists in the possibility that she links it to Darwin's theory of natural selection, which is to be seen as a mechanism affecting *social* change. The critical history on the topic of Darwinism in Wharton's fiction leads one to explore her varied portraits of heredity, which express biological and social inheritance as inextricable. In this respect, Wharton's method assaults the artificiality of manners that represent social heredity solely in terms of tradition and ritual, or, as in Newland Archer's world, "the [fashionable] thing" (AI 4) which *The Age of Innocence* reveals to be a codifying cloak that conceals biological essences. I pursue this topic by exploring the implications, for the fictional portraits of ideological competition, of Claire Preston's claim that "Wharton's sociobiological frame of reference predicts modern social analysis, which has made [. . .] [the] useful analogy between evolution/selection theory and social development, treating the macro-social structure as 'a selection environment'" (54–55).

The fictions I examine oppose the idea that it is not possible to curb the harm to individual equality caused by unregulated natural selection; these works find a politicized interpretation of Darwin, which is actually a form of *cultural selection,* objectionable. In this limited sense the novels tender a model of incremental progress predicated on scouring away from an idealized core of American distinctiveness an aberrant brutality toward marginal and vulnerable people, no matter their class affiliation. Ironically, though, the novels do not offer a clear idea of how to balance nature's positive effect on culture—in the case of Ellen Olenska and Newland Archer, how sexual freedom might lead to a mutually enriching hybridization of American and European cultural practices—with nature's disruptive potential. Individual moral agency holds out the possibility of resisting, even altering, a pervasive "survival of the fittest" ethic. Outside a problematic social Darwinist culture, there exists another interpretation of nature in Wharton's texts, but it is one that must now be acknowledged as having its own distinct political thrust. In this interpretation, symbiosis and cooperation are key words, and mutual dependence between species provides a model for relations between individuals, and between classes.

The narratives find in Darwinian ecology a model for obviating the kind of individual aggression displayed by Undine Spragg in *The Custom of the Country,* and the cultural expansionism depicted in Wharton's statement that "[t]he modern European colonist apparently imagined that to plant his warehouses, *cafes* and cinema-palaces within the walls which for so long had fiercely excluded him was the most impressive way of proclaiming his domination" (IM 22). Intervention is called for in preventing the wastage that is visited on humankind in an uncultured state, and which persists in a "civilized" world that extirpates Lily Bart and Ralph Marvell, causes the social death of Ellen Olenska, and colonizes other cultures. Wharton's participation in the broader literary response to Darwinism, moreover, exhibits a complex and relatively consistent perspective that requires some historical contextualization to understand.

Donald Pizer[3] describes the influence of Darwinism on American literature during the first decades of the twentieth century. He identifies a misinterpretation of Darwinian thought that the novels I examine refute in a systematic way:

[. . .] Darwin's belief that biological change is the product of variation and natural selection was immediately available as a possible means of examining change in other phases of man's experience. The application to literary study of the environmental determinism implicit in the theory of natural selection was also encouraged, of course, by Taine's belief that literature is the product of a nation's physical and social conditions. But the basic pattern of evolutionary change which was joined to Taine's environmental determinism to produce an evolutionary critical system was seldom Darwinian. Rather most critics accepted and absorbed Herbert Spencer's doctrine that evolution is, in all phases of life, a progress from the simplicity of incoherent homogeneity to the complexity of coherent heterogeneity. [. . .] The combination of Taine and Spencer is therefore the basic pattern in most evolutionary critical systems of the 1880s and the 1890s. (*Realism and Naturalism* 88)

Born in 1862, Wharton came of age intellectually in the period Pizer identifies. She once wrote that "Taine was one of the formative influences of my youth, the greatest after Darwin, [and] [. . .] Spencer" (*Letters* 136). Frederick Wegener relates that "her criticism generally bears little resemblance, on the whole, to Taine's famous deterministic method" ("Enthusiasm Guided by Acumen" 31), but the influence of Taine's method exists in the "environmental determinism" present in novels such as *The House of Mirth*, which Carol Singley views as documenting "the effects of an increasingly consumer-based culture, shifting sexual relations, and changing urban and rural demographics on women of all classes" (*Historical Guide* 8). In Wharton's sustained focus on change in culture that does *not* lead to coherence, one finds that her evolutionary fictional and critical system combines Taine and Darwin and, mostly, rejects Spencer; by 1902, in fact, she viewed Spencer's thought as "the popular superstition" ("George Eliot" 73).

Despite her stated earlier enthusiasm for Spencer's thought, Wharton grew to be skeptical of the optimism implied by his doctrine, which viewed evolution as a goal-directed process. In *Social Statics* (1851) he had written "so surely must evil and immorality disappear; so surely must man become perfect" (31). Informed as she was in these matters, Wharton would have encountered criticism of Spencer's views on evolution. He had, for instance, come under attack from the American sociologist Albion Small who wrote that "biological sociology" (qtd. in Bannister 45) had unfortunate ethical and social consequences. In 1897 Small charged that Spencer's alleged "principles of sociology" were really "supposed principles of biology prematurely extended to cover social relations" (qtd. in Bannister 45). A strikingly similar exception to Spencer's work is a prominent feature of Wharton's writing between 1905 and 1920, and, to a lesser extent, in later work too; signs of the esteem in which a young Wharton held Spencer, and then the growing dissatisfaction with his views, are present in her fiction and non-fiction.

Wharton's confrontation with social Darwinist derivations of Spencer's teleological evolutionism exists in her representation of characters such as Lily Bart, an "organism" with "inherited tendencies" (HM 301). Though highly moral, Lily, by the novel's end, is eliminated because what T. H. Huxley called "the cosmic process" in his 1893 essay "Evolution and Ethics" (327) is reckoned with ineffectively. Some today view Huxley as the originator among Darwin's defenders of the idea that progress toward a preordained goal is an element of natural selection, something absent from Darwin's original concept. Colin Tudge argues, "Huxley (and Herbert Spencer, and many others since) did not simply espouse Darwinian evolution. They promulgated evolutionism—which effectively conflates progressive evolution in nature with social progress" (29). But one must also acknowledge that Huxley perceived Darwin's original concept clearly, and that Huxley sought to address the dilemma evolution presents to beings capable of moral reasoning. "Now when the ancient sage [. . .] looked the world, and especially human life, in the face, he found it as hard as we do to bring the course of evolution into harmony with even the elementary requirements of the just and the good" ("Evolution and Ethics" 315). Huxley made political points with Darwin's work, and Wharton fictionally assesses the conflict between evolution and the "requirements" of which Huxley writes. She is sympathetic to Huxley's belief that the "conscience of man revolted against the moral indifference of nature" ("Evolution and Ethics" 316), and she locates in Darwin's work a material basis for conscience.

Wharton is critical of Spencerian evolutionism for its promulgation of the idea, as the philosopher Daniel Dennett expresses it, that the "'survival of the fittest' [. . .] is not just Mother Nature's way, but *ought* to be *our* way" (461). She finds in an adaptive moral sense a viable basis on which to base her view, shared with Huxley, that mitigation of the "cosmic process" is possible. It is arguable, moreover, that Huxley was not so much an evolutionist as he was a thoroughgoing materialist who viewed ethics as an adaptive feature of humans and their collectives, a possibility suggested by his claim that

> the sum of tendencies to act in a certain way, which we call 'character,' is often to be traced through a long series of progenitors and collaterals. So we may justly say that this 'character'—this moral and intellectual essence of man—does veritably pass over from one fleshly tabernacle to

another, and does really transmigrate from generation to generation. ("Evolution and Ethics" 317)

These complexities are addressed in *The Custom of the Country*, for example, in Wharton's portrait of Undine Spragg as signifying a recurrence of an earlier stage in social evolution. Undine finds her "impulses" (39) untrustworthy in an upper-class context desultorily battling the ethos of individualism and the isolation that kills Lily in *The House of Mirth*. But Undine soon gravitates to the ambitious Elmer Moffatt's sphere, which exists apart from the world of the gentry—until Moffatt begins to buy it; here she can release her primal power. As an anti-heroine, Undine is the logical outcome of a Spencerian interpretation of Darwinian theory that downplays Huxley's view, and that of Darwin in *The Descent of Man*, that moral "character" has evolved in response to environmental factors. Wharton's depiction of Undine's aggression illustrates a contemporary "scientific" devaluation of moral agency and judges it negatively.

In Thomas Kuhn's *The Structure of Scientific Revolutions* he discusses one radical aspect of *The Origin of Species*, clarifying what were difficult and important aspects of evolutionary theory for Wharton to present:

Though evolution, as such, did encounter resistance [. . .] it was by no means the greatest of the difficulties Darwinians faced. [. . .] All the well-known pre-Darwinian evolutionary theories—those of Lamarck, Chambers, Spencer, and the German *Naturphilosophen*—had taken evolution to be a goal-directed process. The 'idea' of man [. . .] was thought to have been present from the first creation of life. [. . .] Each new stage of evolutionary development was a more perfect realization of a plan that had been present from the start. [. . .] *The Origin of Species* recognized no set goal either by God or nature. [. . .] What could 'evolution,' 'development,' and 'progress' mean in the absence of a specified goal? (171–72)

The "idea of man" present in these "pre-Darwinian evolutionary theories" views the human species, in its biological and moral dimensions, as subject to a process of perfectibility supposed to exist—and which was a sign of divine presence—in natural law; Wharton must have been skeptical of the pre-Darwinian theorists of evolution, for she depicts the version of evolution that was linked to the concept of perfectible humankind, but only in terms of the resultant damage to characters like Lily Bart. This misconception contributes directly to Lily's fate by fostering the notion that an individual's lack of adaptation to the social environment yields one unable to contribute to

the realization of the "plan" Kuhn describes. A nineteenth-century teleological view of the evolutionary process, one that Wharton was conversant with,
thus presented her with a working example of assumptions about a perfectible society *her* biological reading of culture had to dislodge.

Evolution argues for invisibly slow yet inescapable change, an idea that
assaults not only theological principles, but, as Dorothy Ross notes, the ahis-
torical tenor of an American society that saw itself in Wharton's time as
exempt from the political dialectics of the old world (23).[4] This sense of the
special quality of the United States was under siege. As Ross writes: "American social scientists understood the laws of nature as Europeans had in the
eighteenth century, as the rules through which God governed the world.
[...] In the Gilded Age [...] secular naturalism would begin to undermine
this early modern conception of natural law" (50). Wharton illustrates that
social evolution progresses by chance variation, and so questions the proposition that the United States can make progress toward a pre-ordained ideal
holding that self-interested individuals can pursue enrichment under the
assumption that success is a sign of God's plan. An ideology of progress
attributes the growth of wealth to the activities of "many estimable citizens
trained to all the advantages of self-government" (HM 120), which nevertheless disempowers the vulnerable. Jennie A. Kassanoff forcefully illustrates
Wharton's concern with social Darwinism when she reports that, "[e]choing
the work of the American neurologist George M. Beard, who had declared in
1881 that 'the lower must minister to the higher. [...] Millions perish that
hundreds may survive' [...] [*The House of Mirth*'s Lawrence] Selden theorizes that 'a great many dull and ugly people have been sacrificed to produce
[...] [Lily Bart]'" (62). In another fictional context, the "business instinct"
(CC 212) of Undine Spragg's father, according to Beard's model, can produce benefits for the wider collective, which will inevitably suffer losses.
However, according to the texts discussed here, the ideal will yield nothing
but a collocation of blinkered individual interests.

Spencer's influential interpretation of evolution as "a general law,
applying outside biology as well as within, provided a justification for ethical
action" (Ridley 368). This was "ethical action," though, that could extin-
guish those at the margin and, from the perspective of social Darwinists,
consider it natural, and thus right. Wharton's evolutionary themes draw
from Darwin and Spencer, but at the core of her relation of human animals
to the organizing principles of their world, Wharton resists granting validity
to a general application of Spencerian evolution, for it ignores the human
capacity for moral reasoning which might strike at the action of evolution
within society. Wharton, that is, agreed with the Spencerian principle that

biology was a factor in social relations, but she was adamant that the unfortunate consequences that followed from an existing "biological sociology" could be remedied.

Wharton focuses on the profound limits of goal-directed progress, which would have to overcome the universal human character she implies when she writes in *The Fruit of the Tree* (1907) that "human relations [are] [. . .] a tangled and deep-rooted growth, a dark forest through which the idealist cannot cut his straight path without hearing at each stroke the cry of the severed branch: '*why woundest thou me*'" (624). Hence, it is difficult to make the argument that her fiction, in the context of "the history of literature" Pizer outlines, can be affiliated with "progress toward a democratic individualism in expression and subject" (*Realism and Naturalism* 88). She commented negatively on contemporary literary naturalism that represented determinism neutrally, without moral comment; such fiction did little to discourage the unsound Spencerian "ethical action" of allowing a mechanistic universe to winnow vulnerable individuals.

Outside of scientific works, Wharton encountered in her reading of fiction different responses to developments in biology and evolutionary theory. One type of response was present in a realist and naturalist affinity with "secular naturalism," which Wharton shared. She admired Dreiser's *An American Tragedy* (1925), a key work of literary naturalism, when she read it in 1933, and was evidently struck by "his compassionate vision of the human being trapped and doomed to disaster by the very nature of things" (qtd. in Lewis 520). So, too, did she respect Robert Grant's *Unleavened Bread* (1900), a model for *The Custom of the Country* (Lewis 148), and Norris's *McTeague* (1899). These were "great novels" which had a "bitter taste" of causality unalloyed by metaphysics ("The Architecture of Humanism" 132). Wharton was dissatisfied, though, with presentations of determinism that portrayed society as necessarily reflecting natural processes, for this only fed back into the perception that social Darwinism described a relation between nature and culture that was absolute.

Approaching Wharton's fiction from this angle can demonstrate the consistency with which she evades reproducing in her fiction a positive valuation of the ideology of progress she viewed as baneful. While Darwin "never ceased to admire the clearness and condensed vigor of Huxley's prose" (Desmond 313), it is clear that Darwin's bulldog made a similar impression on Wharton, for she sought an "economy of material" (WF 56) that is at least partially responsible for the critical perception that "objectivity is practically a hallmark her realism" (Garlepp-Burns 39). Attentive to Huxley's standard of proof, Wharton copied into a notebook his refusal "to put faith in that which does not rest on sufficient evidence" (qtd. in Lewis 229–30). Her remark that dialogue "should be reserved for the culminating moments, and regarded as the spray into which the great wave of narrative breaks in curving toward the watcher on the shore" (WF 73) illustrates her pursuit of an "economy of material" with an organic image that makes of the reader an objective observer. The avoidance of subjective and impressionistic fictional representation combines with a focus on claim and proof, to suggest a basis for Wharton's skepticism of the Spencerian evolutionary system that, as Pizer shows, underpinned the linking of evolution and progress.

Huxley's "Evolution and Ethics" appears to have influenced Wharton's formalization of her subject by modeling ways to represent biology as an active force in social change.[5] Similarities exist between a number of Wharton's works and Huxley's essay at the level of figurative language and thematic affinity. Metaphors that make of the social environment a garden or conservatory appear in the novels I focus on, and also in Huxley's essay. The latter finds that "only in the garden of an ordered polity can the finest fruits humanity is capable of bearing be produced. [Yet] [. . .] the garden was apt to turn into a hothouse" (313). "Evolution and Ethics" conjectures social progress that takes Darwinism into account in a way that is not Spencerian, for Huxley will not abdicate to a view that finds humankind unable to engage in moral reasoning. Huxley's biographer Adrian Desmond remarks that the essay exhorts "ethical man [to revolt] 'against the moral indifference of nature.' [. . .] 'Evolution and Ethics' split the world; it separated a wild zoological nature from our ethical existence. 'Social progress means a checking of the cosmic process.' It selects not the 'fittest' but 'ethically the best'" (597–98). The split Desmond suggests, though, must be considered against the fact of Huxley's occasionally obscure view that "ethical man" is a product of natural selection. Huxley's sense that "the cosmic process" must be checked is at odds with Spencer's "belief in universal progress" (Cowley 226) predicated on the triumph of the fittest, and has much in common with Wharton's well-known view that ethics was a shriveled dimension of human life.

Recalling Bourget's remark about Wharton that "there is not a book of Darwin, Huxley, Spencer, Renan, Taine, which she has not studied" (qtd. in Lewis 69), and her interest in imaginatively equating biological and social laws, it is important to look for points of contact between Huxley's essay[6] and her fiction. In *The Age of Innocence,* Newland Archer's observation that May Welland unconsciously "was making the answers that instinct and tradition taught her to make" (82) indicates Wharton's interest in the interplay of "cosmic" forces and the values held by social collectives, exemplified in their traditions. Archer's inability to distinguish between instinct and tradition (for he views the former as socially generated) is distinct from the narrator's understanding, and points to cultural work that remains undone; the gentry must come to understand that their "instinctive recoil [. . .] [from] unusual situations" (108) epitomized by the influx of immigrants, increased mobility, the democratization of high culture,[7] and a surging imperialism in the United States,[8] does little to check the "cosmic process" discussed by Huxley.

In inscribing her place in the literary history of the United States by writing her memoir, Wharton clarified her artistic interests when she asked, "In what aspect could a society of irresponsible pleasure-seekers be said to have on the 'old woe of the world,' any deeper bearing than the people composing such a society could guess? The answer lies in its power of debasing people and ideas" (BG 207). For Wharton, the optimistic and progressive idea that social evolution results in coherence is not a given. Neither is it so for Huxley, who states that "social progress means a checking of the cosmic process at every step and the substitution for it of another, which may be called the ethical process" ("Evolution and Ethics" 327). While Wharton takes exception in her fiction to the association of social progress and evolution by natural selection, she is sympathetic to Huxley's sense that "what we call goodness or virtue [. . .] involves a course of conduct which, in all respects, is opposed to that which leads to success in the cosmic struggle for existence" (327). It will be seen, however, that Wharton locates in Darwin's claim for an evolved morality a wellspring for virtuous conduct; nature is moral, but so-called social Darwinist progress, so ready to concede masses of people to the "refuse heap" (HM 313) of the marginalized, is not. That her fiction concerns itself with arresting the debasement of "people and ideas" by "pleasure seekers" is not a new idea, but what requires exploration is the contention in many of her narratives that the frivolity of the established elite illustrates an unwillingness to come to terms with the ramifications of biology for human culture.

Wharton draws together Huxley's "cosmic process" and her notion of the "old woe of the world" to present specific qualities of their relatedness. Her figurative language sees the "gestures" of humans as the reflexes of lower-order animals, but in this Wharton presents the negative example of how a disordered world she inhabits sees individuals through a Spencerian lens. Such an extension of biology over "social relations" and their actors finds Lily Bart to be a fly banging "irrationally against a window pane" (115), and she is also described as a "sea-anemone" (301). Undine Spragg is "instinctive" (355) and "primitive" (470). In *The Age of Innocence,* Newland Archer sees himself as "a wild animal" (67). However, he feels that this is a "coarse view"

(67), demonstrating that his class makes a careful distinction between biology and culture that the narrative counters. To progress morally, even in a limited sense, Archer's class must reckon with the *affiliated* spheres of nature and culture. The novel negatively assesses Archer's aversion to the idea that he is an "animal" by positively viewing sexual selection as a basis for pairing, even though such a basis is potentially disruptive. All three narratives assert that culture grows from its biological foundation, but must control the hazards to equality posed by natural law, much as Huxley contends in his essay.

"Evolution and Ethics" articulates an idea that becomes a central metaphor in each of the novels I investigate: "if our hemisphere were to cool again, the survival of the fittest might bring about, in the vegetable kingdom, a population of more and more stunted and humbler and humbler organisms, until the 'fittest' that survived might be nothing but lichens [. . .]. They, as the fittest, the best adapted to the changed conditions, would survive" (327). Huxley's statement opposes the idea that change will result in "progress." He is skeptical of the claim that "men in society, men as ethical beings, must look to the same processes [the struggle for survival] to help them toward perfection. I suspect that this fallacy has arisen out of the unfortunate ambiguity of the phrase 'survival of the fittest.' 'Fittest' has a connotation of 'best'; and about 'best' there hangs a moral flavour" (327). Wharton's fiction combats the same fallacy by detailing a downward trend, or devolution of culture that she finds to accompany the embrace of this misleading notion. *The Custom of the Country* presents as the medium of cultural heredity an ideology of gentility and ritual that governs Ralph Marvell's caste. Distinguishing an oppositional ideology is the market orientation, lack of ritual, and encouragement of the aggression that guides the business dynamo Elmer Moffatt and those like him. If one reads Huxley's "hemisphere" as analogous to the social environment Wharton depicts, the triumph of the lichen-like, culturally vacant socioeconomic elite invalidates the idea of inevitable progress toward any single ideal. "Progress," in the sense Wharton and Huxley mean, lies first in a retreat from finding advantage in the destructive force of natural selection.

Adaptation to changing environments is the key to survival in nature, not complexity. Wharton imports this idea into her fictional social analysis where "the best adapted to the changed conditions" of *culture* believe falsely that their success is due not to an altered social environment, but to their fulfillment of a distinctly American idea of progress. The idea supplies a justification for social conditions favorable to a less morally oriented, individualistic model of the path to economic success. By representing the damage caused by what Wharton views as the application of incorrectly interpreted Darwinism to social evolution, the novels urge the recognition of the ways nature and culture interact. The degradation suffered by Lily Bart, and the awful triumph of Undine Spragg in *The Custom of the Country,* expertly describe the problem posed by an overt biological sense of social "progress." In these novels, Wharton portrays the eroding authority of an older class that imagines a society wherein "the cosmic struggle for existence, as between man and man, would be rigorously suppressed, and selection, by its means, would be as completely excluded as it is from the garden" ("Evolution and Ethics" 293). In *The Custom of the Country,* Ralph Marvell does not initially recognize the relationship between the social gardening Huxley describes and the facts of nature that necessitate such careful tending. Marvell's is a world that has lost sight of the hazards posed to social evolution by instinct. One such hazard is Undine Spragg, who exemplifies Huxley's characterization of the struggle for existence as "the unscrupulous seizing upon of all that can be grasped" ("Evolution and Ethics" 311). In her instinctive appetite for resources, she displays a lack of the qualities ideally possessed by members of Marvell's class. His stratum, forgetful of its obligations, has yielded to her, and become "frivolous" (BG 207).

Similarly, in *The Age of Innocence* the financier Julius Beaufort transgresses on establishment morality in his relationship with Fanny Ring. From the perspective of those he offends, his behavior does not require suppression as outlined by Huxley, only casual remonstrance. His actions are interpreted as an affront not to social integrity, but to style, for "few things seemed to Newland Archer more awful than an offense against 'Taste,' that far-off divinity of whom 'Form' was the mere visible representative and viceregent" (14). Divorced from real instinct by the system of signification used to control it, Newland Archer finds his established world displaced because of a focus on "Form" that excludes the chaotic energies of aggression and libido. Instead of attending to the reality of changed environments and the appearance of a new type of individual equipped to thrive there, Archer makes fetishes of "Taste" and "Form" and loses sight of the instinctive energies they channel, but he is only following his training. Archer's understanding of "Taste"—depicted as morally disengaged despite the fact, from Wharton's perspective, that it is a potent aspect of a "stabilizing tradition"—illustrates one potential hazard of Gautier's "art for art's sake" principle and the Aesthetic Movement of the 1870s, the period during which the novel is set. *The Age of Innocence* has in common with *The Custom of the Country,* then, a concern with the inheritance of values so important to a gentry nonetheless "doomed to rapid extinction" (CC 78), values which order primitive impulses and longings. And Archer's receipt of what he thinks is "a wonderful new volume called 'The Renaissance' by Walter Pater" (69) is an efficient stroke of characterization that puts Archer into contact with Pater's advocacy of intense experience at the time of a culture-wide loss of understanding—in the narrative's view—regarding an important connection between values and their embodiment in cultural forms.

Each of these novels describes characteristics of the gentry and the socioeconomic elite through the materialism of a biological viewpoint concerned with sexual selection, mutation, extinction, and the possibility of a biologically based moral sense Wharton encountered in an implicit form in *The Origin of Species* and explicitly in *The Descent of Man*. This viewpoint juxtaposes natural selection—a central tenet of scientific texts that are metaphorical seedbeds for Wharton's portraits of social change—against the desire for cultural stasis exhibited by the establishment. In conceiving of Wharton's fiction as literary sociobiology I am borrowing the latter word, and a definition of what such an enterprise entails, from Daniel Dennett's discussion of Nietzsche's *Genealogy of Morals* (461–67). Dennett writes that Nietzsche's "primary target was the historical naïveté of the social Darwinists (Hoy 1986), their Panglossian optimism about the ready adaptability of human reason (or Prudence) to Morality" (462). Wharton's interest in Nietzsche's work has been investigated by William Macnaughton[9] and by Lewis. In his biography of Wharton, Lewis writes that

> [s]he was intently reading Nietzsche's writings—*Beyond Good and Evil, The Will to Power,* and *The Genealogy of Morals* were all in her inventory of favorites [. . .]. What she especially admired was Nietzsche's exhilarating 'power of breaking through the conventions,' and she thought that it was 'salutary now and then to be made to realize *'Die Unwerthung aller Werthe'* ["the re-evaluation of all values"] and really get back to a wholesome basis of naked instinct.' Thus enthralled, Edith Wharton shared for a time Nietzsche's driving hostility to Christianity as an emasculating force and a repressive 'instrument of culture.' She applauded Nietzsche's concept of 'the blond beast,' a mythic embodiment, as it were, of naked instinct: an unfettered animal impulse that Nietzsche believed needed to erupt from time to time in an assault upon traditional culture and upon Christianity's influential distrust of the human body. 'There are times,' Edith wrote Sally Norton, 'when I hate what Christianity has left in our blood—or rather, one might say, what it has taken out of it—by its cursed assumption of the split between body and soul.' (230)

As the representative of biological instinct related allegorically to her innate morality *and* inexpressible sexuality, the failure of Lily Bart's encounter with traditional culture demonstrates the ability of liberal Christian values to repress what is "salutary" about nature. It seems reasonable to claim, then, that the "cursed assumption of the split between body and soul" in part provokes Wharton's recognition and valuation of "naked instinct" outside the context of a metaphysical system she distrusted.

In *The Age of Innocence,* Newland Archer hints at the desire to control social evolution, when he derides "[t]he stupid law of change" (310).[10] Wharton advances the possibility of controlling the chaos and aggression on display in conflicts between increasingly indistinct classes in *The Custom of the Country* and *The House of Mirth,* and the portrait in *The Age of Innocence* of the emerging socioeconomic elite. She identifies in eroding gentry values a traditional and conservative counterforce able to act centripetally against nature's contingent essence. But she also illustrates ways these timeworn values, by being intolerant of difference, foreclose the positive change that allows controlled transformation—a dynamic evident when Newland Archer's mother remarks that "people should respect our ways when they come among us" (86–87). To Archer, stability is simultaneously repressive, desirable, loathsome, and ultimately impossible to maintain.

In Wharton's view, social evolution can be constrained to a degree. It will not happen by embracing social Darwinism, which is shown to rest on an economically exigent interpretation of evolutionary theory, but by considering and acting on Huxley's statement that the "optimism of philosophers [. . .] prevented them from seeing that cosmic nature is no school of virtue, but the headquarters of the enemy of ethical nature" ("Evolution and Ethics" 324). Wharton's representation of "ethical" nature's suppression shows a social field increasingly controlled by the socioeconomic upstarts. The material success of this group has little collective benefit where Wharton's "impalpable dust" of culture is concerned, despite the good uses to which capital might be put; social Darwinism is a sham model of the culture's biological foundation that disregards the potential of the human collective to grow toward a virtuous limiting of "cosmic nature."

Darwin claims in *The Descent of Man*[11] that "an advancement in the standard of morality [. . .] will certainly give an immense advantage to one tribe over another" (166), and Wharton addresses this possibility in her fiction. Cooperation and mutuality among individuals is a concern Wharton detects in the fiction of George Eliot too. When Wharton expounds on the way "Eliot's noblest characters shrink with a peculiar dread from any personal happiness acquired at the cost of the social organism" ("George Eliot" 76), she gives a positive valuation of Darwinian symbiosis in the human sphere of action. Indeed, each of the major novels addressed in this study shows Wharton to be engaged in fictional theorizing about social equity and the biological foundations of culture. In doing so she anticipates contemporary criticism of the kind mentioned by Joseph Carroll, a key figure in the study of Darwinism and literature, who remarks that, "[a]rguing from a Darwinian perspective, James Q. Wilson has proposed that the evolved human capacities for social interaction include the instinct for fair play—for reciprocity and equity—and contractual arrangements" (156). The vitiation of such capacities in the novelistic settings demonstrates the clear importance to Wharton of their viability.

Contemporary skepticism toward the idea of connections between, for example, contractual arrangements and adaptive traits, exists in the work of Harvard biologist Edward O. Wilson, who cautions that while there is evidence for a "hereditary human nature. [. . .] it is still risky to [see social practices] as evidence of the linkage between genes and culture" (149). In creating fiction and not scientific knowledge, Wharton is free to imagine connections unproven by the available evidence, but clear enough to a writer asserting that instinct coerced into submission for the greater good results in misery for some. And while it may be risky to do so, Wharton links culture and genes, or at least her understanding of what is meant today by the latter term, aligning her thematic interest in this linkage with Huxley's contention that "man, physical, intellectual, and moral, is as much a part of nature, as purely a product of the cosmic process, as the humblest weed" ("Evolution and Ethics" 290). For Huxley, and for Wharton, the premise is similar to Spencer's inclusion of social relations in the sphere covered by biology. The novelist, however, follows Huxley, despite the inconsistencies to which I have alluded, to find in the moral *instinct* a way to imagine a modern, humane, and more authentic picture of the relation between nature and culture that works from the best evidence available.

That this idea was clear to Wharton in the years before she wrote *The House of Mirth* is evident in her previously mentioned 1902 review of Leslie Stephens's biography of George Eliot. Here, Wharton defends Eliot against the charge "that she was too scientific, that she sterilised her imagination and deformed her style by the study of biology and metaphysics" ("George Eliot" 71). Troubled by a perceived split between literary and scientific disciplines that she views as overlapping, Wharton objects to the "belief that scientific studies have this [sterilizing] effect on the literary faculty" ("George Eliot" 71). Years later, she opined on art in a generalizing comment that demonstrates her tendency to thresh from her intellectual labours in natural history metaphors that joined the best ideas her society produced—in her view—to a biological substructure:

The natural processes go on in spite of theorizing, and the accumulated leaf-mould of tradition is essential to the nurture of new growths of art, whether or not those who cultivate them are aware of it. All the past seems to show that when a whole generation misses the fecundating soil stored for it by its predecessors its first growth will be spindling and its roots meager. ("Tendencies in Modern Fiction" 170)

In other words, tradition is natural in the arts; the obvious organic metaphor strikes one first—tradition is fertilizer, but more to the point, "the leaf-mould of tradition" is cultural "germ plasm," or from a Mendelian perspective, the genetic content of culture. Expressed in this way, the generation that "misses" the nutritive history of the past, one supplied by a "tradition" of wealthy elites, is consigned to a "spindling" and faulty germination.

In her discussion of the Eliot biography,[12] Wharton finds the shoots of "new growths" of art rising from a metaphorical soil in which biology inhabits culture at a foundational, or to extend her metaphor, a cellular level. A scientific perspective on art will enhance our understanding of it; employed as a method, though, the perspective risks alienating the reader. As it is used by characters such as Charles Bowen in *The Custom of the Country*, and Newland Archer, science is an instrument with which to describe and control destabilizing sexual desire and aggression, especially in the case of traditions of taste and form, which exhibit these forces in permitted guises. Wharton might criticize as amateurish Newland Archer's objective scrutiny of Ellen Olenska early in *The Age of Innocence* as a monitoring of her dangerous sensuality, and as a way for him to control his unauthorized attraction to her, but Wharton's omniscient scientism risks narrowing the reader's perception of Archer's thwarted impulse by constricting the figurative means with which she creates her biosocial analysis. However, she refutes the principle implicit in "Darwin's well-known statement that, as he grew more engrossed in his physiological investigations, he lost his taste for poetry" ("George Eliot" 71). Wharton's reply to Darwin argues that

there is more than one way of studying the phenomena of life [. . .] the fixity of purpose and limited range of investigation to which the scientific specialist is committed differ totally from the cultivated reader's bird's-eye view of the field of scientific speculation. George Eliot was simply the cultivated reader, and her biological acquirements probably differed in degree, rather than in kind, from those, for instance, of Tennyson, who is acknowledged to have enlarged the range of poetic imagery by his use of metaphors and analogies drawn from the discoveries of modern science. ("George Eliot" 71)

Putting her observations about Eliot into practice, Wharton's metaphors and analogies unite organisms and human individuals in what can seem like a conceit derived from casual scientific reading; but hers is an act of serious intellectual labor directed toward defusing "the cultural vulnerabilities of class and gender," as Kassanoff writes in a discussion of race in *The House of Mirth* (61).

The resulting narratives reflect a refusal to be limited by disciplinary boundaries, for Wharton's capitalization on the imagery of "modern science" is necessary to her "studying the phenomena of life" in fiction. Her multi-disciplinary analysis will proffer evolutionary mechanisms as being impli-cated in individual psychology. In discussing the possible reasons for George Eliot having "not the slightest leaning toward creative work" until "chance [. . .] threw her into the society of George Lewes and Mr. Herbert Spencer," Wharton asks, "[w]hat was so likely to free such a spirit from the bonds of ethical pedantry as the contact with that vast speculative movement which was just then opening countless new avenues into the mind of man and the phenomena of the universe?" ("George Eliot" 72–73). The yoking into a subject for fiction of "the mind of man" and the material "phenomena of the universe" emerges from Wharton's own contact with that which stimulated Eliot's imagination.

Promoting her own combination of scientific method and social criti-cism in the review of Stephens's book on Eliot, Wharton differentiates her work from the narrower concerns of science without excluding the use of its methods. Even in a statement on the scientific theory that was for her an intellectual touchstone, one detects Wharton's appreciation of the persuasive uses to which it can be put: "No one can deny," she writes, "the poetic value of the evolutionary conception [. . .] almost all the famous scientific hypotheses have an imaginative boldness and beauty" ("George Eliot" 72). This "beauty" lies in the metaphorical richness and transferability to social evolution of Darwin's "conception."

Gillian Beer relates one reason for this metaphorical richness in reminding us that the "readerly community of the educated mid-nineteenth century in Britain assumed that it could rely on gaining access to whatever knowledge was current even within specialist groups. It was, consequently, often taken for granted that words retain the same signification across widely divergent fields" (*Open Fields* 203). As Wharton systematically educated her-self in the science of the period subsequent to having read her way through her father's library as a young woman,[13] the author-scientist who complained about the difficulties of Mendelism was driven forward in her studies by the perception that scientific writing was mostly accessible.

Whereas Beer's remark provides one reason why a literary writer might feel able to impose scientific language on a social field seemingly removed from the study of natural selection, Wharton's novels do posit real connections between the development of human culture and biological processes. Such connections call for a consideration of Wharton's use of metaphor to combine the biological and the social. Considering this issue Karin Garlepp-Burns claims that Wharton's "use of scientific jargon remains essentially symbolic, and as such, unscientific" (40); it is arguable, however, that Wharton deploys the biological and social metaphor for her own stylistic and socially critical ends—that is, as a way to create authoritative fictional social analysis that has a scientific tone *and* binds nature and culture through the use of metaphor, which if not scientific has the virtue of hypothesizing connections between biology and society beyond what science imagines. Wharton creates from biological figurative language a subtle polemic that advances the idea of interconnectedness between human culture and natural realms, catapulting facts at the religious and ideological walls that separate them.

II. "BETWEEN SOCIAL ORDER AND INDIVIDUAL APPETITES"

In 1953 Blake Nevius addressed the difficulty of charting the relation between evolutionary theory and Wharton's "naturalistic tragedy," concluding that "it is impossible, perhaps, to calculate [. . .] but it has never been considered" (56). The past decade has seen scholarship take up the task of considering the relation of Wharton's writing to the fields of biology and evolution, as well as to anthropology and sociology. These disciplines are now visible as defining constituents of Wharton's fiction.[14] Nancy Bentley, for example, has persuasively shown that Wharton's fictional framework peers "[t]hrough an ethnographic lens, [to find that] manners become the keys to the secrets of social control and cohesion" (*The Ethnography of Manners* 70). That the locks turned by these "keys" bar the fulfillment of desire, and substitute a socially constructed "instinct" at variance with biological impulse, suggests that Wharton represents the diminishment of instinct by manners, and in so doing delineates her position in "the literary controversy over [. . .] sexual reality" (Bender 317) as one set against excessive controls over *Eros*. The novels enter into this controversy, to cite two examples, by associating equality with the expression of female sexual choice in *The House of Mirth,* and by depicting the linguistic nullification of sexuality in conversations between Archer and May Welland in *The Age of Innocence.*

Nevius's early study is still valuable for its implicit claim that ideology is a subject of *The House of Mirth.* This is evident in his reference to Lily's loose "theoretical grasp of the principles which enable Selden to preserve his weak idealism" (57). Nevius writes, furthermore, that Lily Bart "is as completely and typically the product of her heredity, environment, and the historical moment which found American materialism in the ascendant" (57). In choosing the word "heredity," Nevius does not distinguish between biological and cultural heritage, demonstrating a failure to perceive Wharton's concern with their commonalities. In Wharton's fiction, heredity is an aggregation of both biological and cultural inheritance conceived of by characters, whether consciously or not, in a way that often ignores the former. One valuable element of recent scholarship on this issue has been to illustrate historical attitudes about heredity, which, as Kassanoff shows, can conflate cultural memory with genetic inheritance: "the writer Forbes Phillips queried in 1906, 'Is it not possible that the child may inherit some of his ancestor's memory? That [. . .] flashes of reminiscence are the sudden awakening [. . .] of something we have in our blood; [. . .] the records of an ancestor's past life?'" (60–61). Wharton's analysis of social and biological heredity represents social change within the terminological framework of Darwinism. Consequently, ideology becomes visible as the medium of cultural transmission and is analogous to the claim of early twentieth-century science that "germ plasm" functioned as the medium of physical heredity. Wharton's application of theories from the physical sciences to a sociological domain considers social change to proceed from a biological base. The resultant narratives, however, can appear to offer a natural basis for social conservatism, as when the easy availability of divorce and the resultant transformations to marriage and family, as depicted in *The Children* (1928), for example, are judged as retrograde.

Nevius's basic suggestion that evolutionary theory and ideology are aspects of Wharton's fiction directs one to consider Lawrence Selden's idealism in *The House of Mirth* to be a trait of the class to which he belongs, and a core principle that he inherits. He is an agent of a social stratum that asserts, as one definition of ideology expresses it, "concepts and categories that distort the whole of reality in a direction useful to the prevailing power" (Makaryk 558), which he diligently serves as a lawyer. Yet he also has a sense of the way he is limited by his class values, and how the price of stepping out of his role is the termination of the privilege he enjoys. Compared to Lily, he is a different species, and she recognizes that he belongs "to a more specialized race" (65).

Nancy Bentley's claim that "Wharton, at certain fictional extremes, make[s] the exchanges of drawing-room culture indistinguishable from acts of coercive force" (*The Ethnography of Manners* 70) compels one to view such coercion as a patterning of biological imperatives such as competition for resources and sexual partners. The "exchanges of the drawing-room" also contain and limit the visibility of the biological reality represented in strictly prescribed social relations. Manners imply a process of signification that intrigues Lawrence Selden, yet as an observer of habit, he often fails to connect normative behavior to the concern over preserving his hereditary caste that manners represent. Selden has forgotten that the ability to perpetuate his own class values is at stake. Blinded to passion and enervating desperation in ways Lily Bart is not, he is "as much as Lily, the victim of his environment" (152).

In *The Age of Innocence,* Newland Archer is insensible to impending social change. Whereas he can foresee life in the house that his father-in-law will build for May Welland and himself, "beyond that his imagination could not travel" (71). The exchanges of the drawing room offer rites and forms that restrict the imagination in a way that disrupts access to instinct. In *The House of Mirth,* Selden finds Lily to be "a captured dryad subdued to the conventions of the drawing room" (13). Mannered exchanges signify victimization by an ideology that shrinks the horizon of the imagination. Bentley's comment thus directs one to consider *why* force must be used in the drawing-room, opening the subject of manners in the novels to an examination of their relation to disruptive instincts that the novels depict as poorly understood, and whose potential to ignite social renewal is undervalued.

My readings of Wharton's fiction build on Bentley's relation of her stories to anthropology and ethnography, and on Nevius's suggestion that Wharton's interest in evolution is an issue in her depiction of the principles of idealism relied upon by Selden's class. I look beyond the limits of anthropological influences for a narrative remainder that can only be addressed by investigating Wharton's knowledge of biology and evolutionary theory. Dale Bauer provides one rationale for my approach in her elaboration on Wharton's response to "the nineteenth-century anthropological model, [in which] culture functions as an imposed restraint upon the primitive and unlimited impulses and desires" (*Brave New Politics* 16). Bauer's work offers a way to interpret Newland Archer's reading of books on "Primitive Man" (AI 44) as contributing to his analysis of his world, giving him insight into the ways he is controlled. Restraint of the primitive affects Lawrence Selden, Ralph Marvell and Newland Archer, redirecting the barely discernible "naked instinct" of each character into aesthetic pursuits. For all three men, sexual matters vaporize in an aesthetic fog where cultural narratives envelope the "impulses and desires" they encode, control, and dematerialize.

Wharton's own literary criticism also displays her interest in "impulses and desires," and evolution and biology. In discussing the weaknesses of early novels in her 1934 essay "Tendencies in Modern Fiction," she observes that "most of the characters in fiction were either 'stylized' abstractions or merely passive subjects of experiment, or both" (170). She states too, however, that "presently someone [. . .] noticed the impact of surrounding circumstances on every individual life, [. . .] the religious and atmospheric influences, and those subtler differences produced by the then scarcely apprehended law of variability" (171). On the subject of variation, Darwin writes that "[n]o one supposes that all the individuals of the same species are cast in the very same mould. These individual differences are highly important to us, as they afford materials for natural selection to accumulate, in the same manner as man can accumulate in any given direction individual differences in his domestic productions" (*Origin* 110). Notable in Wharton's comment is the suggestion that only recently had material reality, or "circumstances," been viewed as connectible to the "law of variability" so central to Darwin's work. Fiction, according to this passage, can represent the complex interaction of social environment and natural law, a claim further evidenced by her belief that "[d]rama, situation, is made out of the conflicts [. . .] produced between social order and individual appetites" (WF 13–14).

This book's examination of the aforementioned novels, and other works, through the framework of Wharton's scientific knowledge is not exhaustive. Janet Beer indicates opportunities for further work in this area when she writes that a "structural principle, used repeatedly in Wharton's later fiction, is also established in the novella [1900–1907] where she draws powerful contrasts and imagery from language usually found in other contexts, for example in the law, commerce, science, anthropology" (*Edith Wharton* 99).[15] The presence of this principle in *The House of Mirth*, *The Custom of the Country*, and *The Age of Innocence* has guided my choice of these works, where one finds a weaving together of evolutionary science and social criticism which assumes that culture cannot be understood in full without accounting for its biological foundations.

Literary criticism that explores how other writers were affected by advances in evolutionary theory has also contributed to my investigation of tension between order and appetite in Wharton's writing. Gillian Beer's *Darwin's Plots* (1983), which elegantly demonstrates the explanatory potential of evolutionary theory for late nineteenth-century literature, is a case in point. In another work by Beer—*Open Fields: Science in Cultural Encounter* (1995)—she quotes the well-known final paragraph of *The Origin of Species* as an epigraph. This passage serves to describe Wharton's tenuous and prospective delineation of the human psyche: "In the distant future I see open fields for far more important researches. Psychology will be based on a new foundation, that of the necessary acquirement of each mental power and capacity by gradation. Light will be thrown on the origin of man and his history" (3). Darwin's statement is relevant to Wharton's extension of his ideas into a cultural space, for it postulates that processes described by evolution were active in the development of capacities for conceptual thought that define human beings. The affinities between the passage Beer cites and the work I investigate frame Wharton's interest in an American citizenry's gradual acquisition of "mental power and capacity," and a resultant cultural capital that might curb contingent evolutionary processes.

Beer mentions *The House of Mirth*'s "condensation of sang-froid and violence, private and public [. . .] where the highly polished surface of Lily Bart's milieu is crazed with dirt" (*Open Fields* 281), and she recounts "[a]n engrossing question" explored in *Darwin's Plots* that asks "what happens when unforeseen readers appropriate terms and texts" (1). Wharton was one of these readers, employing Darwinian language to serve her response to social Darwinists (among others) whose own appropriation of "terms and texts" signals a political perspective that she confutes with the literary tools of the realist and a ready confidence in her objectivity. While not focused on Wharton's fiction, *Darwin's Plots* demonstrates what evolutionary theory offered her in terms of a model for an ecological interrelation of individuals that might be conducive to social equality. When applied to Wharton's fiction, *Darwin's Plots* helps to focus the implied argument in the novels that biology is needed to explain cultural change. Paradoxically, though, the novels contend that repressive social codes channel libidinal energies, directing them into the creation of culture, even as the redirection of these energies is portrayed neutrally or negatively in its effect on desexualized male aesthetes such as Newland Archer. Wharton, it seems, can be Freudian, despite her hostility to Freud's work,[16] in her analysis of the sublimation of drives.

Beer's work compels a consideration of the exchange of ideas between science and social criticism that occurs in Wharton's fiction. Beer writes that Darwin struggled "to find a language to think in. He was working in a milieu where natural theology had set the tone for natural historians" (*Darwin's Plots* xviii). In her narratives, Wharton entered into a conversation with a national literature shaped by sentimental bestsellers, and overlapping realist and naturalist strains of fiction that included the varied representations of determinism found in the work of Dreiser and others. She "would have seen that the new psychology" she was exposed to when Egerton Winthrop introduced her to Westermarck's *The History of Human Marriage* "was reiterating what her American predecessors in the fiction of courtship and marriage had known since the 1870s, that 'many of the psychic facts in human courtship point directly to that of animals'" (Bender 317). In turning to Darwinism to find her own "language to think in," she located a scientific ground from which to extend existing fictional considerations of the "animal" aspects of human culture.

The forms in which this knowledge manifests itself show Wharton's facility with the literary traditions she inherited. Her novels confront an American literary scene with a biological view of love evidenced by attractions between Lily Bart and Lawrence Selden, Peter Van Degen and Undine Spragg, and Newland Archer and Ellen Olenska that are less socially useful than based on sexual attraction. From this perspective, the individual's search for sexual fulfillment is one that must contend with erasure of now abnormal vestigial desires by the cultural context. This animal dimension of human courtship, though, is nested inside Wharton's tactical and often ironic use of the sentimental tradition, which clothes her fiction in forms recognizable in the literary marketplace. She gathers her audience to the scene of startling messages about the impossibility of escaping chance, and the dubiousness of contemporary ideas of social progress, even if these messages are obscured by broad strokes depicting solidarity between female moral exemplars such as Lily Bart and Nettie Struther at the end of *The House of Mirth*.

Striated with a descriptive tone found in scientific contexts, the sentimental settings of romantic encounter, and family life, can seem to be sketched in a naturalist's notebook. Of Undine Spragg's father in *The Custom of the Country*, Wharton writes that "it was the hereditary habit of the parent animal to despoil himself for his progeny" (483). This characteristic visioning of individuals as biological entities reinforces a thematic concern with breaking down conceptual divisions between nature and culture, humankind and the animal world. Claire Preston writes in *Edith Wharton's Social Register* that "Wharton's work is difficult to place within the conventions of '*women's*' writing; she is influenced instead by social fictions and by non-fictional work in biology and evolution, anthropology and sociology" (xii). Wharton's redirection of biology and evolutionary theory toward the task of fictional social criticism suggests that the physical laws studied by science play on individual and social bodies in unacknowledged ways. The methods of science help her create work "supplemented by the intellectual range and detachment needed for the survey of culture" ("William C. Brownell" 205). Preston discusses *The House of Mirth's* objectivity, or "detachment," affirming that a biologically framed portrait of culture exists in the novel. Her discussion, moreover, detects social commentary:

> Lily is not a self-supporting organism; she can only live in unnatural, ultimately insupportable conditions. Her dainty ideas of social suitability

are unsustainably specialised: archaic, outmoded, they are more appropriate to an Old New York which social evolution has left behind, impossible in a New York in which 'the purely decorative mission' (HM 487) is no longer a sufficient *modus vivendi*. (50)

According to the values of the text, Lily *should* be able to live.

The old New York left behind by "social evolution" had created a niche in which Lily could thrive, though such an existence limited her options. Whereas old New York aspired to fence itself off from contingency, the socioeconomic elite has dispersed this ideal and thrived in an altered environment that formerly offered sustenance to creatures like Lily. Wharton's depiction of this process is persuasive, not neutral; her method is argumentative, not objective. Preston's suggestion that the conditions Lily *does* live in are natural is a striking observation. Yet this must be qualified by stating that Lily succumbs in an environment where the predatory activities of Wall Street seep into a social sphere that, given the allegiances of the narrative, ought to offer some protection. Lily has been "fashioned to adorn and delight; to what other end does nature round the rose-leaf" (301), but this trait has flourished in the context of an *idea* of nature symbolized by the hothouse, conservatory, and garden which appears, in at least one of these guises, in each of the novels addressed here. Wharton is clear in showing that Lawrence Selden's view of Lily as artificial is correct, but only to the extent that her delicate beauty is a product of an older interpretation of nature that finds little difference between her flowering face being inside the glass wall of a conservatory, or outside in a sympathetic culture. This possibility is dissolving in the acid of a new idea; nature is not only uncontrollable, but should be allowed into the enclosed garden of New York as something that will invigorate "the blind inherited scruples" (104) of Selden's desiccated world. As I show in my chapter on *The House of Mirth*, Lily would be a "self-supporting organism" in a social context that acknowledged the example of a natural world wherein Darwin's "ecological image of the 'inextricable web of affinities'" (Beer *Darwin's Plots* 19) serves as a model for social relations. Preston's articulation of "the severe logic of natural competition" that has penetrated "the social hot-house" (51) of *The House of Mirth* is, then, an insight to which I add the claim that the "logic" she mentions is itself not absolute, but is produced by a politically self-serving scientism.

Despite Preston's claim about the difficulty of placing Wharton's work "within the conventions of '*women's*'" writing, Hildegard Hoeller has argued for the presence of "a dialogue between the realist and sentimental voices in Edith Wharton—who is praised for her mastery of the former and deplored

for her lapse into the latter" (10). Hoeller asks, "What, aesthetically and ideologically, did the sentimental tradition have to give to Wharton?" (10).
Hoeller's identification of a dialogue between women's sentimental writing and
a realist masculine-gendered tradition is particularly valuable for its assertion
that Wharton's fiction drew on both modes. Although the novels examined
here are aesthetically superior to the sensational and sentimental romances of
an author such as E. D. E. N. Southworth, for example, they draw from the
tradition Southworth helped to shape. It is evident that Wharton's sentimental
"lapses" are counterweights to her scientific realism, but Lily Bart's nostalgic
inspection in her boarding-house room of fine dresses that are "survivals of her
last stage of splendour" (317) is but one example of moments that are at once
deeply ironic in their use of sentimental convention, and eager to be carried to
the market by the same fictional mode.

Wharton criticized the literary tastes implicit in the "facile sentimentalism of the early Victorian public" ("George Eliot" 74) and assumed the presence of the same tastes in her own day, an attitude evident in her story "The
Descent of Man," which I discuss in chapter two. Her biologically influenced depersonalization of Lily classifies the character as a cultivated and
"rare flower grown for exhibition" (317), but Wharton alternates such narrative instances with passages indebted to literary sentimentalism. In many
sentimental writers, Harriet Beecher Stowe perhaps most notably, there exists
a realist project devoted to many of the same concerns Wharton had: an
acute observation of bodily affect, an interest in the experiential formation of
character, a puzzling over the degree to which biological categories like race
explain behavior, a recognition of the commodification of the individual,
and a concern to preserve distinctions between gentility and wealth as a basis
of class. Hoeller describes another feature of the tradition Wharton evidently
drew from, finding that "[t]he sentimental vision [. . .] adopted by Susan
Warner and Harriet Beecher Stowe, could be said to look at characters as
signs of abstract qualities and feelings" (Hoeller 27). This is the case with
Lily Bart's signification of morality and marginalization. Hoeller's unassailable view of Wharton as a writer whose work shared key interests with sentimental literature provides a basis for suggesting that its popularity gave
Wharton another reason to capitalize on its "realist project." Wharton classes
Stowe as one of the "pleaders of special causes" but at the same time admits
that "that unhappy hybrid, the novel with a purpose" could be "immensely
remunerative" ("Permanent Values in Fiction" 175). It is evident that *The
House of Mirth* is a "novel with a purpose," and that Stowe's subject matter
and Wharton's, in a general sense, are related. Certainly, Stowe's success in
the marketplace caught Wharton's attention.

Hoeller claims that Wharton's *The Writing of Fiction* is her "most self-conscious attempt to place herself inside the critically approved, and predominantly male, realist tradition" (12). Yet once inside, Wharton looked to the possibility that the individual acting in concert with his or her society can take saving action in a hostile environment "against which only genius can prevail" (WF 133), differentiating her perspective from Stephen Crane's naturalist portrait of chance and nature in "The Open Boat" (1894), for example.[17] Representing, in the psychology of her characters, a potential to respond to indifferent forces, Wharton's beautiful failures (Lily Bart, Ralph Marvell and Newland Archer, among others) diagnose their society's malaise for the reader by coming to naught. Yet each character gamely plays out his or her straitened options: Lily by trying, uselessly, to work, Marvell by playing the market to purchase the custody of his beloved son from Undine, and Archer by moving as far toward Ellen Olenska as his tribe will allow him. Drawing upon another "predominantly male" tradition, that of science, Wharton represents tensions between agency and determinism, and she portrays the way incursive social Darwinist attitudes remake the social context her realism depicts, something contemporary criticism of Wharton's fiction acknowledges, even if it has not explored the topic in sufficient detail.

Wharton's affiliation with, and skepticism toward, aspects of American realism and naturalism intersect with my interest in building on the work of the critics I have discussed because, as Daniel Borus notes, those "who have tried to answer the question of why realism emerged in the late nineteenth century have often pointed to the prevailing cachet of science and its stress on observation and exactness" (9). Many of Wharton's pronouncements on naturalism are harshly critical, even though she was clearly interested in "observation and exactness" in her own work. While she shows a lack of sympathy in her criticism for fiction unwilling to represent the potential response of the individual to deterministic forces, critics have found in her fiction links to Crane, Dreiser, Howells, Norris and Robert Grant. In praising Grant, Wharton reveals one dimension of her literary method in a letter to him when she writes, "I am so great a believer in the objective attitude that I have specially enjoyed the successful use you have made of it" (*Letters* 40). Pamela Knights has noted the periodic appearance of this "attitude" in *The Age of Innocence,* in which "[f]requently we meet objective narrative commentary, often at the start of a chapter, which suddenly relocates itself in Archer's focalizing vision: 'These things passed through Newland Archer's mind'" (21). Wharton was acquainted with Howells through Henry James and Charles Norton. She "had a great admiration for 'A Modern Instance' and 'Silas Lapham'" (BG 146–47). One can identify similarities in the grain of

Wharton's representation of determinism in comparison to these writers. *The House of Mirth* demonstrates, in the consequences of Lily's repayment of the money she has received from Trenor, the harm of a purely instrumental model of human relations, showing that such an implicit "[c]ontract might, as *A Modern Instance* dramatizes, undermine appeals to a higher standard of equity" (Thomas 33). Wharton, then, presses the case that biological models that bypass a "higher standard" are uninformed regarding the facts of evolutionary theory. It is to this subject that I now turn.

III. "THAT UNHAPPY HYBRID, THE NOVEL WITH A PURPOSE"

Wharton's critical writing depicts naturalism as a mode in which "the novelist exchanged his creative faculty for a Kodak [. . .], statistics crowded out psychology," and writers who did not represent the full vision of determinism "beat their brains out against the blank wall of [a] 'naturalism'" ("Tendencies in Modern Fiction" 171) which did not foresee any possible response to a deterministic universe. Her negative characterization of naturalism in literature chides writers inattentive to the ability of disenfranchised subjects to assert that where there is no meaning, meaning can be made. Wharton counters realist and naturalist themes that mute the actions of higher perception by, in one instance, portraying in *The Age of Innocence* the outcast Ellen Olenska's ability to identify "the blind conformity to tradition—somebody else's tradition—that I see among our own friends" (240). Ellen's difficulties present the effects of tradition, but her reaction demonstrates her capacity to respond with reason. Ellen's rational judgment confirms the soundness of the narrative's probing of tradition, for Wharton articulates the attempt to control difference that conformity serves.

The focus on the socially useful response to determinism of individuals expelled or extinguished by it differentiates Wharton's characterization from W. D. Howells's depiction of moral salvation through independent action in *The Rise of Silas Lapham*. Although Wharton admired the novel, Howells's hero makes a redemptive decision despite the fact that he is characterized as a man whose acts exemplify economic individualism. In Wharton's fiction, no ghost in the machine of social mechanism facilitates unrealistic combinations of hyper-competitiveness and moral agency. The effort at self-redemption in Lily Bart's repayment of her debt to Gus Trenor, or Ralph Marvell's attempt in *The Custom of the Country* to regain the custody of his son, ends in failure and death that both narratives view as a collective abdication to a model of interpersonal competition that renders the moral impulse irrelevant. This model, however, does not exhibit the relation between nature and morality in the sense outlined in Darwin's *The Descent of Man:*

> The moral nature of man has reached its present standard, partly through the advancement of his reasoning powers and consequently of a just public opinion, but especially from his sympathies having been rendered more tender and widely diffused through the effects of habit, example, instruction, and reflection. It is not improbable that after long practice virtuous tendencies may be inherited. With the more civilised races, the conviction of the existence of an all-seeing Deity has had a potent influence on the advance of morality. Ultimately man does not accept the praise or blame of his fellows as his sole guide though few escape this influence, but his habitual convictions, controlled by reason, afford him the safest rule. His conscience then becomes the supreme judge and monitor. Nevertheless the first foundation or origin of the moral sense lies in the social instincts, including sympathy; and these instincts no doubt were primarily gained, as in the case of the lower animals, through natural selection. (394)

Refuting the notion that moral progress can spring from the cultural politics of social Darwinism, Wharton instead avers the naturalness of cooperation in the human context. In her discussion of Dreiser, Rachel Bowlby notes that his "reading of Herbert Spencer is evident in a picture of an individual wholly subject to distant 'invisible forces'" (53). As much as this description might seem to apply to Lily Bart, Gerty Farish, or Nettie Struther in *The House of Mirth,* Wharton does not emulate Dreiser's judgment in *An American Tragedy,* that a Spencerian model of social progress—which finds that incurring casualties on the road to prosperity strengthens the American stock—is unanswerable. The popular understanding of evolution Wharton challenges is facilitated by a popular ignorance of *The Descent of Man*'s affirmation of reasoning *and* natural selection as the sources of "conscience."

For all her respect for the American realists whose work she read, Wharton believed that "copying can never be a substitute for creative vision" ("Tendencies in Modern Fiction" 171). Her realism extended beyond depicting the material effects of determinism, taking her French masters as its model. In *The Writing of Fiction* she relates how "Balzac was the first not only to see his people, physically and morally, in their habit as they lived [. . .] but to draw his dramatic action as much from the relation of his characters to their houses, streets, towns, professions, inherited habits and opinions, as from their fortuitous contacts with each other" (5). One explanation for Wharton's sensitivity to the presence of social evolution implicit in the hereditary system of values she notes in Balzac is the fact that "she had immersed herself in the skeptical sciences, especially in evolutionary Darwinism, and she understood both manners and morals to be evolved products of slowly altering social and ethical conventions" (Tuttleton "*The Fruit of the Tree*" 165). But even this insightful comment doesn't take one far enough into Wharton's conception of an evolved "manners and morals," for she beheld a biological basis for them.

Interested in more than the metaphors Darwinism offered, she saw its principles alive in the social sphere. Ellen Olenska's will to evade the effects of "inherited habit and opinion," seen in her wish to ignore the instruction offered by "our little social signposts" (AI 122), deviates from a social code that is more than just figuratively related to biology. Wharton read in *The Descent of Man* that

> [t]he development of the moral qualities is a[n] [. . .] interesting and difficult problem. Their foundation lies in the social instincts, including in this term the family ties. These instincts are of a highly complex nature [. . .]. [T]he more important elements for us are love, and the distinct emotion of sympathy. These instincts are not extended to all individuals of the species, but only to those of the same community. As they are highly beneficial to the species, they have in all probability been acquired through natural selection. (391)

In the context of this passage, the stripping of Ellen's blood-based membership in the elite, provoked in part by her European upbringing and her consequent difference, presents her exclusion as the action of "social instincts" that withdraw sympathy when it becomes clear that she is not of the same mind as her putative community. Wharton offered "a much more complicated notion of selfhood and human agency than they [realists] are given credit for" (Thomas 23). One aspect of this notion is the adaptive sociality, functioning as Darwin describes, that banishes Ellen because she is not a member of the community, despite the fact that she is of the same "species" as Archer, something suggested by her blood relation to his group.

Ambivalence toward fiction that lacked an affirmative perspective on the individual's search for meaning beyond the horizon of the normative is evident, too, in Wharton's sympathetic recollection of Henry James's attitude toward naturalism. James, she recalls, noted that in such writing whatever was "smelt, seen, tasted, or touched, was given precedence over moral characteristics" ("Tendencies in Modern Fiction" 171). This recollection of James's opinion on the subject admits the importance of a moral dimension in literature, which in Wharton's fiction is apparent in the response of individuals to that which "seizes the characters in its steely grip, and jiu-jitsus them into the required attitude" (WF 133). In "Henry James in His Letters" she writes that "[f]or him every great novel must first of all be based on a profound sense of moral values ('importance of subject'), and then constructed with a classical unity and economy of means" (144). In *The House of Mirth*, Lily's casting into the fire of Bertha Dorset's letters to Selden is, notwithstanding the important critical work of distancing Wharton from James's formal influence, a Jamesian moment. It is less an impulsive or unpremeditated act as one that is deliberate, the negative consequences of which are clear to Lily even as she acknowledges the potential "triumph" (104) her possession of the letters represents. Although it is evident that Wharton reifies in her work the pessimistic determinism she denigrates in her pronouncements on naturalism, it is the active response to coercive circumstances of characters like Lily Bart, and Charity Royall in *Summer* (1917), that inspires a sense of control, despite the fact that such acts can be self-abnegating.

Looking at the matter from this angle helps to clarify Wharton's statement that "real drama is soul drama" (WF 132). Indeed, acknowledging the role of "soul drama" in her writing can help the reader avoid one interpretive trap in particular. The critic who would see in a fictional lens ground from biology and evolution the belief that for Wharton biological and social determinism are unanswerable, must keep in mind that she tempers her realist "novel[s] of manners" with a sensitivity to less tangible human psychological faculties. This sensitivity results in the depiction of the "crowded stage" of each tale, where a "continual interweaving of individuals with social analysis" (Wegener "Enthusiasm Guided by Acumen" 14) reveals her interest in representing her characters' *desire* to transcend a rigidly determined fate as perhaps the only consolation available to them. This desire is also one way in which a deterministic environment might be transformed.

The narratives I focus on make the case that nature and culture exist on a continuum, and that, similarly, as Wharton wrote, "[e]ach of us flows imperceptibly into adjacent people and things" (qtd. in Wegener "Enthusiasm Guided by Acumen" 6). The theme of interconnectedness is palpable in Wharton's fiction. Natural selection operates in social evolution; instinct and manners, and even fiction and science, are richly connected. Wharton pleads against the central Darwinian principle that "many more individuals of each species are born than can possibly survive" (*Origin* 68), by suggesting that what ought to stand against the ideological reconstruction of unfettered natural selection within a rapacious elite culture in these novels is a collective capacity for reason that can preserve manners, traditions, and rites as stabilizing influences in an increasingly complex civilization. Despite the fact that Wharton is a materialist in her recognition of the realities of class, capital, and labor, the politics of these novels argue—through insisting that agency and choice can buffer natural phenomena—that ideas *and* biology are destiny. The novels attempt to represent and comment on the contemporary emergence into broad consciousness of a "Darwinian ecosystem" (Preston 50), which downplays the potential for individual moral agency. Yet they face great difficulty in suggesting a way to address the social problems that flow from a social Darwinist model of social evolution unwilling to confront the moral questions it generates.

Each of these novels finds that biology and culture are not separate spheres, though such a claim would trouble Wharton's sensitive males: Lawrence Selden, Ralph Marvell and Newland Archer. Before these characters experience passions that will redefine them, they believe something like the following contemporary description of what is currently seen to be an erroneous view of the relation between nature and culture: "Whereas animals are rigidly controlled by their biology, human behavior is determined by culture, an autonomous system of symbols and values" (Pinker qtd. in Dennett 490). The assault by the modern on the assumption that nature and culture are separate results in the exposure of these characters to the fact that "[w]hereas animals are rigidly controlled by their biology, human behaviour is *largely* determined by culture, a *largely* autonomous system of symbols and values, growing from a biological base, but growing indefinitely away from it" (Pinker qtd. in Dennett 491). Wharton's corrective to the view implicit in gentry manners calls for an awareness of biology as an ineradicable element of culture.

Wharton, of course, was not alone in seeing commonalities between nature and society. I have already presented Thorstein Veblen's claim that "[t]he life of man in society, just like the life of other species, is a struggle for existence, and therefore it is a process of selective adaptation. The evolution of the social structure has been a process of natural selection of institutions" (147). The idea bears repeating, for Wharton depicts class as subject to "a process of natural selection" that sustains institutions best suited to a modern political environment favoring the "fierce interplay" (CC 195) of the forces of capitalism. The tension between Mayflower descendants and *arrivistes* is real enough in Wharton's world and in her narratives. But the question of the scientific correctness of figuring intra-class competition as "selection" is unsettled and open to politically motivated interpretation by oligarchs and plutocrats alike.

Joining the spheres of nature and culture in the novels are two kinds of instinct. One is social instinct, which motivates characters who act out behavior scripted by manners. Lily Bart's halfhearted attempts to secure a husband of means, and Newland Archer's happiness in conforming to tradition by marrying May Welland, are two examples of behavior driven by this type. The second type is biological; unconstrained by manners, Undine Spragg personifies it. My analysis of these varieties of instinct finds the sundering of their sociobiological fullness to be one way Wharton signals a gentry division of nature and culture, which short-circuits sexual selection in favor of socially approved matches. Wharton's portraits of a socially mediated concept of instinct establish a broader understanding of it similar, again, to Freud's, who wrote, "The concept of instinct is thus one lying on the frontier between the mental and the physical" (*Three Essays on Sexuality* 83). The novels, however, remain within the Darwinian context in figuratively depicting the borderland between biological materialism and the motivations of social actors.

Two Darwinian concepts Wharton allegorizes are natural selection and sexual selection. Darwin defines natural selection when he writes, "This preservation of favorable variations and the rejection of injurious variations I call Natural Selection" (*Origin* 131). In *The Descent of Man,* he summarizes sexual selection as follows:

> Sexual selection depends on the success of certain individuals over others of the same sex, in relation to the propagation of the species; whilst natural selection depends on the success of both sexes, at all ages, in relation to the general conditions of life. The sexual struggle is of two kinds; in the one it is between the individuals of the same sex, generally the males, in order to drive away or kill their rivals, the females remaining passive; whilst in the other, the struggle is likewise between the individuals of the same sex, in order to excite or charm those of the opposite sex, generally the females, which no longer remain passive, but select the more agreeable partners. (398)

In an undated essay titled "Fiction and Criticism," Wharton offers some insight into the way her understanding of Darwinian principles might be formally signified in her novels:

> The doctrine of 'art for art's sake,' of the fixed gulf between art and ethics, which was enunciated with so much confidence thirty years ago, and is still a terror to the simple-minded critic, was merely a reaction

against the tendency to sacrifice character drawing to a thesis. It cannot be too often repeated that every serious picture of life contains a thesis; what differentiates the literary artist from the professed moralist is not a radical contradiction of purpose, but the fact that one instructs by his observation of character, the other by the general deductions drawn from such observation. [. . .] The novelist ceases to be an artist the moment he bends his characters to the exigencies of a thesis; but he would equally cease to be one, should he draw the acts he describes without regard to their moral significance. (295–96)

The character, or values, of a figure such as Elmer Moffatt in *The Custom of the Country* exhibits his digestion of half-truths about natural and sexual selection at large in the broadening informational context made possible by mass culture. The authorial effort to refine the reader's understanding of Darwin's concepts, however, works from the "thesis" that they are misunderstood. According to Wharton's pronouncement on the need for the fiction writer to be a "moralist" that avoids "deduction," characters must reflect, as they do in the case of Lily Bart, the presence and actions of local "moral complications" (196). Such complications do, in the novels, reflect the broad misapprehension of natural laws, and such complications also iterate a politically invested disparagement of cooperation that receives attention from Wharton's search for the "moral significance" of her subject.

It is possible that Wharton bridges "the fixed gulf between art and ethics" by focusing on the moral significance of the "serious picture of life" she presents, but the question of whether her readers perceived her sociobiological "thesis" with clarity is open. Wharton was, of course, not alone in her desire for sales that would reward her work. American realists and naturalists who were Wharton's contemporaries—William Dean Howells, Henry James and Frank Norris—"[c]ollectively [. . .] fashioned a theory of how to write a novel under the conditions imposed by the mass market in literature" (Borus 10). Wharton was no less compelled by these conditions, as her correspondence with her editors confirms.[18] One obstacle Wharton had to surmount in achieving popular success was what W. D. Howells articulated when he acknowledged that "what the American Public wants is *a tragedy with a happy ending*" (FW 65). Valuable for its snapshot of the way Howells saw the serious writer's predicament, Wharton's reference to his comment in *French Ways and Their Meaning* also demonstrates her concern with the literary tastes of the American reader. These tastes, which made a bestseller of Thomas Dixon's *The Clansman: An Historical Romance of the Ku Klux Clan* (1905) in the same year *The House of Mirth* was published, are not fully accommodated in the three novels examined here; instead, one discovers Lily Bart, Undine Spragg and Ellen Olenska to be subject to misapplied natural laws that cause the elimination of the unfit, the triumph of aggression, and the expulsion of difference respectively. Bender observes that in Wharton's fiction, she faces the dilemma that "[n]atural and sexual selection pose grave threats to liberal ideology, in general—to the ideal of democratic equality and to possible moral or social reform" (4). However, Wharton implies that with knowledge of the biological underpinnings of culture, particularly what she gleaned from *The Descent of Man,* a meaningful collective response to natural and sexual selection is possible. Keeping in mind that "'justice and order,' [. . .] was Edith's chief passion, according to her own notation" (Lewis 388), the overlapping subjects of social equity and natural and sexual selection in the novels were reconcilable through an appeal to Darwin's principles, and her perfect pitch in crafting popular fiction.

Bender's important expression of Wharton's interest in "the threats to liberal ideology" posed by natural and sexual selection focuses her antagonism to Spencer's biological view of human culture. The problem was not Spencer's assumption that nature was operant in culture, but rather that his materialism seemed to demote the potential of human moral agency to mitigate the inequality inherent in natural competition. Nevertheless, one also finds that Wharton was indebted to Spencer for his articulation of mind as

> an adaptive function [that] was also a crucial influence on the development of the pragmatic philosophy and functional psychology of William James and John Dewey. James said that 'few recent formulas have done more real service of a rough sort in psychology than the Spencerian one that the essence of mental life and of bodily life are one, namely, 'the adjustment of inner to outer relations.' (Young "Herbert Spencer's Concept of Evolution" 276)

Insofar as Wharton represents the psychology of her characters by examining the effects upon them of class ideologies, she finds value in William James's statement that Spencer's work is important because he showed that "since mind and its environment have evolved together, they must be studied together" (qtd. in Young "Herbert Spencer's Concept of Evolution" 276).

Spencer's interpretation of Darwin, as I discuss in the upcoming chapters, offered a biological theory that applied to human culture, and provided a way to view social progress as just another natural process. My investigation reveals Wharton's recognition that Spencer's view "was not Darwin's view of evolution—he [Darwin] dismissed the distinction between lower and higher animals as meaningless. [. . .] natural selection is a contingent, short-term process that works with accidental, rather than progressive, variation" (Ridley 3). Social complexity will not be equated with progress in these novels, and Wharton takes aim at the moral authority of Newland Archer's class by painting an unreasoned and ineffectual morality or "niceness" as a "negation" (212) of culturally obscured biological instinct, and by depicting the sacrifice of individuals to a "collective interest" (111) that is portrayed as frivolous. Hence, the narratives render as inadequate, and badly informed in matters of evolutionary ethics, an ideology that does not confront the new elite's biological justification for expansion and dominance.

In *The House of Mirth, The Custom of the Country* and *The Age of Innocence,* the principle of chance, often figured as the speculative economic activities of financiers and industry titans, exists in opposition to a gentry adherence to order and stasis; the nouveaux riches embrace the idea that nature underwrites the relation of the individual to the social collective, and Wharton agrees with this view in a general way. Within this set, accumulation is more valued than philanthropy, and advantage is taken whenever it is glimpsed, as when Simon Rosedale buys "the newly finished house of one of the victims" (HM 121) of a stock-market crash. In *The Custom of the Country* in particular, the aristocratic Marvell, who invites the upstart Undine Spragg into his circle and eventually marries her, does not anticipate that introducing a new species into his environment will result in disaster.

The Dorsets in *The House of Mirth,* and the Marvells and Dagonets in *The Custom of the Country,* obsess over a process of cultural heredity existing in the passing on of rites and values. Newland Archer's distinction between his social sensibilities and his biological instincts exhibits a belief that cultural heredity delivers its ideological content without the potential for mutation that occurs in "coarse" nature. The preoccupation with ritual of these characters, who have slight but significant differences in class affiliation, displaces interest in the plain facts of biological inheritance and the variations it introduces, and the possibility that the inheritance of values is subject to similarly disruptive laws. This attitude appears from Wharton's viewpoint completely to mask an undervalued "naked instinct" (*Letters* 159) that asserts itself in the unfulfilled desire shared by Lily Bart and Lawrence Selden in *The House of Mirth,* and Newland Archer and Ellen Olenska in *The Age of Innocence.*[19] Unsurprisingly, the passion of these characters carries them outside the pale of the permitted, something Wharton makes concrete in the geography of empty houses and distant shores where forbidden expressions of sexuality surface only to be repressed. Acknowledging instinct as an ineradicable facet of culture, Wharton suggests, is a step toward accounting for, and limiting, powerful and disruptive natural laws at work on social groupings.

Clearly, desire is portrayed as an instinctive quality. Sexual longing enters the lives of Selden, Marvell and Archer as in, Wharton commented, "Butler's great novel, 'The Way of All Flesh,' [. . .] [in which Butler deals] soberly but sincerely with the chief springs of human conduct" (WF 50). The reader learns that the symbols of high culture that these characters obsess over signify something utterly true but inaccessible about themselves—their status as biological entities called upon to forge out of primitive energies a coherent society. They are the agents of their class, cleaving to existing "symbols and values," and they possess the tools to refine the forms that shore up an existing order, even if they are unable to. Although it is important to use caution in invoking the book as an indicator of Wharton's attitudes,[20] *French Ways and Their Meaning* (1919) insists that "we should cultivate the sense of continuity, that 'sense of the past' which enriches the present and binds us up with the world's great stabilizing traditions of art and poetry and knowledge" (97). Ideas and instincts are destiny; they form the content of cultural heredity that in turn stabilizes and then upsets the social medium in which ideas are transmitted. These might stand for a time against Veblen's "selective adaptation" of institutions, but the social garden will be populated with new species nevertheless. "Knowledge" is a "stabilizing tradition," but knowledge is contested. Even the science Wharton uses to buttress the significance of "continuity" in stressing the importance of "stabilizing traditions" must face revision.

When one considers Wharton's ability to assert in best-selling novels a biologically informed interpretation of social evolution, her narratives seem directed at moving beyond existing realist practices in terms of method and content. Her attempts to exceed the tools of cultural analysis she inherits from her literary forerunners, moreover, have consequences for our understanding of the cultural politics portrayed in this grouping of novels. These stories demand the dispersal of interpretive tendencies and prejudices they associate with social Darwinism and existing definitions of nature that obfuscate the complexity of biology's interactions with society. Wharton remarked that "intellectual honesty, the courage to look at things as they are, is the first test of mental maturity" (FW 58). As an instructor of "intellectual honesty" to a wide readership, she sets the plank of biology as she understood it[21] into the platform of her fictional efforts to represent class conflict and the reproduction of political ideologies in each new generation of Americans.

Chapter Two
"Blind Inherited Scruples": Lily Bart's Evolutionary Ethics

I. "THE REQUIREMENTS OF THE PUBLIC"

Many readers have noted Wharton's delight, mentioned in *A Backward Glance,* in reading Darwin, Huxley, Haeckel, and other "various popular exponents of the great evolutionary movement" (94), including Herbert Spencer. But her youthful enthusiasm turned to a questioning of Spencer's social Darwinist precepts. This shift calls for a detailed account of *The House of Mirth*'s negative portrayal of social Darwinism's belief in "an accord between moral fitness and the ability to survive" (Beer *Darwin's Plots* 64). Depicting cultural practices that lead to the elimination of unfit individuals such as Lily Bart, the novel questions the position that natural selection and other laws theorized in *The Origin of Species* should be permitted to apply to New York society. Accompanying an often-implicit dialogue with Spencer and, at a further remove, the American social Darwinist William Graham Sumner, are Wharton's frequent allusions in *The House of Mirth* to the writings of Darwin and Huxley. The novel draws too on her knowledge of contemporary books on evolution, which provide a conceptual framework for individual variation of the kind Hildegard Hoeller describes as "Lily's specialization, Rosedale's 'impossibility,' Trenor's 'carnivorous' bestiality, and Gryce's boring mediocrity," which together comprise the novel's "boundaries of race, taste, and morality" (133).[1] *The House of Mirth,* moreover, was composed during a period in which Wharton seemed increasingly occupied with the crucial responsibility of ethical leadership to be carried out by a class that, in her view, had failed to fulfill this role, and this issue is a concern of the novel.

Wharton referred to the damage caused by wealth without responsibility in a letter written shortly after *The House of Mirth* was published:

> New York society is still amply clad, & the little corner of its garment that I lifted was meant to show only that little atrophied organ—the group of idle & dull people—that exists in any big & wealthy social body. If it seems more conspicuous in New York than in an old civilization, it is because the whole social organization with us is so much smaller & less elaborate—& if, as I believe, it is more harmful in its influence, it is because fewer responsibilities attach to money with us than in other societies. (*Letters* 97)

Her observation highlights, with a suggestion of physical and mental feebleness, that the class Selden as a lawyer serves, and is nominally tied to, has defaulted on unnamed responsibilities that "attach to money." Such blitheness has consequences, for what is high can be brought low; alterations to a social environment reconfigured by economic or demographic change may favor a different class. When Selden envisions "the great gilt cage in which they all were huddled for the crowd to gape at" (54), aristocrats become zoological exhibits, and lower-class spectators view the elite social fray from objective heights. The environment in which social evolution occurs is changing, and *it* will determine which class species is fittest; but as Wharton shows, the "atrophied organ of [. . .] idle & dull," its former power of cultural transmission notwithstanding, relaxes control over the environment with the result that the tendrils of change invade the ecosystem of an old order.

The novel's commentary on what is wrong with the excesses permitted by such porous boundaries proceeds through the presentation of Lily Bart's destruction by four elements: her socialization or "training" (HM 301), which creates in her an unbearable "second and abhorrent self [. . .] produced by a patriarchal society and a capitalist economy" that compels her to compete for a wealthy and socially appropriate husband (Showalter "The Death of the Lady (Novelist)" 14), her vulnerability to being "ruthlessly sacrificed" by Bertha Dorset (HM 227), the complex influence of Lawrence Selden and his "republic of the spirit" (HM 68), and an instinctive sensibility that drives Lily's non-adaptive choices, and ultimately resembles Selden's idealistic personal philosophy. Lily's training is especially significant, for it forms part of an education that suppresses "instinctive" tendencies—such as a habit of personal display that never "forsook her" (17), and her emergent morality—which the available modalities for self-interpretation make "obscure" (105).

The novel's diction interleaves the social and the natural, and offers the latter not as an absolute, but as a site of conceptual dispute between different, quite politicized understandings of what should or should not happen in the "great gilt cage" of culture. I focus here on allegories in *The House of Mirth* that demonstrate the ways a biological underpinning of culture complicates the maintenance of a sustainable framework for equality. These allegories make problematic Spencer's biological view of collective human relations and counter it by suggesting that biological determinism must be reckoned with in a way less damaging to the instinctive, yet reasoning, individual. Investigating this set of issues seems particularly relevant given the contradiction evident in my description of Wharton as a writer interested in social and biological determinism, but who also claimed to be a student of a Spencerian sociobiology. Hence, the arguments made here on this subject extend Michael Nowlin's insight that "[o]ne can hardly think of a body of literature more hostile to feminist premises than the social Darwinist sociology and anthropology that Wharton apparently learned so much from" (227). My interpretation of what Wharton might have learned from social Darwinism finds *The House of Mirth* fastening on bad science as both a cause and a correlative of those attitudes in the "big & wealthy social body" she found most damaging.

*   *   *

Although Wharton copied passages from Herbert Spencer's *First Principles* (1875) in her Daybook in the 1890s (Howard 145), by the time she came to compose *The House of Mirth²* her enthusiasm for Spencer's work had evidently faltered. The shift in Wharton's response to popular scientific works of the kind authored by Spencer, one visible in *The House of Mirth*, is also illustrated in her short story "The Descent of Man" (1904), a work whose date aligns it with the novel. The story satirizes the influence on serious intellectual pursuits of the market for popular books, depicting the perilous interaction of an eminent biologist named Professor Linyard with the world of bestsellers. "The Descent of Man" is also an early depiction within Wharton's corpus of the audience for popular books, a subject that appears in *The Custom of the Country*'s detailed representation of mass culture and its effect on its consumers.

"The Descent of Man" portrays a public acceptance of a brand of science made digestible through a suspect synthesis of fact and faith, and a literary marketplace wary of works that offer unadorned truths about the biological origins of life. Such unsweetened facts have the potential to disturb, as Wharton put it, "a public long nurtured on ice-cream soda and marshmallows" ("The Great American Novel" 153). Linyard is a rationalist who "felt within himself that assurance of ultimate justification which, to the man of science, makes a lifetime seem the mere comma between premise and deduction" (DM 360). But he writes a book in which his commitment to the method of "premise and deduction" seems to bend to a popular metaphysics. The sequence of events surrounding this apparent "change of front" (353) is the focus of the story.

The Professor is alarmed at a popularization of science that obscures the difference between facts laboriously attained, and the way such facts are interpreted by newspapers, magazines, and best-selling books that equate science with metaphysics.[3] Linyard notes that "[e]very one now read scientific books and expressed an opinion on them. The ladies and the clergy had taken them up first; now they had passed to the school-room and the kindergarten. Daily life was regulated on scientific principles; the daily papers had their 'Scientific Jottings'" (349). It is not, however, the popularity of a scientific way of thinking Linyard objects to most strenuously:

> The very fact that scientific investigation still had, to some minds, a flavour of heterodoxy, gave it a perennial interest. The mob had broken down the walls of tradition to batten in the orchard of forbidden knowledge. The inaccessible goddess whom the Professor had served in his youth now offered her charms in the market-place. And yet it was not the same goddess after all, but a pseudo-science masquerading in the garb of the real divinity. (349–50)

In discerning an alignment between the "marketplace" and "pseudo-science," the story attributes a misleading quality to representations of scientific fact sponsored by the former. The "flavour of heterodoxy" possessed by "scientific investigation" creates the prospect of strong sales for works that exploit this fact, but the focus imposed on scientific subject matter being framed for popular consumption renders the material unscientific.

In its portrait of how the predilections of a spiritualized public that has seized on science affect what passes for fact, "The Descent of Man" defines one objection Wharton has to popular interventions into the realm of the specialist. Yet she was herself one of those "ladies" that read scientific books, though her reading was perhaps more rigorous than that of the women disparaged by Linyard. "The Descent of Man" thus invites one to ask whether the signs of Wharton's intense interest in science are those of a specialist's attempt to create a higher standard for mass-culture products such as her own serialized novels, and to what extent she sought to counter the trend noted by the protagonist of her story. That these related questions raise issues pertinent to the novels I discuss is augmented by a claim made by Gaillard Lapsley, Wharton's close friend and literary executor, who in an unfinished introduction to her critical writings wrote that she "disliked & disbelieved in metaphysics" (qtd. in Wegener "Enthusiasm Guided by Acumen" 43).

Wharton found herself in the position of reconciling her low opinion of metaphysics with the tastes of her audience, whose belief in religion and simultaneous interest in science are carefully reproduced in "The Descent of Man." Hence, one can also assign Linyard's lack of sympathy for "pseudo-science" to his creator. Wharton's intolerance of such thought is further evident in her comment that "[t]ranscendentalism owes much of its perennial popularity to a reverence for the unintelligible, and its disciples are largely recruited from the class of readers who consider it as great an intellectual feat to read a book as to understand it" ("The Vice of Reading" 103). In the story's disapproving depiction of the interpretation of science through the prism of faith, and the seductive compensations of a market unsympathetic to Linyard's wish to write a "real book" (362), "The Descent of Man" foreshadows the challenges faced by Wharton in achieving commercial success on her terms. Among these challenges was her wish to reach a wide audience with "real books," that critically addressed popular "pseudo-science" with a reductive materialism. This materialism rejected metaphysics, positively valued the pursuit of truth through science, and yet questioned the terms of Spencer's desire to find "for the principles of right and wrong a scientific basis" in evolutionary theory (qtd. in McCosh 607),[4] which granted insufficient credence to the possibility of an evolved moral faculty.

In her story "The Descent of Man," Wharton defined specific problems posed by non-professional science for achieving a clear articulation of how nature and culture interact. Examples of the kind of thinking Linyard attacks in the story can be found in Spencer's work itself. In *First Principles*, the book from which Wharton copied passages in the 1890s, Spencer argues that "a civilized society is made unlike a barbarous one by the establishment of regulative classes" (317). Spencer's reasoning is of interest here for Wharton's exception in "The Descent of Man" and *The House of Mirth* to the methodology Spencer exhibits in the passage.

To make the case that the establishment of "regulative classes" will result in "a civilized society," Spencer moves from the microscopic biological level to a broad sociological perspective by first describing how the mammalian embryo is reliant upon nutrition supplied by surrounding tissue. This is, we are told, an illustration of the way "organisms are made dependent on one another" (315). Spencer's observation echoes Darwin's point that plants and animals "are bound together by a web of complex relations" (*Origin* 124–25). In *First Principles,* Spencer's description of the primitive dependency of organisms on one another naturalizes hierarchies, as the argument describes the workings of dependency among more complex animals. This is evident in Spencer's statement that "creatures who hunt in packs, or that have sentinels, or that are governed by leaders, form bodies partially united by cooperation" (315). As Spencer moves in his discussion from lower to higher organisms, his anthropomorphism surfaces in words such as "governed" and "cooperation," which accent instinctive behavior with the vernacular of human politics, making his description of non-human mammalian behavior inexact. Higher organisms, humans among them, naturally sort themselves out by competence, according to this reasoning. In 1884 Spencer's American counterpart, the social Darwinist William Graham Sumner, was more assertive: "we see that so soon as the exigencies of life are felt, men are differentiated according to their power to cope with them into 'better' or 'worse' with reference to personal and social value" ("Sociological Fallacies" 578). Civilized society, in Spencer's account, is natural to the extent that it reflects mutual dependency, but Spencer's conclusion that the appearance of "regulative classes" makes "a civilized society" unlike a "barbarous one" is countered in *The House of Mirth,* where what defines and maintains classes is destructive to Lily Bart.

Wharton's literary reiteration of an ecological model of class relations derived from Darwin reenacts Spencer's methodology of drawing parallels between natural and social processes, but does not draw the conclusion that progress toward "regulative classes" might protect *The House of Mirth*'s protagonist. Lily's trials depict a society that has not incorporated one of Darwin's key points: "[l]et it be borne in mind how infinitely complex and close-fitting are the mutual relations of all organic beings to each other and to their physical conditions of life" (*Origin* 130). It is in the phrase "mutual relations" that an ethical dimension lurking in *The Origin of Species* awaits fuller articulation in Darwin's *The Descent of Man.* Wharton's depiction of the applicability of Darwin's comment about mutual relations bends biological theory to social commentary, dramatizing her subject in terms that would present a positive alternative to the dispersive effects on interdependence wrought by wealth without responsibility, and by an aristocratic denial of instinct.

"The Descent of Man," punning on the title of Darwin's work as it depicts collective intellectual decline, goes on to relate the genesis of the Professor's reply to the "pseudo-science" that he finds so ubiquitous in American culture:

> This false goddess had her ritual and her literature. She had her sacred
> books, written by false priests and sold by millions to the faithful.
> [. . .] they filled him with mingled rage and hilarity. [. . .] the hilar-
> ity remained, and flowed into the form of his idea. And the idea [. . .]
> was simply that he should avenge his goddess by satirizing her false
> interpreters. (350)

Linyard's new work will be "a skit on the 'popular' scientific book; [. . .] it
should be the trumpet-blast bringing down the walls of ignorance, or at least
the little stone striking the giant between the eyes" (350). To realize this goal
he takes the completed manuscript to Ned Harviss, an old friend who has
become one of the nation's "purveyors of popular literature" (350). Further
revealing the story's juxtaposition of profitable faith and less remunerative
fact, Harviss "looked as if he had been fattened on popular fiction; and his
fat was full of optimistic creases" (351).

   Wharton's production of popular novels[5] that exploit the popularity of
science becomes interpretable as an act of social intervention when one recognizes how in "The Descent of Man" she portrays the ability of the market
to undermine "the objective faculty" (WF 78) that is as important to the scientist as it is for Wharton the novelist. The tale retains the virtue of "objectivity" by characterizing the audience who make Linyard's book a
blockbuster as inferior, and by containing Linyard's satire within its own.
Wharton critically brings to the attention of her audience their own tastes,
though it is also arguable that she would have thought her readers different
from the more credulous consumers of popular writing depicted in her story.
In considering *The House of Mirth* from this angle, though, one senses the
need for an assessment of whether Wharton made compromises similar to
those entered into by Professor Linyard, who believed that the "elect would
understand; the crowd would not" (354). I want to suggest that in *The House
of Mirth* Wharton attempts to negotiate this strait between the demands of
the market and her belief that the serious novelist is an agent of cultural
change.

   During the initial meeting between author and publisher, Harviss, not
having read the manuscript, suggests that Linyard take it to an educational
house, adding that "[y]ou're a little *too* scientific for us. We have a big sale for
scientific breakfast foods, but not for the concentrated essences" (360).
When he does read Linyard's book, its satire evades him. Harviss, instead,
sees unlimited commercial potential in the work. In welcoming the Professor
for their second meeting he exclaims, "I don't know when I've had a bigger
sensation [. . .] you've brought it so exactly to the right shop" (352). Harviss

takes the book to be Linyard's "apologia—your confession of faith, I should call it" (352). What makes the book a potential bestseller in Harviss's opinion is that it is "full of hope and enthusiasm; it's written in the religious key" (354). This scene resonates with Wharton's call in *The House of Mirth,* and other novels, for the modification of an American "hope and enthusiasm" that, ironically, extirpates Lily Bart, elevates the atavistic Undine Spragg in *The Custom of the Country,* and in *The Age of Innocence* expels Ellen Olenska, despite her understanding that personal relations cannot evade social control. Wharton's depiction of the marketplace's fact-altering purveyance of a national ethos of progressive improvement indebted to spiritual faith is thus an element of her fiction one can trace to the period immediately prior to the publication of *The House of Mirth.*

When Linyard finally overcomes Harviss's belief that the book represents a "shifting" of "stand-point" (353) and reveals to the publisher "the very core of the joke" (353), Harviss reacts by saying, "I don't pretend to be up in such recondite forms of humour" (353). Such satire, to a man who claims to "represent the Average Reader" (354), lies beyond the margin of intelligibility. As Harviss's eye for opportunity adjusts its focus, he suggests that the author not "insist on an ironical interpretation" (354). The "book is susceptible of another" reading (354), something proven by Harviss's initial reaction. Claiming that the work "is just on the line of popular interest," he convinces Linyard that "it'll sell like a popular novel if you'll let me handle it in the right way" (354). The Professor agrees, and the book, now titled *The Vital Thing,* goes to market.

Wharton perceived that the expansion of mass culture constituted a threat not only to the authority of literature, but also to the integrity of fiction's capacity to express the private voice. She retreats, via panoramic social chronicles, from "the nightmare weight of the cinema close-up" (BG 97) that makes a fetish of the individual at the expense of representing the social bond. Her comment on the way a "universal facility of communication" ("The Great American Novel" 154) erodes idiosyncrasies, and makes society as a fictional subject difficult to depict, also suggests that in her writing the cultural work of literature and the reader's capacity to become critically aware of his or her world are connected. "[O]nly when mediocrity has achieved universal diffusion," she writes, "does it become completely unpaintable" ("The Great American Novel" 154) and, one imagines, invisible to author and reader alike.

Wharton's satire in "The Descent of Man" on works in which "ancient dogma and modern discovery were depicted in close embrace under the lime-lights of hazy transcendentalism" (DM 350) depicts Linyard's own mock-metaphysics as being subverted through misinterpretation by popular taste. Yet the story is noteworthy too for its foreordination of Wharton's narrative practice in one of her most commercially successful novels, for the tonal darkness of *The House of Mirth* obviates the connection in *The Vital Thing* between bestseller status and the optimistic tone favored by the publisher of this tale within a tale. While "The Descent of Man" and *The Vital Thing* are both satirical, Wharton dissuades her reader from interpreting the former as a parable of a morally barren science in which "the recantation of an eminent biologist, whose leanings had hitherto been supposed to be toward a cold determinism" (355) marks a victory for irrational metaphysics. She blocks this reading by equating such faith with a superficial, selfish philosophy that caters to a public ready to follow the reasoning of writers like Spencer.

The House of Mirth reveals the author to be faced with a conundrum similar to Linyard's desire to take issue with the misrepresentation of how one arrives at facts when practicing science. There, Wharton depicts the social Darwinism that extinguishes the unfit Lily Bart as one result of a popular misinterpretation of natural selection that has become a cultural tenet. To make her point, though, Wharton must negotiate with the market for her work, a market represented by men like Harviss. To succeed, she redacts unsentimental biological interpretations of social relations that would otherwise be perceived to run against the grain of popular scientism, relying in the process on established modes of popular fiction to increase the palatability of her product.

Of course, sales of *The Vital Thing* are strong. The book is compared by Harviss with the "'How-To-Relax' series, and they sell way up in the millions. [. . .] he drew the Professor a supplementary cheque" (358). Once a solitary walker in the pursuit of truth, Linyard becomes a celebrity:

> Presently his head began to figure in the advertising pages of the magazines. Admiring readers learned the name of the breakfast-food in use at his table, of the ink with which 'The Vital Thing' had been written. [. . .] These confidences endeared the Professor to millions of readers, and his head passed in due course from the magazine and the newspaper to the biscuit-tin and the chocolate-box. (360)

Linyard eventually feels the pull of his real work. The Professor proposes a serious scientific book to Harviss, but the publisher refers to it as "a little harmless amusement. When you want more cash come back to us" (362). The story ends with the Professor's decision to put off for six months the scientific study he wants to write. Instead, he'll do another volume for Harviss, which will be included in a boxed set with *The Vital Thing* that "will take tremendously in the holidays" (362). Although this rational man justifies the decision to himself when he muses, "I can do better work when I get my new instruments" (363), the reader is left with the sense that the Professor's scientific career is over.

Echoing her protagonist, Wharton had rigorous standards regarding intellectual integrity, but she also believed that "[t]he greatest writers have made concessions (if unconsciously, yet inevitably) to the requirements of the public" (qtd. in Wegener "Enthusiasm Guided by Acumen" 25). Whether or not she made concessions that inadvertently rendered the sociobiological aspect of her fictional social analysis illegible is a question that, in being addressed, can illustrate the extent to which Wharton's desire to change her culture was overshadowed by the marketplace in which she labored. The "microscopist" (DM 355) of "The Descent of Man" understands his scientific pursuits to comprise social action as well. Linyard the scientist takes "a sociological view of his case, and modestly regarded himself as a brick in that foundation on which the state is supposed to rest" (348). Like the author, Linyard associates the pursuit of unalloyed fact with political action. In this way, the tale grants the seriousness of its protagonist's dilemma, one that is also Wharton's, in being faced by a "gross crowd" (DM 350) whose avid consumption of mysticized science represents a turning away from a reinforcement of the state's foundation through the pursuit of truth. Like Wharton, Linyard looks up from his loom to take the measure of his readers: "[f]rom this first inspection of the pattern so long wrought over from behind, it was natural to glance a little farther and seek its reflection in the public eye" (349). This passage is similar to an observation Wharton shared with Bernard Berenson regarding the "wonderful sensation [. . .] [felt] when one comes out from behind the [. . .] frame of the story-teller, [to see] that one's picture lives to other lives [. . .] the picture so blindly woven from the back of the frame" (*Letters* 398). The difficulties in addressing the mass market for fiction that Wharton perceived in the "reflection in the public eye" called for a careful and programmatic use of the scientific knowledge that would carry her social criticism to a reading public which took its fact with a strong dose of fancy.

II. "NEVER DO A NATURAL THING"

I have argued that Wharton was a serious reader of Darwin,[6] and that she gleaned from his work certain implications for interrelations amongst species, which she transforms into interrelations amongst classes. I want also to propose that her depictions of class competition between the gentry and socioeconomic elite dramatize a statement made in Darwin's masterwork: "[a]s species of the same genus have usually, though by no means invariably, some similarity in habits and constitution, and always in structure, the struggle will generally be more severe between species of the same genus, when they come into competition with each other, than between species of distinct genera" (*Origin* 127). *The House of Mirth* laments the impediments to a symbiotic model of interrelatedness between different species of the elite at odds with a contractual view of relations that finds human feeling is converted to a mode in which a "mutual accommodation" (HM 259) is the gold standard for conduct. Wai-Chee Dimock has shown convincingly that fair play is not part of the deal. Dimock argues that in *The House of Mirth,*

> [b]usiness, in the social world, operates by what we might call the commodification of social intercourse. Everything has a price, must be paid for, just as—on the opposite end—everything can be made to 'count as' money, to be dealt out and accepted in lieu of cash. Dispensed in this manner, social gestures lose their initial character and figure only as exchange values. (784)

Scratch the surface of the novel's presentation of Lily acknowledging her debt to Gus Trenor—and paying it despite the fact that this act impoverishes her—and one finds in the misery that results a negative judgment of the lost character of "social gestures" positively represented in Nettie Struther's rescue of Lily late in the novel. The competition Wharton attends to finds species of the same genus (bodied forth in the novel as interbreeding classes of elites) struggling for resources in a setting defined in part by a commodified and reformulated cooperative impulse. It should be noted, too, that Wharton in this way participates in sentimental fiction's tradition of attributing moral sensibility to the feminine, by continually illustrating that her "characters are products of their inner feelings" (Hoeller 25). These feelings, particularly in the case of Lily Bart, are qualified as natural, right, and beyond criticism by their grounding in Darwinism.

A strict adherence to a brutal mode of social relations will not address the moral dilemmas the novel presents. Lily is less a person with a soul than a woman constructed by her context as a biological entity. She has fallen afoul of a social Darwinist belief in its own program, one evident in D. D. McCosh's 1898 statement that "as the fittest, [social Darwinism's philosophy] will survive, and as a force will persist till it brings all the [sociocultural] environments in accordance with it" (607); her extinction is a function not just of natural selection, but also of its unanalyzed acceptance as a model for social relations. The novel's biologizing metaphors and allusions, therefore, represent faithfully a zeitgeist formed in part by "Mr. Herbert Spencer's philosophy," which *The House of Mirth* presents as what Wharton elsewhere termed "the popular superstition" ("George Eliot" 73). Confronting the reconfiguration of individuals as organisms, she holds out to her audience a portrait of an atypical character whose fate is consistent with a popular understanding of biological and social fitness, but she also describes the damage to individuals caused by allowing Spencer's "philosophy" to foster a radical *laissez-faire* shirking of its consequences.

The biological characterization of Lily the story develops, and describes as an activity of the environment she occupies, conforms to the views of those who might believe in "the popular superstition" *and* demonstrates the abandonment of moral social relations by those who merely look on as Lily fails. But in staying true to social Darwinist imperatives by permitting Lily to spiral toward her end, the dictates of gentry manners limit her power of sexual selection. Lily, it seems, cannot *fully* be an "organism." Selden's heightened consciousness contrasts with Lily's nature, which is multifaceted in being socially conditioned to pursue a place in the preserve of the elites, and in driving her desire for a life unconstrained by the tradeoffs that accompany her training, which compels her to "marry the first rich man she could get" (84). She demurs marriage, and her rejection of a string of potential husbands manifests a variation from standard ideology. In Preston's view, Lily is a "non-viable mutation" (51). This insight reveals Wharton's Darwinian metaphor, and leaves for others the examination of her defining mixture of evolutionary theory and sociological interests; for it is in depicting the expediency of thinking that natural selection is applicable to human collectives that Wharton shows its political dimension. This mixture views a Spencerian interpretation of evolutionary theory as supporting cultural attitudes that permit Lily to be viewed as disposable; and it is Wharton's fictional sociobiology that makes visible the popular interpretation of scientific theories as an activity that affects individual lives.

Alluding initially to the Malthusian principle of excess population so useful to Darwin in formulating his theory of natural selection, and thereby aligning her social analysis with biological science, Wharton characterizes her brand of tragedy in an introduction to the 1936 Oxford edition of *The House of Mirth,* as focusing on lost opportunities for intervention by the privileged into the conditions that destroy Lily Bart:

> The fact is that nature, always wasteful, and apparently compelled to
> create dozens of stupid people in order to produce a single genius, seems
> to reverse the process in manufacturing the shallow and the idle. Such
> groups always rest on an underpinning of wasted human possibilities;

and it seemed to me that the fate of the persons embodying these possibilities ought to redeem my subject from insignificance. This is the key to *The House of Mirth,* and its meaning; and I believe the book has owed its success, from the first, as much to my picture of the slow disintegration of Lily Bart as to the details of the 'conversation piece' of which she forms the central figure. ("Introduction to *The House of Mirth*" 266)

Here, "wasteful" nature manufactures many who are "shallow" and who might otherwise create the conditions wherein "possibilities" such as those possessed by Lily would not result in her death. In rendering Lily's vulnerability and extermination, Wharton depicts with intense irony the rotten fruits to be harvested from the promulgation of social Darwinist views. That the novel's ending confirms the efficacy of the social mechanisms it depicts places Lily's fate in concord with the spirit of her times.

As Wharton presents it, tragedy is a diminished aesthetic category that in the novel's contemporary setting contrasts minimally with a social world wherein natural selection is unhindered by decaying social controls. The context in which the trampling of a "rare flower" (317) like Lily elicits a sense of loss is out of phase with the teleology of social progress that includes the idea that only the fittest should survive. This is a prospective, cautionary narrative thread, for the book's audience did find the story at least incipiently tragic, a fact evident in a review in *Spectator* which suggests Lily is "a figure which has at least the possibilities of a tragedy in it" (*Reviews* 113). If the social Darwinist ethos relies on only half the evolutionary story by ignoring the significant role of cooperation in human adaptability, as Wharton maintains, social Darwinism must be discouraged. Even as her fiction negotiates with popular ideas about evolution by partly validating social Darwinism (Lily is unsuited to her environment and does perish), it coexists with psychological textual spaces in which Wharton offers individual volition and imagination as a path away from the domination of reason by nature. Although Wharton refers to the novel as "a simple and fairly moving domestic tragedy" ("Introduction to *The House of Mirth*" 267), her comment understates her ambition for the book in this thematic area, which is to upset the truism, as she wrote, that "traditions and conventions were unassailed, and tacitly regarded as unassailable" ("Introduction to *The House of Mirth*" 268).

Nancy Bentley's insights about manners as agents of coercive force safeguarding tradition, which were discussed in chapter one (*The Ethnography of Manners* 70), enable one to view Lawrence Selden's preoccupation with social forms as playing a causative role in his interpretation that Lily's every move is part of a "carefully-elaborated plan" (5). His expectations regarding

Lily's wishes mislead him; he knows that she must marry to survive, but he doesn't comprehend her desire to do the "natural thing" (15). Lily wants to choose whom to love. She tells Selden that in being compelled to find a rich husband, "she despises the things she's trying for" (189). In this way, Lily reacts to traditions and values that direct the reader's attention to the imperfection of Selden's world. He, though, interprets even Lily's weeping "as an art" (72), and could "never be long with her without trying to find a reason for what she was doing" (11) because "his own view of her was [. . .] colored by any mind in which he saw her reflected" (159). But where Selden conventionally sees Lily as a grasping and artful marriageable woman, she "had never been able to understand the laws of the universe which was so ready to leave her out of its calculations" (27), illustrating her assumption that nature and her social world, the latter of which she understands as her "universe," are coterminous.

Juxtaposed with Selden's opinion of Lily is her sense that she is, by the novel's end, "rootless and ephemeral, mere spindrift of the whirling surface of existence" (319). The "exchanges of the drawing-room" do a disservice to them both; social forms displace instinct, yet Selden has little understanding that their functioning denies him a part of himself. Acted upon by these same exchanges, Lily is badly served by the formal social categories of wife, mistress, and worker that standard ideology makes available. The coercive force Bentley assigns to manners polices a blue-blooded ordering of not only female sexuality, but self-awareness as well.

This claim can be tested by considering whether Lily behaves in ways ruinous to her social self when doing so fulfills her sexual will, something that often results in admonition. "Why could one never do a natural thing without having to screen it behind a structure of artifice" (15), Lily wonders as she lies unconvincingly to Rosedale about the reason for her visit to Selden's apartment building. Her first impulse checked, she almost regrets being with Selden in his apartment. Yet her desire to engage in "intercourse" with Selden (88), to enact the "imperishable flame" of her love for him (309), or serially to reject potential husbands, is not entirely modified by social considerations that are repressive when they are concerned with the fact that a woman must marry. Lily resists having her habit of "measuring distances and drawing conclusions with all the accuracy needful of [. . .] [her] welfare" (115) reformulated by the demands of her "training and experience" (16). But it is for the welfare of a self apart from the demands of her social world that she seems concerned. The marriage market would break her desire to evolve, and confine Lily's definition of what is best for her to "marrying well." However, her urge to fulfill her nature is signified by the word

"Beyond!" on her signet ring, which implores her to do the "natural thing" so problematic in her social environment.

The word "Beyond!" hints at Lily's belief in another state of being. The Lamarckian notion that behavioral adaptation can produce physical changes that subsequent generations inherit is an idea Erasmus Darwin, the grandfather of Charles Darwin, considered some years before Lamarck in *Zoonomia* (1794, 1796). Erasmus Darwin wrote that "all animals undergo transformations which are in part produced by their own exertions, in response to pleasures and pains, and many of these acquired forms or propensities are transmitted to their posterity" (qtd. in White and Gribbin 44). Lily undergoes her own transformation in becoming aware of her innate moral sense, but she does not survive to reproduce. Within the framework of adaptation, Lily's morality is an unfavorable trait. The fact of her childlessness, particularly given her great beauty and ability to attract potential mates, indicates antipathy in her world to renewal or change along the lines her behavior and statements advocate. In this antipathy one detects what can be termed cultural selection, for values, and even attitudes, are a determinative part of her environment.

Along with depictions of Lily's psychology as an unviable variation that will not be passed down to a new generation, *The House of Mirth* often depicts her as a biological entity compelled to move in a human social world where she

> was less to blame than she believed. Inherited tendencies had combined with early training to make her the highly specialized product she was: an organism as helpless out of its narrow range as the sea-anemone torn from the rock. She had been fashioned to adorn and delight; to what other end does nature round the rose-leaf and paint the hummingbird's breast? And was it her fault that the purely decorative mission is less easily and harmoniously fulfilled among social beings than in the world of nature? (301)

Being "torn" from her native environment endangers Lily the "sea-anemone." The Darwinian assertion that "[n]atural selection did not demand that life continually progress, only that animals anchor themselves into niches" (Desmond 258–59) finds its analogue in Lily's "narrow range," which is disappearing. Her difficulties signify, in the novel's cultural politics, a failure of the organizing principles, viewed in the passage as unnatural, created by the "social beings" amongst whom she lives. Wharton juxtaposes the battleground of New York society, where inter-species and intra-species competition is a philosophy of life, with the "world of nature" in which Lily might otherwise survive, rendering a culture shaped by social Darwinism artificial. The phrase "fashioned to adorn and delight" reflects an overlapping biological and social determinism in which her manufacture by "social beings" through "early training" combines with her "inherited tendencies" to demonstrate the inseparability of nature and culture, despite the flaws of her training. Gentry social codes might resist this implication, but they are undermined by the novel's blurring—through figurative language in which Lily is a "rose leaf," among other things—of the lexical distinctiveness of the word "heredity" in social and biological contexts. Wharton writes a biological lesson into the signifying manners of social heredity, demonstrating that "social training" denervates Lily by blocking her sense of herself as an "organism." Thus desensitized, Lily's adaptive morality is debarred, or "torn," from the social setting.

Carol Singley states that there exists in Wharton's fiction a "moral dimension" (*Matters of Mind and Spirit* 6). To the critic who reviewed *The House of Mirth* for *Outlook* in 1905, Wharton seemed to have "escaped the danger of setting up moral sign-posts on the road, and [to have] given her novel a concentrated and tragic moral significance" (*Reviews* 111). Her system of evolutionary metaphor displaces into the terms of scientific discourse a moral analysis of "fashionable New York" (BG 207) intent on showing the damage to the social fabric wrought by a class possessed with great resources, but no sense of social responsibility. Wharton's clothing of "[a] world in which such things could be" (HM 27) in metaphors and language grounded in evolutionary thought does the cultural work of "moral sign-posts" without being overtly moralistic.

The House of Mirth's representation of the social determinism that guides Lily Bart toward her fate is a central feature of a novel intent on showing how a "frivolous society" debases "people and ideas" (BG 207), associating such debasement with the favorable valuation of ruthlessness in business and personal relations which flows from the capitalist viewpoint the novel details. Underwriting this perspective is a fixed idea about the primacy of nature over culture. The view held by Selden and his class, that nature and culture are separate spheres, errs in its belief that the latter does not derive from biology; conversely, the view of the socioeconomic elite that nature is a model for culture, or might just make culture in its image, regardless of efforts to the contrary, is also misguided from the perspective the novel proposes. The resulting representation of a stratified New York condemns and satirizes a materialism that diminishes socially useful abstractions like equality. This was recognized by another contemporary reviewer who commented on how "[i]t seems to me that she creates a very high ideal by her masterly presentation of the absence of all ideals" (*Reviews* 119).

The novel converts into literary capital a turn-of-the-century fascination with popular Darwinism by using evolutionary and biological metaphors. There are nearly thirty instances in *The House of Mirth* of the word "instinct," or a variant of it. Over a dozen uses of "inheritance" or "inherit" accrue, conflating class values and capital—both of which are passed from one generation to the next—with biological heredity. This mixing of social and biological registers facilitates Wharton's dissolution of a division between nature and culture in the reader's mind, the latter of which, again, might seem to align the novel's perspective with the object of its criticism. *The House of Mirth,* though, combines the social and biological through allegory: that is, random occurrences like Lily's encounter with Rosedale outside the *Benedick* represent chance variations in nature. Lily's social progress, such as it is, suffers reversals at many points; in this minor way her experience suggests goal-directed change in the sphere of human relations is more fanciful than factual. Lily's bad luck at cards and her decision to drink the chloral despite "the one chance in a hundred" doing so might kill her (322) denotes the ineradicable presence of the accidental. Chance is a constituent of ordered, upper-class New York despite the fact that gentry ideology sees contingency as intolerable. Wharton's realistic presentation of social mores contests that a "frivolous society" ignores the possibility that an absence of ideals is an absence of knowledge of a possible material basis of ethics.

That Lily views her world from a perspective anchored in the material world is clear. She sees different character types as "species" (49); in a strong invocation of natural selection, she admits to the belief that "a slowly accumulated past lives in the blood" of her parents (319). The psychology of individuals, moreover, is made up of "inherited passions" (319) that suggest a tie between emotional makeup and biological heredity. Something similar to what the biologist E. O. Wilson calls "gene-culture coevolution" (136), wherein the "two forms of evolution are linked" (138), is present in a rough way in the organic metaphors that describe Lily, and the way they draw her social milieu as a "whirling surface of existence" (HM 319) subject to unpredictable natural selection. It is not poverty from which the heroine turns "with the greatest shrinking," but "inner destitution" (318) and the sense that she is "mere spindrift [. . .], without anything to which the poor little tentacles of self could cling before the awful flood submerged them" (319). Although it is the narrative's objective, omniscient register that most often describes Lily in evolutionary terms, even Selden (reader of Spencer that he is) feels "how highly specialized she was" (5).

The novel also articulates how Lily's evolutionary ethics lie at the base of her negation of the marriage market. This makes her self-sabotage in the nuptial sweepstakes an assertive act that exhibits the same confounding set of "inherited resistances, of taste, of training, of blind inherited scruple" (104) that causes her to feel "disgust" and a sense "of personal contamination" when faced with the opportunity of destroying Bertha Dorset by using her letters to Selden. Her "training" infiltrates and nearly obscures, quite normatively, Lily's cooperative impulse. This passage also sets bio-ethical "inherited resistances [. . .] blind inherited scruple" against socio-ethical inheritance, which is, as Wharton has it, a negation of tolerance and equality. Lily's "resistances," in this reading, are another manifestation of her extra-conscious impulsivity, and so resemble "the blind motions of her mating instinct" (319) that cause her rejection of the socially perfect, but otherwise unsuitable, Percy Gryce. Yet even the man who knows her best miscalculates the motivation of her behavior.

The House of Mirth relates that "[i]n judging Miss Bart, he [Lawrence Selden] had always made use of the 'argument from design'" (5). The argument from design, of course, perceives in the complexity of nature proof of God's existence. In Selden's application of this argument to Lily, her complexity proves to him the omnipotence of the social conditioning to which she is subjected, which in his eyes is all-powerful. But as with the argument from design, which, as now, was used to refute natural selection,[7] there is a better explanation for Lily's behavior. Selden attributes to her training Lily's pursuit of what she has been conditioned to want, but when she responds to his vision of freedom "from money, from poverty, from ease and anxiety, from all the material accidents" (68), he does not recognize that what from his perspective is an ideal is in accord with her adaptive though as yet unfelt values. The suggestion that Lily's moral dimension is the result of natural selection strikes the believer in the autonomy of culture from nature as odd, but Darwin does connect the two when he ruminates over "[t]he development of the moral qualities [which] is a[n] [. . .] interesting and difficult problem. Their foundation lies in the social instincts" (*Descent* 391).

Lily initially seems divorced by her training from the "social instincts" that might foster cooperation. She states that her idea of success is "to get as much as one can out of life" (68). Prompted by Selden, though, her instinctive values cause her to repay Gus Trenor, and to refuse to blackmail Bertha Dorset. These values encounter a debasing society that discards unfit individuals. At the head of this newly viable grouping are opportunistic speculators and industrialists. The hereditary elites and members of the gentry encounter the *arrivistes* at the "vast impersonal Van Osburgh 'crushes'" where increasingly indistinct class

lines blur (16). Characters such as Gus Trenor and Simon Rosedale, although
they are from very different backgrounds, and treat Lily quite differently,[8]
possess attitudes reminiscent of J. P. Morgan's statement: "I owe the public
nothing" (qtd. in Morris 30), which though true from a strictly legal perspective in which the corporation is responsible to its shareholders only, denigrates the "development of the moral qualities." Inattentiveness to the
political consequences of "wealth without responsibility" parches the moral
climate. Five years before the novel was published, Wharton scribbled in a
notebook a line regarding Gus Trenor: "[he] dreaded ideas as much as he
dreaded contagious diseases; not that he had ever caught any" ("Donnée
Book 1902"), showing that in her early thinking, Trenor was politically disengaged. Even the thoughtful Selden, though, can't apprehend Lily accurately. Wharton's association of an anti-Darwinian argument from design
with Selden's perspective on Lily reveals him to embrace faulty explanations
of reality. His irresponsibly casual and consequential intermixing of biology
and standards for social relations stands as an authorial condemnation of relativistic class values, which loom starkly when Lily loses her social standing
because it is "convenient to be on good terms" with Bertha Dorset (226),
who is jealous of her husband's affection for Lily.

Wharton's reference to evolution in the context of human social relations results in a literary sociobiology that complicates the idea of moral and
material progress. A 1905 review of the novel recognized her refusal to sustain the progressive note of a forward-looking nation that equated evolution
with advancement toward perfection, remarking that "Mrs. Wharton makes
no concession to the optimistic mood which is supposed to dominate American readers" (*Reviews* 112). Writing, without conceding to such optimism,
for an audience with an inexact understanding[9] of vital aspects of Darwin's
ideas, meant that Wharton had to confront and dispatch erroneous thinking
on the subject. *The House of Mirth* does so by explicitly depicting the dilettantish Selden analyzing Lily in terms analogous to the argument from
design, terms in which he attributes her complexity to the milieu that he
thinks made her. He also repeatedly demonstrates his belief that nature only
exists in culture as an imaginative construct, as when he notes that "the syl-
van freedom in her [Lily's] nature [. . .] lent such a savour to her artificiality" (13). Selden doesn't recognize that Lily has been only partially subdued
by her socialization, and that her "artificiality" is her naturalness misappre-
hended. The novel portrays this misreading of Lily (and its dependence on
Selden's belief that culture is a human invention insulated from nature), even
as it exploits the familiar application of Darwin's work to society so it can
offer an alternative to Selden's view. The effect of this, though it is perhaps

too subtle to register on a reader laboring under misconceptions regarding Darwin's thought, is to demonstrate that the elite are out of touch with the social implications of evolution.

*   *   *

Defining the role in her fiction of Wharton's scientific interests can show the limits of existing criticism of *The House of Mirth*. Elizabeth Ammons argues convincingly that "[p]art of the point of *The House of Mirth* [. . .] is to dramatize how perfectly trained she [Lily] is for the important job society expects her to serve as some rich man's wife" (31). Ammons's discussion of the novel takes up "the predatory economics and sexual politics" (35) that she finds evident, for example, in the crucial episode between Lily and Gus Trenor. While Ammons writes of Lily's failed opportunities to marry that "she does not want to be owned by any man" (35), her feminist perspective is unconcerned with the source of Lily's refusals, seeing as self-evident Lily's resistance to patriarchal institutions. Ammons interprets Lily's actions as hesitance toward entering into relationships in which she is "powerless" (35), but Lily's powerlessness to enact her instinctive tendencies, especially her sexuality, needs also to be considered in theorizing about Lily's attitudes and behavior.

Although the novel encourages Ammons's reading insofar as it portrays the negative effects of marriage on women, Wharton's framework of evolutionary metaphor also introduces factors such as sexual selection, and presents Lily's refusals as the acts of a woman whose "social habits are instinctive" (115) and, consequently, problematic outside of the framework Ammons presents. Wharton portrays Lily as a woman who does not consciously understand her most natural response to circumstances. She therefore lacks the intentional aspect Ammons ascribes to her.[10] While opportunities to marry arise frequently—Percy Gryce, Lawrence Selden, George Dorset, and Simon Rosedale are potential partners—Lily at crucial moments acts in ways that preclude consecration of a match. The question of what causes Lily to defeat her goal of marrying well is more complex than has been advanced in Wharton criticism, and it is complicated by *The House of Mirth*'s ambiguity regarding Lily's intentions. Textual evidence suggests, however, that this ambiguity is a marker of Lily's *lack* of intention, or a sign that inarticulate instinct guides her refusals of (from her perspective) inappropriate pairings. Selden believes Lily's "genius lies in converting impulses into intentions" (67), but she lacks the ability to enact intent, except negatively.

Lily "despises the things she's trying for" (180), and it is clear that she possesses an innate moral sensibility the novel aligns with her half-conscious wishes for herself, which if less mediated would drive her to try for the man she wants. She understands that society and money can be put to good purposes, for they represent "opportunities, which may be used either stupidly or intelligently, according to the capacity of the user" (70). She does not consider her debt to Gus Trenor while she is in Europe because "[m]oral complications existed for her only in the environment that had produced them [. . .] but they lost their reality when they changed their background" (196). The interaction between environment and organism is profoundly determinative of Lily's behavior, and "her two months on the Sabrina [. . .] tended to throw into the extreme background of memory the prosaic and sordid difficulties from which she had escaped" (196). She has listened to Selden wonder "if we're all the raw stuff of the cosmic effects" (70), and the narrator, confirming Selden's speculation, comments that Lily, like a creature able to survive small changes in environment, "had adapted herself to the somewhat delicate conditions" of her trip to Europe (197). Her lack of intentionality is present, too, in her obsession over the question of why her best efforts to secure a husband go awry. She asks herself whether it was "her own fault or that of destiny" (28), but she is unable to discern that her actions are under the sway of sexual selection that patterns her refusal to choose a mate.

The contention that Wharton deploys Darwinian allegory encounters critical estimations of *The House of Mirth* which vary in allowing that Wharton is systematic in her use of evolutionary thought. Maureen Howard finds that the novel "presented a specimen case of evolutionary metaphors. [. . .] Rosedale is 'still at a stage of his social ascent.' Percy Gryce [. . .] feels in Lily's ministrations 'the confused titillation with which the lower organisms welcome the gratification of their needs'" (144). Howard states that these "allusions toy with the evolutionary concerns of the day" (144). Yet, Lily is a "victim of avenging moral forces" (*"Introduction to The House of Mirth"* 269) that are immoral in the judgment of the novel, being class codes that naturalize expulsion of the unfit. This morality—one that finds benefit in expelling Lily's difference—is unwilling to accommodate that which can invigorate it.

Howard writes, "It is not fate, after all, but a fastidious irresolution" (143) that causes Lily's destruction, allowing the interpretation that Lily's fastidiousness lies in a dimly perceived attempt to follow the dictates of sexual selection. Howard does not note Selden's perception that Lily wears "an air of irresolution which might [. . .] be the mask of a very definite purpose" (3). His attribution of intent to Lily is correct, but he doesn't realize that she cannot see through her "mask" either. Lily understands, at least, that infamy will result from her habit of wasting opportunities to marry well, even if this habit asserts a provisional independence. As she contemplates what might befall Bertha Dorset if Bertha's letters to Selden were made public, Lily realizes "that there is nothing society resents so much as having given its protection to those that have not known how to profit by it: it is for having betrayed its connivance that the social body punishes the offender who is found out" (104). Notwithstanding this observation, Lily recalls a sensation—experienced during a youthful romance—that she feels again with Selden, despite the difficulty of their pairing both perceive. It is a "sense of lightness, of emancipation [. . .] that glow of freedom" (65). For Lily, "irresolution" holds at length the hollow alternative of the socially sanctioned match in favor of embracing an attraction that fulfills biological will and is felt bodily. Lily's instinct carries her toward the fulfillment of desire that is blunted by mediation yet not destroyed, but also into conflict with an ideology affiliated in *The House of Mirth* with Selden's actions, but not necessarily his privately held ideals. This system of thought is intent upon suppressing bodily desire, and must increasingly accommodate the socioeconomic elite, particularly Rosedale. Sympathetic to Lily's impulsiveness, Rosedale is, however, intolerant of her habit of lowering her value as social currency. Neither class offers a niche in which Lily might anchor her true self, and it is the competition between the gentry and the socioeconomic elite that prevents the emergence of a "social body" sympathetic to her.

The view that Wharton portrays a form of competition modeled on nature has found acceptance in recent criticism of *The House of Mirth*. Claire Preston "considers Wharton's use of Darwinian metaphors of survival and adaptation [. . .]. Lily's outcasting is, in a sense, impersonal, merely biologically necessary rather than governed by volition or intention; the tragic agent of *The House of Mirth* is thus less human than environmental" (xiii-xiv). Preston's approach prompts a further question: just who is using "Darwinian metaphors" in the novel? One important issue Preston's analysis suggests is the potential for the biased use of such metaphors, which are a powerful tool for the elimination of the unfit and the ideological nonconformist. The novelist who would use such metaphors to present a nonconformist as lacking in "volition" finds instinct fragile, and "Lily's outcasting" less "biologically necessary" than caused by an exigent recasting of Darwinian survival and adaptation as features of a world that refuses to see cooperation as a dimension of instinct. In writing of Wharton's use of Darwinian metaphors, Preston invites one to examine Wharton's distinction between the particular interpretations of evolutionary thought permeating elite New York and the narrative's perspective on its heroine's fate, which delineates Lily's life as one of "wasted human possibilities" ("Introduction to *The House of Mirth*" 266). A social context that creates her as disposable does so through a spectacular use of "Darwinian metaphors of survival and adaptation" countered by the novel's interpretation of evolutionary theory, one no less politically freighted.

Gentry characters that might be venerated caretakers of aesthetic and intellectual achievement become, in the view the novel reviles, a group that has allowed the contours of its social environment to resemble a natural world without a moral center. The tragic movement of the novel portrays Lily as victimized by the fact that her "specialized" (5) traits are ill suited to an intellectual climate in the United States shaped by the view that

> [t]he dogma that all men are equal is the most flagrant falsehood and the most immoral doctrine which men have ever believed. [. . .] Men are very unequal in what they get out of life, but they are still more unequal in what they put into it. The most unequal bargain has always been made by the men who have done the world's thinking for it. (Sumner 578)

Markedly similar to Spencer's thinking, William Graham Sumner's viewpoint supports assumptions deadly to Lily in the shattered hothouse of her world. Moral volition of the kind Lily, to her detriment, eventually practises is an ideal only, one she hears Selden articulate as such: "[w]hy do we call our generous ideas illusions, and our mean ones truths?" (70). Her avoidance of the "personal contamination" (104) she feels in contemplating the fact that she can "overthrow with a touch the whole structure" (104) of Bertha Dorset's life displays non-adaptive, non-competitive behavior that is an insupportable ideal in a social context shaped, in part, by Sumner and Spencer.

Lily's searching reaction to her declining social and economic status, her "vision of the solidarity of life" (319), defines an equally unrealistic desire for interdependence between classes and individuals. This outlook is evident, too, in Lily's "faculty of adapting herself, for entering into other people's feelings, [which] if it served her now and then in small contingencies, hampered her in the decisive moments of life" (53), such as those moments where she might follow through on opportunities to marry. This shape-shifting trait is not uncommon in her set, for even Selden has "tried to remain amphibious" (70); he wishes to retain an ability to function amongst the elite, while maintaining the capacity to breathe "in another air" (70)—his "republic." Yet conventional definitions of womanhood, and Selden's pernicious aestheticism, overwrite Lily's instincts, which have no standing in a realm that defines selfhood through ritual and manners.

The limits of Lily's consciousness show a writer's technique Wharton shared with Henry James. In *The Writing of Fiction* Wharton notes how "James sought the effect of verisimilitude by rigorously confining every detail of his picture to the range, and also to the capacity, of the eye fixed on it" (89–90). In her depiction of Lily's imperfect understanding of how early train- ing betrays her better instincts, Wharton adheres to this principle rigorously while omnisciently describing the factors that condition the range and capacity of Lily's viewpoint. Lily's inability to marry Selden, or her other suitors, may be self-destructive. She's been warned that "the only thing that can save you from Bertha is to marry somebody else" (252), but her bristling refusals temporarily preserve her dissolving sphere of autonomy. Whether or not Lily comprehends the friability of this autonomy is a question readers of Wharton have addressed. William Moddellmog argues that "[j]ust when we think we are getting to know 'the real Lily Bart,' Wharton discards her authorial omniscience and withholds from us central elements of Lily's consciousness. 'Intimacy' seems no more pos- sible between Lily and the reader than between Lily and Selden" (338). This criticism can be made of Wharton at those moments in the novel when Lily seems inexplicably to act in a way that contradicts her goal of marrying well. However, Moddellmog's interpretation doesn't contend with the possibility that Wharton withholds nothing of Lily's consciousness from the reader; warring influences of sexual selection and socialization undercut Lily's desire for Selden, nullifying the latent connection of these characters.

Furthermore, the text "withholds" intimacy between Lily and the reader because Lily is awash in the riptide of her "early training," even as she senses the weak countercurrent of instinct in her physical reaction to Selden. The "central elements of Lily's consciousness" referred to by Moddellmog are in flux, and thus cannot be enunciated or displayed by her except as what Selden calls Lily's "irresolution" (3). For example, while the reader can see no reason why Lily shouldn't blackmail Bertha, it is an action the narrative indi- cates would deeply compromise the protagonist's better self, even as it would save her socially. Lily wavers over whether to use the letters to benefit herself, but her knowledge of the consequences for Selden prevails, and a course of action unmediated by Lily's training ensues:

> Bertha Dorset's letters were nothing to her—they might go where the current of chance carried them. But Selden was inextricably involved in their fate. Men do not, at worst, suffer much from such exposure; [. . .]. Nevertheless, the fact that the correspondence had been allowed to fall into strange hands would convict Selden of negligence in a matter where the world holds it least pardonable. (105)

A second reason for withholding the letters, one that resonates with the Dar- winian metaphor of interdependence, is that saving Selden is an expression of Lily's love for him. Her awareness of the interconnectedness of those from different classes is incomplete at this stage. A few pages earlier she has swept by a charwoman on her aunt's stairs, thinking it "insufferable that Mrs. Peniston should have such creatures about the house" (99), yet her hesitance to use the letters is there. Notable, too, is Lily's sensitivity to the presence of "chance" in the matter of the letters, a process she intervenes in by taking action. Her actions are consonant with the mitigation of the harmful effects of unhindered natural/social selection, and her ruin is a caution regarding an inhumane embrace of biological determinism.

Lily Bart's non-adaptive interest in "solidarity," and the fact that she refuses her opportunity for redemption via Bertha Dorset's letters, recreate a tension between competition and interdependence[11] addressed in *The Origin of Species:*

> The dependency of one organic being on another, as of a parasite on its prey, lies generally between beings remote in the scale of nature. This is often the case with those which may strictly be said to struggle with each other for existence [. . .]. But the struggle almost invariably will be most severe between the individuals of the same species, for they frequent the same districts, require the same food, and are exposed to the same dangers. (126)

Mrs. Haffen's offer to sell Bertha Dorset's letters to Lily presents an exchange-based form of mutual dependence in which Selden's reputation has a cash value.[12] Yet Lily refuses what, in the context of Darwin's statement, would be the natural thing. Here, a working-class woman and Lily, beings "remote in the scale of nature" now transposed to a class system, would fulfill the principle of "the dependency of one organic being on another." Instead, Lily opts to follow Selden's lead and not participate in the exchange. She occupies an environment hostile to her impulse to redefine, through her altruism, "the struggle" detailed by social Darwinism. In this environment, doing the "natural thing" (HM 15), whether enacting her power of sexual selection, or by competing directly with Bertha Dorset, will in the former case upset the sublimation of sexual instinct to class-appropriate behavior, or in the latter, play into the philosophy of intense struggle Lily's omnisciently politicized instincts oppose.

Lily's initial outrage at Mrs. Haffen's offer of the letters is tempered when "an obscure impulse restrained her" (105). The "obscure impulse" is an upwelling of Lily's sense of connection with Selden, which seems both a reversion to Selden's influence on her evaluation of potential courses of action and a manifestation of her hard-wired evolutionary ethics: "[i]f Lily weighed all these things it was unconsciously: she was aware only that Selden would wish the letters rescued, and that therefore she must obtain possession of them" (105). The moral instinct is a psychological phenomenon beyond conscious awareness, and Wharton, unwilling to step into the frame, lightly hints. The most adaptive act in Lily's vacuous world, obtaining the letters for her own protection, is an alternative that if "weighed," assesses not to find advantage in another's vulnerability, but to protect Selden.

Gaining possession of the letters leads Lily to the brink of blackmailing Bertha, which would save her socially but compromise the sense of self established in freeing herself from "what had contented [her] before" (308). This freedom is of Selden's design and cannot sustain Lily, but beyond the consequences for Selden "her mind did not travel" (105). Only later, as her fortunes decline, will Lily understand that her own instinctive ethics, which are quite similar to those Selden derives from his envisioned "republic," enable her to see into the lives of "young girls, like herself [. . .] leading [. . .] a life in which achievement seemed as squalid as failure—and the vision made her shudder sympathetically" (111–12). Sympathy, unfortunately, is incompatible with self-preservation in "a world in which such things could be" (27).

III. "WHAT *IS* YOUR STORY LILY?"

Many years after the publication of *The House of Mirth,* Wharton wrote that women seeking an education might "better stay at home and mind the baby" (qtd. in Benstock 387). Her portrait of the straitened options available to Lily Bart, and the consequences descending on women such as Ellen Olenska in *The Age of Innocence* who make untraditional choices, suggests the statement may be a warning about straying from defined roles rather than an indication of authorial conservatism. When Selden alludes to the effects of determinism on Lily, whom he believes to be "so evidently the victim of the civilization which had produced her, that the links of her bracelet seemed like manacles chaining her to her fate" (7), one senses his narrow view of the choices available to women. Selden does not admit readily that Lily might find a niche for herself by emulating his cousin Gerty Farish, whose lack of a husband has consigned her to the margin. This would be a less compromising path for Lily, whose impecuniousness subjects her to "the shock of the insult" of Bertha Dorset's public humiliation when Lily must absorb the fact that she "'is not going back to the yacht'" (218) and has no place to stay.

While the links of Gerty Farish's bracelet are of the same manufacture as Lily's, around Lily's wrist rests a "sapphire bracelet" which causes Selden to appreciate "the irony of suggesting to her such a life as his cousin Gertrude Farish" (7). Selden's aesthetic appreciation of Lily hinders his realistic assessment of her material circumstances, and shapes the guidance that flows from that impression—until late in the novel when he acknowledges "you and she could surely contrive a life together which would put you beyond the need of having to support yourself. Gerty, I know, is eager to make such an arrangement, and would be quite happy in it" (280). To him, Lily's desire to avoid self-compromise is "like a cry for rescue" (158) that elicits from Selden only chivalric fantasy in which he imagines himself aiding Lily, while she "clings to him with dragging arms as he beats back to land with his burden" (154). That Lily takes Selden's opinion to heart is explicit in her statement that his idealized view of her "kept me from really becoming what many people have thought me" (307). Nevertheless, she demonstrates her awareness that her manacles are of iron, not gemstone, when she asserts, in reference to the period in which she initially met Selden, that, as her circumstances worsen, "[e]ven then her feet had been set in the path she was now following" (304).

Alongside Selden's misinterpretation of Lily is her own confusion about what Gerty has achieved. Lily's barb that Gerty has "no maid, and such queer things to eat" (7) doesn't acknowledge the degree of autonomy Gerty maintains. Lily's disdain is clear, for Gerty's "was a hateful fate. [. . .] but how to escape from it?" (25). Yet in a moment of insight, Lily acknowledges that "she is free and I am not" (7). The straitened extent to which Gerty is free is dependent on her knowledge that "[r]eason, judgment, renunciation, all the sane daylight forces, were beaten back in the sharp struggle for self-preservation" (162–63). Gerty has an acute sense of the limitations placed upon her, and she fashions her life according to her awareness of social restrictions. Having found a niche, she enjoys "the privileges of a flat"; but Lily remarks that it is "a horrid little place" (7). Try as she might, Lily can only ask, "[W]hat else is there" (9) except marriage, even though the alternative presented by Gerty is in plain view. Not until the end of the novel, when she admires the choices made by Nettie Struther, does Lily see a positive aspect to a life in which she might not capitalize on her status as a "marriageable girl" (7).

Despite the conflicting demands of personal integrity and economic salvation through marriage, Lily avoids falling into what is defined within the context of the novel's figurative system as real barbarism: behavior that fails to understand "how infinitely complex and close fitting are the natural relations of all organic beings to each other" (*Origin* 130). Lily refuses marriage offers even though acceptance would transform her from the trapped insect she is into the member of society her training urges her to become.

But she acts, unawares, in ways that run counter to her best interests as a social being. This renders Lily opaque to others: "[a]ll I can say is, Lily, that I can't make you out!" (75) utters an exasperated Mrs. Trenor after Lily has spoiled her opportunity to marry Percy Gryce. Mrs. Trenor is bewildered because Lily wants to do the "natural thing" (15) and choose a partner on the basis of sexual attraction, and sympathies of mind and intellect, independent of the manner in which desire is guided by ideologies of class.

When Selden asks Lily, "Isn't marriage your vocation?" (3), he defines the goal of her social training. His question highlights a prevalent attitude with which Lily must negotiate. Wharton articulates this attitude when writing that "[m]arriage, union with a man, completes and transforms a woman's character, her point of view, her sense of the relative importance of things. [. . .] A girl is only a sketch; a married woman is the finished picture. And it is only the married woman who counts as a social factor" (FW 114). One should not impute social conservatism to Wharton on the basis of this seemingly retrograde comment, for women who do not marry are sympathetically portrayed in her fiction as socially hobbled. A better interpretation is to view the declaration as describing a reality Wharton seeks to alter. This view is supported by the fact that while Lily is unwilling to marry the "right" man, whom in each scenario she sees to be a poor match, her unwillingness guarantees that she will not be a "social factor." From the perspective of the environment Wharton describes, Lily is "only a sketch," which makes it more necessary than the protagonist knows for her to attend to the "sharp struggle for self-preservation" that occupies Gerty.

A critical view of *The House of Mirth* that sees it as an example of a naturalist mode portraying unanswerable social determinism has been qualified by the contention that Lily is a seeking and self-affirming character who demonstrates "that men and women also gain strength and derive meaning from their desires, hopes, and faiths" (Pizer *"House of Mirth"* 244). However, the presentation of Gerty's evasion of the social environment that oppresses Lily describes a path not taken by the heroine. Early in the novel, Lily defines success as getting "as much out of life" as she can (68), but her statement is ambiguous, referring perhaps to a mix of material and spiritual satisfaction— even though the idea of spirit and its suggestion of transcendence is problematic given the material grounding of Lily's character. She will not be like the Wetheralls, who "always went to church. They belonged to the vast group of human automata who go through life without neglecting to perform a single one of the gestures executed by the surrounding puppets" (52). Neither will she consider pursuing Gerty's sacrifices and compromises, even though they grant Gerty a kind of freedom. Instead, the protagonist's negation of the social determinism depicted in the novel, primarily the idea that "a girl must [marry], a man may if he chooses" (12), takes the form of a series of acts which modify, even subvert, her stated definition of success. Lily might make a self-affirming choice in refusing to marry an "ass" like Percy Gryce (83), but in wondering "why she had failed" (28) she doesn't perceive what motivates her actions. What she seeks is driven by mute impulse. While Gerty is maddened because "[t]he provoking part was that Lily knew" how to play the social game to her advantage (16), Lily recognizes what is expected of her, but perceives with less clarity the instinctive avoidance of an inappropriate mate that is making her baulk.

After Bertha Dorset's public sacrifice of Lily, Gerty poses an important question that illustrates the parameters of Lily's understanding of her own behavior and why it is at odds with the social context. Gerty asks, "What *is* your story Lily? I don't believe anyone knows it yet [. . .] I don't want a version prepared in advance—but I want you to tell me what happened from the beginning" (226). The ready-made answer preempted, Lily is not sure how to reply: "My story?—I don't believe I know it myself" (226). Lily continues, remarking that "the beginning was in my cradle, I suppose, in the way I was brought up, and the things I was taught to care for. [. . .] I'll say it was in my blood" (226). What she has been taught to care for and what she has inherited culturally and biologically run together in Lily's mind. In contrast to Selden, she makes little distinction between the two sources of influence. What is in her blood is inexpressible within an environment made up of "a hundred shades of aspect and manner" (234) that suppresses the biological will that Lily displays in refusing to marry someone unsuitable. Control over what is in Lily's blood brings little in the way of ethical advancement.

A 1905 review of *The House of Mirth* praises Wharton for her ability to register "to the last degree of delicacy the jumble of crudity and overcivilization which she finds in New York life of to-day. She describes coolly and patiently [. . .] the interminable race after pleasure which that fierce little world [. . .] engages in" (*Reviews* 117). This remark emphasizes the wide-angle perspective of a novel that can also acutely focus on a single consciousness. Lily's response to the pressures of the marriage market confirms a conflict between an innate sensibility, distinguished by her contradictory, though natural, avoidance of "the things she's trying for," and the deforming emphasis on "the use she made of it [her beauty]" in attempting to marry wealth (49). When she states, "I am horribly poor—and very expensive. I must have a great deal of money" (10), her self-conscious analysis of her situation demonstrates an understanding only of public expectations. Wharton signals that the "obscure" initiative of primal impulses is blunted by this expectation, with the result that Lily suffers in a hermetic social world that gives her only "the doomed sense of the castaway who has signaled in vain to fleeing sails" (229). The connection of this personal suffering to a "race after pleasure" emphasizes the causal sequence of "overcivilization," and its invalidation of Lily's socially redemptive impulse to engage her world on her terms.

Lily's experience with Gus Trenor shows how her inaccurate surmises reflect negatively on the "fierce little world" she lives in, rather than on her own "instinctive feeling" (17). Trenor offers to invest money in the stock market for Lily and, as he reports that her investment is performing well, she comes to believe that the "first thousand dollar cheque" (85) represents a return on her investment. In truth, Trenor gives Lily his own money, expecting sex in exchange. Through the interaction of these characters, Wharton examines multiple interpretations of the word *obligation,* which is understood by Lily early in the novel, before her consciousness-raising dialogues with Selden, only in the sense of a debt that can be settled and erased. Dimock points out that

> [i]n repaying Trenor, Lily is indeed complying with the rules of exchange, but she is also challenging the very basis of exchange. [. . .] By paying back the exact monetary amount [. . .] Lily at once obeys the principle of exchange and reduces it to tautology. Her nine-thousand-dollar debt is now just that [. . .] not some ill-defined and possibly limitless obligation. (787)

After becoming aware of Trenor's intent, and examining the situation from a fresh perspective, she feels that "it was not the sort of obligation one could remain under" (292) because it makes of Lily a courtesan—a categorization she refuses.

This reaction bears the mark of Selden's idealism (and possibly his jealousy) and the former's influence on Lily. His vision of "a country one has to find the way to one's self" (68) directs Lily to act in ways that ruin her. As she becomes enmeshed in his ideals she admits to the fact that "a girl who has no one to think for her is obliged to think for herself" (67), but this illusion of agency is an effect of her "fierce little world," for her interpretive powers are a product of her training. Thus, when she tells Selden that she would "never have found my way there [to the republic of the spirit] if you hadn't told me" (68), Wharton demonstrates that her training is capable of subduing her impulse to find a niche outside of marriage. Lily is less alienated from "the laws of the universe" (27) than she thinks, for she ultimately adheres to them in evading the fate of marriage and enacting her instinctive ethics. Because her training distances the natural, she initially takes social law to be all encompassing. Neither does she understand explanations regarding other aspects of her world with great clarity, finding descriptions of Wall Street machinations to be "slurred" (85). Her assumption that she contends with natural laws is erroneous. Rather, she is subject to interpretations of these laws that originate with Selden, Trenor, Rosedale, and others.

Lily's sense of obligation to Trenor results from her training, her innate Darwinian ethics, and the influence of Selden's idealism. Her decision to pay the debt is spurred by a snub from Judy Trenor and Carry Fisher. Lily assumes they mistreat her because Mrs. Trenor knows of the protagonist's indebtedness to her husband. Although discharging the debt will leave her with "nothing left to live on but her own small income [. . .] this consideration gave way to the imperative claim of her wounded pride" (229). Lily's reaction reveals that maintaining her social standing is supremely important; in this instance, training guides her.

Yet her repayment of the debt cannot be motivated exclusively by a wish to follow her training. Lily receives the money to make good on the obligation only after she has been "cut" (225) by her former friends, and therefore won't benefit from being perceived to conform socially. Repaying the money to Trenor is unnecessary from this vantage, for "what debt did she owe to a social order that had condemned and banished her without trial?" (300). Wharton also makes the hypocrisy of the "social order" clear by showing that had Lily inherited Grace Stepney's legacy, cordial relations might have resulted: "[t]hey were afraid to snub me while they thought I was going to get the money" (225). Selden later tells Lily that "[t]he difference is in yourself—it will always be there" (307), reinforcing the idea that the freedom of the individual to maintain a "republic of the spirit" (68) parallels Lily's instinctive sensibility in moral and sexual matters, which she gradually becomes aware of through her dialogues with Selden. As Lily acknowledges this heretofore unperceived aspect of herself, which overtakes her training, Selden describes her as a "dark angel of defiance" (225) possessed of a "habit of resolutely facing the facts" which "did not allow her to put any false gloss on the situation" of her social rejection (227).

Clearly, Selden's mediating aesthetic, which filters his understanding of Lily, does not consider the actual conditions of her life. This is evident when he defines his "republic of the spirit" as "[f]reedom [. . .] from money, from poverty, from ease and anxiety, from all the material accidents" (68) without acknowledging how inapplicable to Lily it is, for she believes she cannot marry him. Selden's promotion of this ideal has a powerful effect on Lily. She occasionally envisions herself through other characters' frameworks for self-understanding, but she is also at one with her physical environment, as when "the day seemed the accomplice of her mood: it was a day for impulse [. . .]. The light air seemed full of powdered gold. [. . .] Every drop of blood in Lily's veins invited her to happiness" (58).13 Lily is particularly responsive to Selden's vision, and her sympathetic reaction points to an affinity with his ideal. For example, she replies to his statement of principle regarding the republic of the spirit by leaning "forward with a responsive flash. 'I know [. . .] that's just what I've been feeling today'" (68). When she admits to Selden that his love gave her "the help of your belief in me" (308), though, such a belief can only be reckoned as destructive to Selden's protégé.

His shaping influence on Lily stands forth as the product of class values that compel a viewpoint harmful to the woman he loves; Selden cannot see beyond it, making him "as much as Lily a victim of his environment" (152). He is unperceptive of the material circumstances beyond his viewpoint. As a result, he cannot foresee the consequences of his effect on Lily, and he abdicates his upper-class role as a contributor to political order; this is a role Wharton identifies when she writes that "[i]t is a fact recognized by political economists that changes in manners and customs, no matter under what form of government usually originate with the wealthy or aristocratic minority, and are thence transmitted to other classes" (DH 7), but the transmission is garbled in *The House of Mirth*.

Early in the novel, Lily behaves in socially acceptable ways that also display, from the narrator's perspective, an inadequate sense of social responsibility. Her three-hundred-dollar donation to Gerty Farish's charitable enterprise saves the life of Nettie Struther, who subsequently bears the child Lily dreams of as she succumbs to chloral and experiences, finally, the "complete subjugation" that has awaited her (323). The donation returns to Lily in the form of a comforting hallucination of solidarity and motherhood that is a "gentle penetrating thrill of warmth and pleasure" (323) in her dying brain. Sensing the fullness of a connection to the web of humanity that includes altruism and motherhood is a realization rich in irony, for she is close to death. The insight accompanies her sense that "everything will be well" with Selden (323). This unsentimental termination of the possibility of Lily's reproduction, and the adjunctive failure of her connection with Selden, symbolizes arrested progress in the society at large.

On donating to Gerty's charity, however, the still unreformed Lily receives the kind of compensation endorsed by a society that is charitable only when there is personal benefit. But even as Lily gains satisfaction from her generosity, another feeling marks her nascent awareness of a self beyond that modeled by her training:

> The other-regarding sentiments had not been cultivated in Lily [. . .] but today her quick dramatizing fancy seized on the contrast between her own situation and that represented by some of Gerty's 'cases.' [. . .] by some obscure process of logic, she felt her momentary burst of generosity had justified all previous extravagances. [. . .] Lily parted from her with a sense of self-esteem which she naturally mistook for the fruits of altruism. (111–12)

Her "sense of self esteem" is wrongly interpreted as the standard reward for charity. The actual "fruits of altruism" are the collective benefits of cooperation. Lily's "process of logic" is obscure—not examinable—and the narrator details a gap between Lily's perception and another actuality. The conventional compensation for altruism is the "mood of self-approval" that comes from acting on "a sympathetic eye for others" (111). But Lily "mistook" "a sense of self esteem" as the product of an act that fulfills a deeper law of interconnectedness between related species, defined in the text as relations between classes, and between people. By noting the contrast between herself and the recipients of Gerty's good works, Lily reveals her perception of a need for charity. She understands that "money stands for all kinds of things—its purchasing quality isn't limited to diamonds and motor cars" (70), sensing a basis for exchange beyond the economic quid pro quo.

Gerty Farish's generation of a viable niche emerges as a positive counter-example to Lily's experience with values that have a pecuniary basis. Gerty's seeking of funds from the well-to-do for her charitable work acknowledges, within Wharton's Darwinian framework, how "the dependency of one organic being on another [. . .] lies generally between beings remote in the scale of nature" (*Origin* 126). Yet Gerty is marginal and undervalued; for all her nurturing and philanthropy, the civilized denizens of New York cast her off. Gerty's evasion of marriage illustrates that Lily is not so trapped in "the great gilt cage" (54) as she might believe. However, Lily's perception is, for a time, absolute. Lily's belief that her only option is marriage is cast in the same foundry of early training that leads her to believe Selden's preservation of "a certain social detachment, a happy air of viewing the show objectively" (54) marks him as free. In truth, what Selden thinks of as objectivity bars the kind of emotional contact Lily seeks from him. The depth of her belief that she must make the family fortune "back with her face" (28) compels her pursuit of a life unlike Gerty's.

Selden shapes Lily's perception of her choices by refusing to see her in other than aesthetic terms (Wolff xxiv). The depiction of Lily overcomes his assumption that she is a delicate flower carefully fashioned to attract the right man by rejecting the solipsism at the core of his "republic of the spirit." This becomes clear after Nettie Struther rescues the ailing Lily from Bryant Park. Lily's recognition and valuation of interconnectedness suggests that Selden's individualistic republic, if embraced universally, would result in the political disengagement and lack of social action displayed by him when he distantly observes with "aesthetic amusement" and "admiring spectatorship" (68) those he disparages. As a result of her interaction with Nettie, Lily transcends the limitations of false objectivity personified by Selden, to embrace engagement as a foundational principle for social conduct. She learns this from a woman she once thought "destined to be swept prematurely into that social refuse-heap of which Lily had so lately expressed her dread" (313).

Warming herself in Nettie's tiny apartment, Lily holds the daughter of her hostess. The infant penetrates Lily's consciousness "with a strange sense of weakness, as though the child entered her and became a part of herself" (316). The child would not have existed without Lily's donation to Gerty's charity, which saved Nettie (in this, Lily and Gerty can be said to have conceived the child) and the subsequent marriage of Nettie to George. It is clear that the relationship of man and wife depicted in this scene is what is missing from Lily's life. Soon after, Lily becomes aware that an obligation involves an interest in others: "the little episode had done her good. It was the first time she had ever come across the results of her spasmodic benevolence, and the surprised sense of human fellowship took the mortal chill from her heart" (316). This contrasts with the narrative's earlier description of how a responsibility to avoid odious transactions (and the expectation of sexual favors) is occluded by Lily's inability to see beyond her immediate desires after she receives a check from Trenor. "The fact that the money freed her temporarily from all minor obligations obscured her sense of the greater one it represented" (111). Lily acknowledges the interdependence of individuals and classes in her dealings with Nettie, and exemplifies through the evolution of her character the principle of change from which gentry characters avert their thoughts.

Lily's interactions with Trenor show money as an unexamined medium of interpersonal exchange. But the seemingly impersonal, cash-based obligation incurred by Lily, in contrast to her connection with Nettie, depicts the corruption of any meaningful sense of responsibility for the welfare of others among Trenor's class by being directed toward sexual exploitation. Wharton's omniscience is subtle in this respect, for the reader glimpses Lily's naïveté through the heroine's innocent perception:

Trenor and Miss Bart prolonged their drive till long after sunset; and before it was over he had tried, with some show of success, to prove to her that, if she would only trust him, he could make a handsome sum of money for her without endangering the small amount she possessed. She was too genuinely ignorant of the manipulations of the stock-market to understand his technical explanations, or even perhaps to perceive that certain points in them were slurred; the haziness enveloping the transaction served as a veil for her embarrassment, and through the general blur her hopes dilated like lamps in a fog. She understood only that her modest investments were to be mysteriously multiplied without risk to herself. (85)

As the setting sun casts the scene into darkness that symbolizes Lily's confusion over the implicit connection made between sex and cash, Trenor's instrumental attitude toward money bars non-monetary interdependence.

Later, Lily faces foreclosure on the debt of tolerance she has accumulated while squandering her chances to marry. Once Lily is "excluded from those sacred precincts" of the socially acceptable (280), she discovers that "there is very little real difference in being inside or out" of "what we call society" (280–81). This is so, she learns, because both positions require different though equally unacceptable compromises. Access to the resources of the "sacred precincts" comes at the expense of being regarded as pure ornamentation. Outside the margin, however, the acquisition of material comfort requires either a prostitute's dependence on Trenor and his ilk, marriage to an unsuitable man, or the kind of compromise chosen by Gerty Farish. Lily is free, in a qualified sense, to marry a poor man who loves her, but the control exercised by her training over her imagining of this option obscures it. Lily feels compelled to repay the debt to Trenor, who expects that he and Lily will "go off somewhere on a little lark together" (117). But even the act of salvaging her reputation and sense of worth is problem-fraught, for in repaying the debt Lily participates in a monetized system of interpersonal relations which is "bluntly contractual" (Dimock 786).

In a moral climate inhospitable to Lily's once unconscious but emergent sensibility, Wharton's substitution of ethics for the non-adaptive physical traits of a species predicts Lily's biological death, and sketches the demise of an environment that would have supported her as a moral person. Lily's "abstract notions of honour that might be called the conventionalities of the moral life" (300) stand in contrast to the treatment to which Trenor subjects her. Her repressed better judgment, rendered repeatedly as "instinctive," is in this way associated with a past wherein the "rapacity" (229) now exhibited by members of the new socioeconomic elite might have been controlled. Lily's adherence to these notions is, therefore, less an assertion of will against a patriarchal system than a demonstration that her honor is not relative, but rooted instead in what seems authorially intended to be unassailable biology.

Wharton includes much omniscient tracing of the heroine's difficulties with consciously understanding herself in terms other than those suggested by her "training and habit of mind" (278). Early in the novel, Lily's training obscures her view of any *type* of history other than that which bears upon her opportunities to secure a good marriage. She imagines her own social evolution in terms that fuse her development to the commodification of her femininity, but remains at odds with the expectation that she "ought to marry" (9), and she is puzzled by the effects of this expectation. Lily "remembered how her mother, after they had lost their money, used to say to her with a kind of fierce vindictiveness: 'But you'll get it all back—you'll get it all back, with your face' . . . The remembrance roused a whole train of associations, and she lay in the darkness reconstructing the past out of which her present had grown" (28). Her negation of the requirement to marry is animated by an instinctive reluctance to move outside her "narrow range" (301). Lily's awakening to Selden's vision confounds her initially, eliciting confused syntax that is a sign of cognitive disarray: "'[i]t was not that—I was not ungrateful,' [. . .]. But the power of expression failed her suddenly" (306). Silence is the sign of inarticulate instinct as Lily senses the consonance between her nature and Selden's ideal of the free individual. Although Gerty Farish recognizes that "Lily might be incapable of marrying for money" (162), suggesting the presence in Lily of motive urges unconditioned by social requirements, the narrative continually reiterates its vision of Lily as an organism, or "a water plant in the flux of the tides" (53). Determined in numerous ways, Lily is carried by the current of convention toward marriage, drawn back by Selden's vision of personal freedom, and finally pulled under when her true impulses compel a non-adaptive attempt at autonomy.

IV. "THAT TUNING-FORK OF THE NOVELIST'S ART"

Scenes of gambling that appear in *The House of Mirth* figuratively represent the element of chance present in New York society. When Lily takes her place at the bridge table at Bellomont, or experiences the vicissitudes of the marriage market, she feels she has no choice but to play both games. She suffers her losses at cards as "the taxes she had to pay [. . .] for the dresses and trinkets which occasionally replenished her insufficient wardrobe" (26), but she feels justifiably more anxious about the requirement to marry. In her interactions with Selden, coincidence is a form of chance that further complicates her attempt to create a viable life despite her ambivalence toward marriage. When Rosedale spots Lily leaving Selden's apartment, she is disturbed, in having to lie to Rosedale about the purpose of her visit to Selden's apartment building, that she must "pay so dearly for the least escape from routine" (15). She has merely "yielded to a passing impulse in going to Lawrence Selden's rooms" (15). In juxtaposing "impulse" and chance with the routines engendered by "social discipline" (16), Wharton contrasts the unpredictable, for which Lily must disburse her monetary and social capital, and the expected.

The novel contains and counters, through negative examples, an environment in which harm befalls a woman who "knew very little of the value of money" (31). Rosedale suggests to Lily that he will marry her if she blackmails her way back into social favor. He sees the potential transaction as "a transfer of property or a revision of boundary lines" (259) and this approach holds some appeal initially to a woman thinking furiously about how to remain good: "Lily's tired mind was fascinated by this escape from fluctuating ethical estimates into a region of concrete weights and measures" (259). Lily discovers in this encounter that the means she might use to rehabilitate herself—the letters written by Bertha Dorset—can be interpreted in a light different than that cast by Selden's ideals. Coming to her senses, however, she sees "that the essential baseness of the act lay in its freedom from risk" (260); the contract proposed by Rosedale is divisive and ethically deforming, morally relativistic and an instrument that downplays the agreement's harm. Lily is "secretly ashamed of her mother's crude passion for money" (35), so Lily's reaction to Rosedale is consistent with at least one other depiction of her beliefs about money.

Rosedale thinks "it's because the letters are to *him* [Selden]" (260) that Lily declines his offer, but he does not understand her valuation of a lack of "concrete weights and measures" that denominates change to the status quo as a collective benefit. Rosedale is right, though; Lily loves Selden, but she does not react physically to his presence in their early meetings. Selden, for his part, cannot help but note the way "[e]verything about her was at once vigorous and exquisite" (4). Social training restrains her bodily, and Selden displaces his desire into an aesthetic register. Her reaction to Rosedale joins right moral action to a refusal to interpret such matters in a relativistic way, as Rosedale does. Chance produces new combinations of genetic and cultural matter; that is, Lily (the variation) reacts to her socialization in a way that produces a fresh outlook. Rosedale would abort the new, and potentially invigorating, notional progeny of individual psychological variation and environment, and this repulses her.

Wharton's metaphoric fusion of chance and social renewal criticizes a gentry that has segregated itself from change. Despite their adherence to social heredity, with its new Darwinian implication of mutation in cultural transmission, Mrs. Peniston, the Dorsets, and others possess a sense that extinction and change don't exist in their world. These characters "belonged to the class of old New Yorkers who have always lived well, dressed expensively and done little else" (37). Such are the "inherited obligations" (37) of a class unready to place themselves within the dominion of the laws of inheritance and natural selection. But change is upon them.

> The convergence upon New York of newly enriched families and individuals [after the Civil War], in addition to the emergence of New York's own nouveaux riches, put considerable stress upon existing social structures. [. . .] some degree of flexibility was necessary to prevent the elite's complete and utter displacement by those with superior financial resources, and so in the 1870s and 1880s the social mechanisms that were put in place allowed for a controlled merger of old and new wealth. (Montgomery 39)

The House of Mirth depicts the aftermath of the merger of wealth, and it illustrates an accompanying merger of ideas represented by Rosedale's entrance into society. A Jew on the cusp of respectability, he knows social evolution is a dynamic process.

From the perspective of those at the center of New York society, Rosedale is the last person who should ever reach the position he does, having "been served up and rejected at the social board a dozen times within [. . .] memory" (16). Wharton portrays his rise in terms that show the error of the novel's social arbiters, who believe they are immune to the whims of "the terrible god of chance" (26). Ironically, even this deification of chance denies its unthinking essence, casting fate in terms of a higher intelligence. While "[i]t had been a bad autumn in Wall Street" (120), Rosedale senses that he will have the opportunity to be less guarded, to reveal more of himself in a society whose prejudices force his close adherence to convention, for "Mr. Rosedale wanted, in the long run, a more individual environment" (121). The depiction of his gradual social acceptance draws on the evolutionary idea that a shifting environment can result in the success of any species adapted to it.

In subjugating Lily, Selden's circle asserts control over the affiliation of nature with chance she personifies. In her 1905 review of Howard Sturgis's *Belchamber,* Wharton encapsulated a perspective evident in the undermining of Lily's power of "measuring distances and drawing conclusions with all the accuracy needful of [her] [. . .] welfare" (115). Wharton wrote in the review of the way "[a] handful of vulgar people, bent only on spending and enjoying, may seem a negligible factor in the social development of the race; but they become an engine of destruction through the illusions they kill and the generous ardors they turn to despair" (110). The statement aligns Wharton's politics with her triangulation of Lily's natural tendencies, the codes of Selden's class, and the consequent imposition of "the standards by which she was fated to be measured! Does one go to Caliban for a judgment on Miranda?" (HM 135). The literary allusion is Selden's, and demonstrates that his view of Lily is conditioned by his aestheticism. His comparison of New York's elite to Caliban suggests that, from his perspective, moral progress toward a world that might accommodate Lily will not occur, for in Shakespeare's play Caliban is a savage who learns nothing, despite Prospero's efforts to educate him (Orgel 23).

The reference to Caliban also recalls the violence this character is capable of visiting on Miranda, and posits Lily as a potential victim of sexual and psychological violation. Selden attempts to educate Lily, and in this respect one can view this bookish character as a Prospero possessed of a magical idealism that leads Lily to her fate. However, from his perspective Lily is "a captured dryad subdued to the conventions of the drawing room" (13). As a forest spirit—Selden, typically, views her in mythological terms—she is supernatural, and therefore only partially "subdued." As a result, Selden can't take "a sentimental view of her case" (12) because Lily seems to be not entirely helpless. She is an "artist and I [Selden] happen to be a bit of colour you are using today. It's a part of your cleverness to be able to produce premeditated effects extemporaneously" (66). While Selden sees Lily as one whose illusions might be "killed" by the "vulgar people" of his class, he is wary of her too. Although he criticizes society for not possessing fine enough sensibilities with which to judge Lily, his allusive perspective rewrites her in artistic and mythological terms that obscure any realistic vision of her circumstances, and reveals the limits of his ability to engage with a living citizen of his republic of the spirit.

Selden sees intent in Lily's attempts to advance within the framework of marriage, but he doesn't consider the deterministic force of the institution. He tries to show Lily the thinness of what she desires—to "get her foot across the threshold" of the rich—telling her that he cannot "guarantee your enjoying the things you are trying to get" (71). When Lily, tearful, realizes that "the best you can say for me is, after trying to get them I probably shan't like them? [. . .] What a terrible future you foresee for me" (71), Selden imagines that "even her weeping was an art" (72). He attributes intention to Lily's behavior, while she feels swept along by forces outside her control; Lily's "discretions interested him almost as much as her imprudences: he was so sure that both were part of the same carefully-elaborated plan" (5). His attribution of grasping materialism is correct, but only to the extent that it anticipates behavior which his social stratum expects from a marriageable woman.

Selden's lack of engagement with the material circumstances of Lily's plight is caused by his inability to evaluate her situation outside of the ideological framework Wharton attributes to his class. Were he to perceive the relationship between Lily and the mediating power of her training, he might note how he too is caught in the processes that duplicate social beings. This would, perhaps, give him the knowledge to actually save their love "whole out of the ruin of their lives" (329). His limitation arises directly from an epistemological perspective conditioned by an aesthetic native to the class Selden serves, and with which he is affiliated. This aesthetic is depicted most forcefully in the Brys' *tableaux*. Here, one of the paintings represented by the women on stage is by Watteau, an artist who idealized the theme of "courtship" (Hartt 842), not by his contemporary Chardin, who depicted the lives of the French lower middle class. Goya and Titian too, the former an artist "we can hardly call anything but Romantic" (Hartt 880), and the latter, known for his mythological paintings, are authorial choices reinforcing the gentry's preference for representations of their values that materialize an association between beauty and symbolic control over sex and violence.

One sees desire for such control in the way Selden wants to take Lily "beyond the ugliness, the pettiness, the attrition and corrosion of the soul" caused by the expectations forced upon a marriageable woman (154); his desire to do so is shaped by a belief that "Perseus's task is not done when he has loosed Andromeda's chains, for her limbs are numb with bondage, and she cannot rise and walk, but clings to him with dragging arms as he beats back to land with his burden" (159). Selden's mythologizing of Lily sharpens Wharton's portrait of the rift between Lily's sociobiological status as a dead-end variation unequipped for the environment she inhabits, and Selden's aesthetic, one in which a representation of Lily drawn from visual art and myth blooms in the hothouse of his imagination.[14] The narrative generates antipathy toward Selden's skewed perspective, showing that his

Claude-glass[15] view of Lily subdues her and impinges on her psychological freedom.

Selden perceives Lily as his aesthetic would have him do, countering the accidental and random aspect of existence experienced by Lily with the forceful ordering of the world offered by art. His approach to Lily's beauty underscores aesthetic valuations that reflect values present in the popularity of *tableaux vivants*. These performances play out a "master plot" that tells "the story of a woman metaphorically killed by the process of being made into an allegorical figure, an object of art, or her husband's property" (Chapman 31). The ideology of Selden and his caste possesses "a force of negation which eliminated everything beyond their own range of perception" (HM 48). He therefore denies that Lily is subject to those economic and political forces his "republic of the spirit" seeks to forestall, even though he acknowledges her subjection to the norm of "the conventional rich marriage which she had been taught to consider the sole end of existence" (155–56). His perspective on Lily is disconnected from the material reality of her life. He views Lily through a "responsive fancy" that inhabits "the boundary world between fact and imagination" (133). Further evidence that Selden's "fancy" focuses his view of Lily exists in the penultimate paragraph of the novel. Here, one encounters Selden's view that the love he and Lily shared has "been saved whole out of the ruin of their lives. It was this moment of love, this fleeting victory over themselves, which had kept them from atrophy and extinction" (329). Selden's romantic elevation of love at the moment he is faced with the reality of Lily's corpse is telling proof of his inability to see beyond the borders of his individualistic liberal aesthetic.

In contrast to the natural, if self-destructive behavior of the protagonist, the Brys display their wealth and allegiance to the aesthetic encoding of sexuality in expensive *tableaux vivants* that reproduce "a series of pictures" (135). Lily's "inherited resistances of taste, of training" manifest themselves in this central scene when Lily unselfconsciously signals the males gathered at the Brys of her availability by using her "dramatic instinct" (131) to stand out among the other women. The reproduction of pictorial fictions in the *tableaux vivants* expresses the mediated concept of beauty formulated by Selden's class; this is a spell Lily's appearance breaks. Possessed with "an imagination which only visual impressions could reach" (131), Lily presents an image that deflects categorizations of her appearance which would pattern her sexuality as controllable (even though it is ultimately subdued). That Lily has "selected a type so like her own that she could embody the person represented without ceasing to be herself" (134) alerts the reader to the extent to which Lily is willing to exercise her sexual attraction. She has "yielded to the truer instinct of trusting to her unassisted beauty" (134), and one is compelled to consider that Wharton's choice of the word "selected" imputes an agency to Lily that foregrounds for the reader the formal challenge of depicting Lily's actions while reducing intentionality to impulse.

Lily's "instinct" differentiates her from the other women whose selves do not escape from behind the portraits of "Titian's Daughter [. . .] the frailer Dutch type [. . .] a Veronese supper [. . .] and a Watteau group" (134). However, when Selden sees Lily attired as Sir Joshua Reynolds's Mrs. Lloyd he is moved, but characteristically interprets Lily from the perspective of a connoisseur, "catching for a moment a note of that eternal harmony of which her beauty was a part" (135). At the moment Selden feels closest to Lily, the difference between his aestheticism and her instinctive nature is clear. Moreover, the fact that the Brys have chosen the exhibition of "fashionable women" (131), who disguise their sexuality behind reproductions of artistic creations as their means to socially "advance into a strange country" (130), accents the difference between Lily's unnerving display as a path to social betterment and the Brys' highly-coded entertainment as a way to accomplish the same thing.

Alone with Selden, Lily's gestures toward social advancement soften. She desires Selden despite the fact that they both believe they cannot afford to wed. Lily can only imagine a "state of existence in which, all else being superadded, intercourse with Selden might be the last touch of luxury" (88). The two obvious meanings of the word "intercourse" resonate in the statement, of course; conversation about matters unrelated to what separates them, and a sexual connection with Selden are only possible in an unreality. In this state, Lily and Selden would not spend the few moments they have in private talking of "what a miserable thing it is to be a woman" (7). They imagine the distance between them in the unavoidable lexicon of money, wherein Lily is "very expensive" and Selden has "no money to spend" (10). A second hindrance to their love is Selden's inability to perceive Lily outside the framework for evaluating a woman's social suitability. He wonders how he could "lift Lily to a freer vision of life, if his own view of her was to be colored by any mind in which he saw her reflected" (159). His desire to lift her clear of the terms of her existence reenacts the suppression of her will to move "Beyond!" her state. This is so because Selden's coercive aestheticism scuttles Lily's chances of finding an independent existence by assisting in the emergence of her true, but unviable, self.

Lily's self-abnegating scrupulousness in moral matters becomes a way to assert her agency even as it forecloses a certain kind of future. For example, her sense that "the reward" to be realized from marrying Gryce "seemed unpalatable" (28) appears to be a response to Selden's influence. The effect of his personal philosophy is clear enough when Lily remarks that "I have never forgotten the things you said to me at Bellomont, and that sometimes [. . .] they have helped me and kept me from mistakes; kept me from really becoming what many people have thought me" (307). Nevertheless, Lily's turning away from the life she has been trained for marks a refusal of convention that exceeds what one can credit Selden with provoking. Lily's behavior resembles that of another female persona who desires to avoid surrender under terms not of her choosing. In the final stanza of Wharton's 1909 poem "Non Dolet!" (which appeared in *Artemis to Actaeon*) a figurative suicide bestows a sense of ironic control over difficult circumstances. The similarity of the poem's theme to Lily Bart's response to her situation is notable: "'It hurts not!' dying cried the Roman wife;/ And one by one/ The leaders in the strife/ Fall on the blade of failure and exclaim:/ 'The day is won!'" (21–25). The martyrdom of Lily models a future in which the failure of moral exemplars cedes to instrumentalism the standard for human relations.

Preston suggests that if Lily's death is a suicide, it "is her single gesture of self-determination" (72). One difficulty with this interpretation is that if Lily's suicide is intentional it is an act for which the formative influence of her training must also share responsibility, for "[l]ost causes had a romantic charm" for Lily (HM 35). As such, the act realizes preconceptions surrounding the fate of lost women. Her death determines her as a woman under the influence of a presiding model of what must happen to one unable to attain the object of her love. If intentional, Lily's demise fulfills an imagined allegiance to an idealized social order, present in her fantasy that she might be in a position as the wife of an "Italian prince to sacrifice her pleasure to the claims of an immemorial tradition" (35). She sacrifices herself to New York's "tradition" by not defending herself in the Dorset affair, and by not combating the suspicion that she is trying to help Mrs. Hatch marry Freddy Van Osburgh. Lily is sacrificed, too, "to Bertha Dorset's determination to win back her husband" (227), yet Lily won't make her side of the story known out of a sense of "some obscure disdain and reluctance" (227). This reason suggests the fineness with which one must make a distinction between Lily's instinctive ethics, which compels her "disdain," and a training that invites self-sacrifice and motivates her idealization of "lost causes."

It is less important, however, to insist on discovering whether Lily intentionally kills herself, than to recognize that the death scene represents Lily's conversion to the point of view that chance is an elemental aspect of the enduring, *real* natural world in which she lives, one unreconstructed by the optimistic, progressive, and often cruel social Darwinism of the new elite. It is the moment when Lily's true self emerges completely into her hostile environment, and one in which she abandons her adherence to the social order, as she "remembered the chemist's warning. If sleep comes at all, it might be a sleep without waking. But after all that was but one chance in a hundred: the action of the drug was incalculable" (322). Now openly embracing the randomness of nature, Lily dies. Her death, whether from accident or suicide, demonstrates that chance permeates the social order, and will not leave her out of its workings, even though Selden's stratum, which believes its rituals distance disorder, does just that.

The House of Mirth reacts to the view that human agency is an illusion in a Darwinian world, doing so through a response that follows the contours of William James's rejection of Spencer's interpretation of evolutionary theory. James "could accept apes for ancestors, but he could not abide dogmatic extensions of Darwinism which denied free will, the efficacy of consciousness, or the value of the individual" (Meyers qtd. in Howard 145). Regardless of Wharton's glibness in referring to him as "William o' the wisp James" (*Letters* 205), her fiction has a stake in James's argument in *Principles of Psychology* (1890) that human instincts are "specialized neural circuits that are common to every member of a species and are the product of that species' evolutionary history. Taken together, such circuits constitute (in our own species) what one can think of as 'human nature'" (Cosmides and Tooby). The articulation of Lily's dilemma asserts that mechanisms for self-preservation, propagation, and even free will can be understood by attending to guiding instincts that are a function of such circuits, and the perspective has a precedent in James's claim that "however uncertain man's reactions upon his environment may sometimes seem in comparison with those of lower creatures, the uncertainty is probably not due to their possession of any principle of action which he lacks. *On the contrary, man possesses all the impulses that they have, and a great many more besides*" (1013). But interference by manners with cooperative "impulses" that differentiate humans from "lower creatures" impairs an individual's viability in an environment sympathetic to "dogmatic extensions of Darwinism." "Because a blue-bottle bangs irrationally against a window-pane, the drawing room naturalist may forget that under less artificial conditions it is capable of measuring distances and drawing conclusions with all the accuracy needful of its welfare" (HM 115). Illustrating this, Lily moves in an "artificial" environment in which her inability to compromise herself morally is unsustainable.

Given the opportunity to marry George Dorset, Lily recognizes, as I've shown, that "revenge [against Bertha Dorset] and rehabilitation might be hers at a stroke" (245). At this moment, however, "fear possessed her—fear of herself, and of the terrible force of temptation" (245). Lily's alienated intelligence is a handicap in a social environment that equates the ability to thrive with unethical action. For a society that does not limit the potential of natural selection to be an agent of social evolution, the negative implications are evident in the way Lily becomes a victim of material accumulation divested of social responsibility. This illustrates Wharton's view of "the moral sensibility, [as] that tuning-fork of the novelist's art" (WF 120). *The House of Mirth* fulfilled Wharton's wish to write "the type of fiction wherein the adventure grows [. . .] out of the development of character and the conflict of moral forces" ("George Eliot" 75). As Lily becomes a moral agent as a result of being shaped by Selden's views and then realizing her possession—at an instinctual level—of what he advocates, she repays her debt to Gus Trenor.

In the last chapters of the novel Lily discovers the value of interdependence, and of symbiosis, in Nettie Struther's kitchen, when the latter remarks how "it's so lovely having you here, and letting you see just how you've helped me" (315). Outside the domestic setting, the formal means Wharton uses to express the vicious rules governing the social hierarchy positions it at a distance from the organic figurative language she employs to describe Lily, and the language of cooperation present in Lily and Nettie's dialogue. The social sphere is unnatural, even inorganic. In one instance a mechanical metaphor contrasts Lily with her environment: "I can hardly be said to have an independent existence. I was just a screw or a cog in the great machine I called life" (308). But while this statement would indicate that *The House of Mirth* depicts social determinism which denies Lily agency, her attempts to transcend a fate that would provide "a future of servitude to the whims of others, never the possibility of asserting her own eager individuality" (101) stands as a valuation of the impulse to take action on the prospect of social renewal. Such a possibility, though, is sacrificed by the lockstep "race after pleasure" depicted in the novel.

*   *   *

Published two years after *The House of Mirth*, Wharton's novel *The Fruit of the Tree* (1907) portrays relations between workers and capitalists in an early twentieth-century industrial context. *The Fruit of the Tree* features a reform-minded factory manager named John Amherst caught between "the abstract standards of honour and their practical application" (311). Despite its weaknesses—R. W. B. Lewis writes that Wharton "seems not to have been quite sure what she was up to [. . .], and one sign of uncertainty was the succession of unrelated alternative titles she proposed" (181)—the novel continues her analysis of impediments to, and possibilities of, "converting impulse" (HM 67) into social cohesion, or what *The Fruit of the Tree* describes as one's "personal relation to the people [. . .]—the last thing that business considers" (192). Published the same year Wharton told Sara Norton, "[t]here is nothing like the joy of a good scientific book" (qtd. in Lewis 82), *The Fruit of the Tree* moves outside the setting of New York and its elite classes to address with fitful objectivity "the conditions under which the mill-hands work and live" (77) at the Westmore textile factory near a small New England town.

John Amherst, the manager of the mill, carries forward *The House of Mirth*'s focus on the unfulfilled possibility of cooperation and equality, when he urges that "the conditions of the operatives could be improved" (qtd. in Tuttleton "*The Fruit of the Tree*" 159). Amherst cites "the baneful paternalism which was choking out every germ of initiative in the workman" when he argues that "the floorspace of the mills must be enlarged, and the company must cease to rent out tenements, and give the operatives the opportunity to buy land for themselves" (194). Yet, when he marries the mill's owner, Bessy Westmore, and comes to feel that "Bessy's interests in Westmore should be regulated by her interest in it—in its welfare as a social body, aside from its success as a commercial enterprise" (189)—it becomes clear he wants to subject her to his reformist vision. Amherst "means he prefers her social concerns over her financial ones. In doing so, he confuses the difference between the individuating interest he has imparted and the decidedly pecuniary investments she represents. [. . .] [Amherst] plans to reform her" (Bauer "Addiction and Intimacy" 132). Depicting a capitalist ethic that reconstitutes interpersonal relations as economic relations, the novel finds that "each particular wrong could be traced back to a radical vice in the system" (112). But changes to the system must be enacted by individuals like Amherst who are no less flawed than the system they serve and help to perpetuate, as this domineering but reform-minded character shows.

In her book on the politics of Wharton's fiction, Dale Bauer remarks that *The Fruit of the Tree* "fails to weave together the complicated issues of reform, scientific engineering, and medicine and the effects of those on the inner lives of the main characters. It focuses on the binary opposites of labor

and leisure" (*Brave New Politics* xiii). While Bauer's criticism accurately highlights the failings of the novel, the Taylorized industrial environment Wharton depicts defines the attitude of the bosses efficiently enough. Capitalists
need to "get the maximum of profit out of the minimum of floor space"
(11), and care little that it "costs more to increase the floor-space than to
maim an operative now and then" (11). John Amherst has a "hope of bettering
things" (17), but despite his efforts, no radical changes occur at the mill. The
mythology of social progress degraded by Wharton in *The House of Mirth* is in
this way criticized again in *The Fruit of the Tree*. The question of whether civilization rests on the suffering of workers such as those at the mill—who might
wonder whether Bessy's "white chin [would] have nestled in such rich depths of
fur [. . .] if thin shoulders in shapeless gingham had not bent day in, day out,
above the bobbins and carders" (49)—seems settled, for the mill workers are
"dim creatures of the underworld" (64), and the underclass, that support Bessy
and her kind. Amherst wishes a "yellow reporter would go through these mills,
and show them up in headlines a yard high" (71). The popular press, Amherst
evidently assumes, has a role in reporting the inequities of factory life, the workings of capital, and the social ills they produce.

When the idealistic Amherst meets Bessy, he is strongly attracted to
her. A romance plot intersects with the genre of the business novel when one
finds him wanting to "bring her face to face with her people [in the factory]"
(47), only shortly after "Bessy puzzled at the unannounced appearance of a
good-looking young man [. . .], while Amherst felt his self-possession slip-
ping away into the depths of a pair of eyes so dark-lashed and deeply blue
that his only thought was one of wonder" (41). After they marry, Bessy
breaks her back in a riding accident, lingering while attended by the mill's
nurse, Justine Brant. Justine's "work among the poor had developed her
interest in social problems" (19), and she is, therefore, more knowledgeable
than Bessy of the problems Amherst agitates to change; Justine's awareness
flows from her experience amongst people Bessy does not know. After the
accident, the subject of euthanasia becomes prominent and the ethics of two
views on the matter are juxtaposed. "Christianity recognizes no exceptions"
(407) where mercy killing is concerned, but the scientific Justine Brent sees
things differently. Justine cannot bear to watch Bessy's suffering, and she
"heard an inner voice, and its pleading shook her heart. She rose and filled
the syringe—and returning with it, bent above the bed" (433) to administer
a fatal dose of morphine to Bessy. Later, she argues with Tredegar, asserting,
"cruel instances are necessary for the general welfare" (418), justifying her
action on grounds that would appeal to a social Darwinist. Justine reckons
with the consequences of her action when Amherst discovers how Bessy

died. The two of them agree never to talk of the matter, but their relationship is irrevocably altered. Enacting her idealism has cost Justine dearly; like Lily Bart, she "had paid—to the utmost limit of whatever debt toward society she had contracted by overstepping its laws" (605), which for Lily meant not exploiting her chances to marry.

A praiseworthy aspect of *The Fruit of the Tree* is its portrait of "human relations [as] [. . .] a tangled and deep-rooted growth" (624) of such complexity that social mores reckon with them impotently. Social Darwinists such as William Graham Sumner recognized such difficulties in concluding that the "principles of social evolution negated the traditional American ideology of equality and natural rights" (Hofstadter 59), even if the offered solutions contributed to the problem. For Amherst, aware of the desires and motives of the workers and the elite, both classes are connected by the dichotomy of the profit motive and an "ideology of equality." Amherst does not "believe in the extremer forms of industrial paternalism" (FT 110), and he hopes that the workers might achieve self-reliance. For the administrators of the mill, Truscombe and Tredegar, the working-class hands live off capital, while the workers see themselves as the host of parasitic capitalists: "[the operatives] knew she [Bessy Westmore] was the new owner, that a disproportionate amount of the result of their toil [. . .] would hang a setting of beauty about her eyes" (61). In conversing with Tredegar over working conditions at the mill, Amherst states that the unfair treatment of the workers has "its roots in the way the business is organized" (78). Amherst is not suggesting that workers should have a stake in the factory. He's no socialist, as Tuttleton makes clear ("*The Fruit of the Tree*" 159), but Amherst attempts to balance his ideals with a capitalist attitude that normalizes exploitation. Amherst encounters this attitude when Tredegar asks him, "In what respect do you think the Westmore hands unfairly treated?" (78), even though he is aware that a worker named Dillon was mangled by the machinery because "a man must be an automaton to be safe in the carding room" (102).

Like *The House of Mirth*, Amherst's story features an authorial linking of environment and character. Like *The Custom of the Country, The Fruit of the Tree* contemplates the effects of divorce, which "has grown almost as painless as modern dentistry" (280) and is "an expensive but unhazardous piece of surgery" (329). *The Fruit of the Tree* develops *The House of Mirth*'s interest in an ideology of equality at odds with exploitation and the material rewards attending aggression and dominance, and in this way looks forward to *The Custom of the Country*'s focus on this subject. Featuring diverse settings—the factory floor, a cotton operative's home, a hospital, and rooms hung with wealth—*The Fruit of the Tree* deals with disparate themes, forecasting the social panorama and thematic inclusiveness of *The Custom of the Country.* Wharton's perspective on the role of mass media in addressing relations between classes, which is touched on in *The Fruit of the Tree,* is also a subject that receives fuller treatment in the later novel. In the tale of Amherst's attempts at reform, Wharton depicts countervailing elements such as equality and profit, human nature and the requirements of social organization that straiten impulse, which are effectively staged in *The Fruit of the Tree,* but fictionally assessed in a systematic way in *The Custom of the Country.*

Chapter Three

The Incoherence of "Progress" in
The Custom of the Country

I. "THE NEW SPIRIT OF LIMITLESS CONCESSION"

In 1935 Edith Wharton expressed her high opinion of *The Custom of the Country* in a letter to H. S. Milford at the Oxford University Press. Milford hoped to publish an edition of *The House of Mirth,* but the author suggested otherwise. Wharton replied through her secretary, who wrote that "Mrs. Wharton is disappointed that you should have fixed on *The House of Mirth.* She thinks *The Custom of the Country* a much better book" (*The Uncollected Critical Writings* 269–70). This is a curious comment if the appraisals of Wharton's critics are to be used as a guide, for their consensus has been that *The House of Mirth* is the more unified novel.[1] Taking a review of the novel as a starting point, this chapter argues that *The Custom of the Country* expands the range of subject matter Wharton represents through her scientific frame of reference.

An appreciation of the effect on *The Custom of the Country* of Wharton's devotion to scientific study has emerged slowly. The *Atheneum*'s 1913 review states that "Mrs. Wharton, by [. . .] laying stress upon the sequence of environment, upbringing, character, has made her character a natural and pathetic figure" (*Reviews* 209–10). While one takes the word "natural" to mean realistic in this context, ample evidence exists in the novel to indicate that its main character, Undine Spragg, is also to be seen as natural in a biological sense. She is an "organism" (CC 64) from the remote Apex City, adrift in a strange, upper-class environment where "all was blurred and puzzling to the girl in this world of half-lights, half-tones" (48). Wharton's characterization of Undine as a biological specimen coexists with a detailed rendering of the "puzzling" social environment she eventually dominates.

The fully gentrified Ralph Marvell and his kind, through their bifurcation of nature and culture, elicit Undine's confusion; "organisms" and social "abbreviations" are incommensurable in their world. The old-money families and the gentry together express their interpretation of the relation between nature and culture in a way that reveals their interest in moderating "impulses" (39) and in channeling base energies represented by the "grotesque saurian head" of the lascivious Peter Van Degen (58). Less than two decades later, Freud would write that "[s]ublimation of instinct is an especially conspicuous feature of cultural development" (*Civilization and its Discontents* 51), and, indeed, instinct tears at the restraints that control it in the sphere Undine Spragg, Elmer Moffatt, and Van Degen move in and redefine. So while the contemporary review of the novel published in the *Atheneum* identified "the sequence of environment, upbringing, character" as a central concern that reflects the novel's attempt at objectivity, links between natural and social environments explored in the novel escaped the scrutiny of the reviewer.

Three sections follow this overview of how *The Custom of the Country* continues the program of work begun in *The House of Mirth*, and what new directions the later novel takes in developing Wharton's sociobiological viewpoint. In section two I examine the role of mass culture in Undine Spragg's socialization and the way it affects her response to tradition. In doing so I explore Wharton's representation of mass culture as a new medium of cultural inheritance that competes with, and displaces, gentry ideology, for mass culture's influence in the novel analogizes environment in a Darwinian sense. Section three investigates the question of cultural heredity as it is posed in the novel in order to argue that one significant feature of *The Custom of the Country* is its implicit theory of the way class-bound traditions are based in one or another interpretation of natural law. I argue that in making this representation, the novel expresses concern about the maintenance of tradition by depicting the gentry's sense of invulnerability to a process of social selection their class cannot elude. Here, too, I address *The Custom of the Country*'s nuanced criticism of the socioeconomic elite's assumptions regarding social Darwinism. Section three positions different class-based assumptions regarding the tension between nature and culture evident in the novel alongside works of evolution and biology whose ideas provided Wharton with a fertile metaphorical field. Section four considers Ralph Marvell's encounter with mass culture and the market as a confrontation with contingent processes of change that his ideals cannot survive, and contrasts his experience of being "in all the papers" with Undine Spragg's (CC 97). Throughout these sections, this chapter addresses Wharton's claim to authoritativeness in the area of social criticism, which relies on an intermixing of biology and fictional analysis that cannot conceal her interest in controlling the mutability of the social world she portrays.

*   *   *

In *The Custom of the Country*, New York is a "new environment" in a social and a biological sense (27). While *The House of Mirth* relates the ways Lily Bart's expression of an instinctive ethics modeling an idealized moral code would benefit a country dealing with the disruptive technological and social changes already mentioned, *The Custom of the Country* represents competing classes more comprehensively than the earlier novel by fictionally analyzing in greater detail their respective ideologies. In important ways, however, *The Custom of the Country* carries forward the project of *The House of Mirth* by depicting the sympathy enjoyed by social Darwinism in a culture increasingly enthralled by individualistic tycoons represented by Elmer Moffatt.

Foremost among these similarities between the two novels is *The Custom of the Country*'s linkage of Undine Spragg's negation of the tradition of equality and natural rights[2] with her achievement of material success viewed as a sign of progress by the socioeconomic elite. Where Undine symbolizes the idea that the fittest should survive, in her devastation of any obstacle she perceives—even her parents fear "the darkening of her eyes" (50)—Wharton places before the reader images of an ecological Darwinian interdependence of species in the social realm that Undine violates.[3] In this thematic scheme, action directed at the presence of natural processes within society can maintain provisional equilibrium and compensate for a "primitive impulse to hurt and destroy" that Undine personifies (470).

Another similarity between the two novels exists in the way Undine's negation of the aforementioned traditions reflects her lack of awareness of a social and historical context that would otherwise preserve and transmit "that impalpable dust of ideas which is the real culture" valued in *The House of Mirth* ("The Great American Novel" 156). Whereas Lily Bart's death illustrates the effects of dispersing a "real culture" premised on equality that might sustain her difference, Undine Spragg is a product and instrument of social evolution that atomizes a society "of continuity and choice" (CC 243). When the story relates, referring to Undine, that "allusions to pictures and books escaped her" (46) while she listens to a dinner party conversation, she is distinguished as a character unable to understand that values can be, according to Wharton, concentrated in art. This motif reappears some pages later when Undine, having been to an art gallery where she sights "Peter Van

Degen, the son of the great banker, Thurber Van Degen" (58), finds that "she could not remember anything about the pictures she had seen" (59). Undine is immune to the teachings offered by art.

The Custom of the Country gives form to competing ideologies of the gentry and the socioeconomic elite that govern each class. Establishment characters such as Ralph Marvell, the Dagonets, Charles Bowen, and the Fairfords, are the bearers of a tradition that is the transmission medium of culture; Marvell and Clare Van Degen "are of the same blood and [have] [. . .] the same traditions" (195). Distinct yet joined, Wharton tracks the relation of "blood" and "tradition" by inflecting gentry norms with biological meaning through the use of Darwinian language and metaphors present also in *The House of Mirth*. *The Custom of the Country* casts social relations as biological "inherited intimacy (Undine had noticed that they were all more or less cousins)" (48). Moreover, the figurative conflation of social change and processes such as natural selection familiar from *The House of Mirth* is present too. An eroding upper-crust system of maintaining order contrasts with the pernicious habits of the socioeconomic elite—divorce, aggression, and financial speculation—that compete with and modify old forms of social governance.

Yet one must be cautious about calling the ideology of the socioeconomic elite in this novel a "system." The ideas of this class reflect instead a thematically significant "incoherence" (CC 243) of recombined signs of old-guard tradition. The adoption by the new elite of culturally significant forms such as dress, language, and architecture is a sign of ideological expansionism in Wharton's hands. Such outward movement resonates with the biological metaphors of a novel that charts the movement of a new species into an unexploited aristocratic environment. Thus, Undine views the opportunities for exploitation of her new milieu as opening "ampler vistas" that afford her an avenue of expression for the fact that "her pioneer blood would not let her rest" (64), tying her historically regressive character to national traits of exploration and domination.

Members of the gentry rely on tradition to prevent uncultured individuals like Undine from entering their class enclave. She is "primitive" (470) and emblematic of a contingent natural world that spurs gentry regulative practices. She is the opposite of her second husband, Ralph Marvell, and an agent of the demise of his class in the historical sequence the novel chronicles. This process begins when she aligns herself with an economically elite social stratum distinguished by an absence of tradition, wherein families are not settled, but live transiently in places like the loudly decorated "Hotel Stentorian" (21) in one of its Versailles-like "Looey suites"

(21). Such appropriation of cultural forms defines Undine's type. In depicting her transformation from prairie girl to paragon of café society, the novel aligns her with Elmer Moffatt, the art-loving predator who by novel's end becomes a "billionaire Railroad King" (502). Marvell and Moffatt epitomize old and new money attitudes respectively. Wharton also introduces the ancient cultural practices of the French aristocracy in her characterization of Undine Spragg's third husband, Raymond de Chelles. These characters define the novel's spectrum of class-based attitudes toward tradition.

The novel revels, for example, in detailing the way Marvell's romanticism blinds him to the need to rigorously suppress the struggle for existence that social Darwinism encourages. He sees Undine through a scrim of myth, and fantasizes about lifting her to his own level of aestheticism. From his vantage he "seemed to see her like a lovely rock-bound Andromeda" (86) and not the recurrence of vestigial American violence that she represents. While Marvell criticizes a brand of capitalism associated with ungoverned nature that buoys the rise of the socioeconomic elite, he doesn't divine the danger it presents to his way of life. Behind the new capitalism is a destructive "Wall Street code" (233) fostering a "chaos of indiscriminate appetites" (78). Undine, Marvell discovers too late, is a mutation immune to a character-moderating socialization, which would soften her tendency to "assert herself as the dominant figure of the scene" (48). In this way, Wharton portrays a sequence in which an altered social environment produces and confirms the viability of Undine by what must be called ideological selection. Her rise occurs within a social environment now subject to evolutionary forces no longer acting exclusively on "the plants and bushes clothing an entangled bank" (*Origin* 125), for the socioeconomic elite have dismantled the old stone walls of insular values to build palatial monuments to capital. Representative of this reality is the displacement of a familiar class species that is the repository of cultural memory and aesthetic achievement. Charles Bowen, Wharton's "sociologist" in *The Custom of the Country* (249), calls this established creature of the New York landscape "Homo Sapiens Americanus" (188). The suicide of Marvell, the representative of this species, personifies its extinction.

In *The Custom of the Country*'s programmatic reinforcement of its cultural politics through scientific metaphor, the individualism of the new rich is a surging tide of chaotic nature that must be countered. Undine embodies this elemental tide: "she felt a violent longing to brush away the cobwebs and assert herself as the dominant figure of the scene" (48). Moreover, her "strange sense of lucid resistance" (127) to Peter Van Degen, a gentry scion unable to resist the delimitation of manners offered by the new elite, suggests the operation of sexual selection beyond conscious control. Wharton juxtaposes the natural aspects of Undine's character with the latent capacity of Ralph Marvell's class to address the tension between social chaos and the pursuit of continuity, the former of which historically has been controlled by coercively confronting "the new spirit of limitless concession" (CC 269) with rites whose past authority is represented in *The Age of Innocence,* which is set in the 1870s.

New mass-culture forms undermine the stewardship role of Marvell's class. Wharton had a degree of contempt for a market-driven and mechanized form of American cultural colonialism that obscured the value of probity, gentility, and artistic achievement "[t]he whole world has become a vast escalator, and Ford Motors and Gillette razors have bound together the uttermost parts of the earth. The universal infiltration of our American plumbing, dentistry, and vocabulary has reduced the globe to a playing field for our people" ("The Great American Novel"[156]), she wrote in 1927. Against Marvell are arrayed the mechanisms of the new, embodied in the productive capacity of ideological assembly lines which reproduce subjects through mass culture, exposing the "hidden hereditary failing" of the inflexible "conventions of his class" (378). Such conventions cannot compete against the full-color advertisement, nor the barrage of messages made possible by mechanical reproduction. The novel finds gentry class ideology to be subject to natural selection by charting how unviable the former is in the social environment engendered by a broad embrace of disposability and novelty.

Accompanying Wharton's depiction of Undine's shallowness and her relation to mass culture is a commitment to social analysis as one way to examine and reply to that which defines the age. Charles Bowen manifests this impulse. He comments on "human nature's passion for the factitious, its incorrigible habit of imitating the imitation" (243) as he observes how the new rich model themselves on socialites who vaguely resemble the real-life Astors. These characters borrow the signs of the gentry. Bowen also embodies an analytical perspective that views objectively that which it criticizes. As in *The House of Mirth,* this trait defines the biases and assumptions of characters; Bowen's blind spot is his passive intellectual acuity, which though one aspect of a tradition dependent on knowledge, generates no social action, something that is evident when, sitting in the restaurant of the fashionable Nouveau Luxe Hotel in Paris, Bowen observes

> what unbounded material power had devised for the delusion of its leisure: a phantom 'society' with all the rules, smirks, gestures of its model, but evoked out of promiscuity and incoherence while the other had been the product of continuity and choice. [. . .] and their prompt

and reverent faith in the reality of the sham they had created, seemed to Bowen the most satisfying proof of human permanence. (243)

This "reverent faith in the reality" of a falsehood describes a socioeconomic elite whose forms owe much to the "promiscuity and incoherence" of a mass culture unable to contribute to the "continuity" Bowen deems valuable. His account of the new rich resonates with Wharton's comment that "[s]ocial conditions as they are just now in our new world, where the sudden possession of money has come without inherited obligations, or any traditional sense of solidarity between classes, is a vast and absorbing field for the novelist" (*Letters* 99). The seeming neutrality of Bowen's depiction of this subject, which in his case is made possible by the "perpetual exercise of his perception" (243), demonstrates the novel's focus on the forms by which the socioeconomic elite defines itself, but also shows that Bowen's viewpoint is unable to deflect the forces overtaking his perspective.

Bowen's clinical tendency to look on matters "impartially from the heights of pure speculation" (187) is founded on the cultural capital of a class that Wharton draws from. But his highly discerning viewpoint is limited by the inability of observation to compel positive social change. Bowen's perspective contrasts with the lack of correspondence between social forms and traditional continuity he associates with a "phantom" society. Although the new rich ape the forms of the gentry, the crowd Bowen watches does not share gentry values. Thus, the novel's method is more than only generally sociological, for it persuades one of the perspicacity of its method by objectifying its impartiality in Bowen's measured insights, and exceeding them by depicting the flaws of his perspective. Fictional methodology becomes a subject for authorial self-reflexivity as the limits of Bowen's viewpoint become clear, and this is a feature of *The Age of Innocence* as well. The dependency of Wharton's method on a scientific frame with its own shortcomings is clear at that moment when Bowen "felt the pang of the sociologist over the individual havoc wrought by every social adjustment" (249). Rational analysis alone cannot generate social action, but the novel, at least, can foster awareness of how vital it is to address the "havoc" wrought by social evolution.

Social adjustment in *The Custom of the Country* consists in interaction between traits such as class affiliation, wealth, and adaptability, the latter of which Undine excels at, and the selection environment that is New York. Here Wharton strengthens *The House of Mirth*'s contention that culture grows out of nature, and is not an autonomous human-made system, by allegorizing individual traits viable in the novel's social environment as primitive impulses of domination and aggression requiring control. One finds modern

pressures exerted on Lawrence Selden's idealistic individualism—the dehu-
manization caused by a social Darwinist interpretation of human relations—
to reconstitute a primitive social environment, the qualities of which are
favorable to some individuals, and not to others. Undine, an "intruder" in
the gentry garden (69), is powerful in her capacity to "adjust herself" to the
conditions in which she thrives (67), but her character has only recently been
acknowledged, by Cecilia Tichi, as one indicator of "arguably Wharton's
most thoroughgoing socially Darwinian narrative" (90), even if the valuable
analysis Tichi offers does not sufficiently distinguish between Wharton's attitude to those works of Spencer and Darwin on which Wharton draws.

Dale Bauer observes that "Wharton critics have typically divorced her
work from larger ideological issues implicit in the act of writing fiction and
have denied her politics, in part because her views are often conflicting and
in part because her works have not been read in light of the relevant intellectual debates of her day" (qtd. in Wegener "Form, 'Selection,' and Ideology"
138n). In *The Custom of the Country* the portrayal of natural selection as an
agent of social change exceeds the achievement of *The House of Mirth* by
incorporating a more detailed examination of ideology's role in social inheritance, a dimension of the novel difficult to interpret without appeal to the
intellectual debates to which Bauer refers. By refining a method of present-
ing political content through biological allegories and metaphors, Wharton's
handling of ideology foregrounds the subject of change while maintaining an
oppositional stance toward misunderstandings of Darwinism. Louis Menand
maintains that

> [o]ne reason for the relatively rapid acceptance of Darwin's theory of
> natural selection was that it seemed another example of order underly-
> ing chance [. . .]. It was therefore tempting to conclude that the world
> must be set up in such a way as that things regulated themselves, and
> this was taken as a kind of cosmic seal of approval on the political doc-
> trines of individualism and laissez-faire. Herbert Spencer titled his
> philosophical defense of laissez-faire, published in 1851, *Social Statics*.
> Darwinism, too, seemed to justify political laissez-faire. (194–95)

However, self "regulation" deprived of doctrines that control individualism, as depicted in the results of Undine's actions, is a disaster in *The Custom of the Country*. In "The Influence of Darwin on Philosophy" (1910),
John Dewey writes that the evolutionist's influence "resides in his having
conquered the phenomena of life for the principle of transition" (qtd. in
Dorothy Ross 316). Wharton's focus on competing systems of thought

captures this principle for the novel's challenge to Spencer's promotion of laissez-faire, and her opposition to the idea that individualism might foster order.

As in *The House of Mirth*, two questions to be asked of *The Custom of the Country* are, first, whether the presence of scientific ideas in the novel is a narrative strategy intended to endow it with authority in the minds of the reading public, and second, whether there is an attempt to demonstrate that principles of evolution have not analogues, but real equivalencies in the historical dialectic that gives rise to ideological systems and sees them falter. In *The Custom of the Country*, both questions must be answered affirmatively, for Undine Spragg and Elmer Moffatt are agents described in biological terms that live a system of belief in which material gain is equated with progress, and indeed theirs is "a costly expression of a social ideal" (CC 243). Undine's "instinct of adapting herself to whatever company she was in, of copying 'the others' in speech and gesture as closely as she reflected them in dress" (150), though, shows that those who equate change with progress premise their actions on a "confusion of ideals" (34) that corrodes the system it copies. Undine emulates gentry rites and forms that facilitate a "gestureless mute telegraphy" for which she has no code key (79). This mode of communication is an attribute of a social context in which Mrs. Fairford is figured to be "harmonizing and linking together what [. . .] [her guests] said" (46), making a social occasion one for reaffirming the efficacy of the spoken language and symbolic forms that bind the class. Undine's attempt to copy these forms results in her feeling an insecure "mistrust" toward her hosts (46), suggesting that her "confusion of ideals" alienates her from the vital connection between social forms and the complex ameliorative process a tradition based on choice represents to Wharton. In using these forms at the same time she is divorcing Marvell or abandoning her son, however, Undine distorts their meaning and contributes to the breakdown of the values they reference.

Elmer Moffatt is similar to Undine in that "something in his look seemed to promise the capacity to develop into any character he might care to assume" (107). Both Moffatt and Undine are akin to embryonic stem cells harvested from the historical protoplasm that would produce an ambitious and destructive American character. One finds Moffatt "sharpening his weapons of aggression" (180), while Undine's "inherited prejudices" (279) compel her to ignore "the strength of [. . .] social considerations" (375). Like Undine, Moffatt is a new species exploiting an ecosystem possessed of no natural defenses with which to combat him, for "no one seemed to know from whence he came" (195). Deals hammered out by this

cutthroat primitive don't mix with the deference to the past involved in preserving outmoded traditions, no matter the cohesiveness fostered by doing so.
When Moffatt says of Raymond de Chelles, "[h]is ancestors are his business,
Wall Street's mine" (492), the novel distinguishes deference to a way of life
built up over time from Moffatt's "epic effrontery" (227), which derogates a
Fifth Avenue premise that one can moderate change; still, Moffatt's attitude is
valid because it acknowledges flux and chance as governing principles.

Ralph Marvell's clan believes in what Moffatt disdains, for juxtaposed
with the gilt surfaces associated with the new elite are the worn, lived-in
spaces occupied by the gentry. These spaces represent the constructed unity
of a society that attempts to minimize the effects of change. This effort
requires knowledge and, indeed, the Fairford's house contains "rows of books
from floor to ceiling" (44). Relying on the books at the foundation of its
own fictional analysis, the novel views organic and social evolution through a
lens that focuses both into a portrait of their bonds. This is an important
characteristic of Wharton's method that illuminates her novel's resistance to a
point of view in which "God would not create the living world by random
variation and the survival of the fittest [. . .]. Even to think of the human
condition in such a manner [. . .] is intolerable" (Wilson 37). Wharton's
materialism sees the human condition in just this, to some, intolerable way, a
trait of *The Custom of the Country* signified in one early instance by the
description of Undine as a "tremulous organism drifting helplessly" (64).
Wharton's reduction of the spiritual to the material makes the biological
basis of culture unavoidable. This serves a politics that seeks to mitigate the
entropic force of chance, a perspective at once nostalgic for and critical of
ossified gentry forms dissolving in an acidic mass culture.

II. "ALL THE HINTS IN THE SUNDAY PAPERS"

Undine Spragg has provoked critical reactions that are in agreement about
her superficiality. Mary Papke comments on Undine's "voracious materialism and [. . .] her limited consciousness" (142), while Candace Waid
insightfully proclaims the character's "absence of interiority" (132). Claire
Preston offers the following interpretation: "there are only two or three elements in her success (principally her beauty, her naïveté, and her blankness,
her readiness to accept the imprint of projected idealising by deceived
men)" (110). Undine is a young woman of "lovely lines" (CC 22), and her
vivid beauty, which "defied the searching decomposing radiance" of the
brightest light (36), parallels the eye-catching designs of the superficial
tabloids she reads. Like the popular papers, she is all surface. Undine can

reformulate her persona to appeal to those who would consume her, and for this reason stands forth as an example of Darwin's observation that "[w]e see beautiful adaptations everywhere" (*Origin* 87). As she mimics traditions, Undine displays her adaptability through a changeling nature attributable in part to the mass-culture products this depthless character consumes.

Gossip sheets and dime novels present a new medium of acculturation in *The Custom of the Country*, and in this respect they can be said in part to define what is new about the material environment the novel depicts. Habermas states that the public sphere "was supposed to link politics and morality in a specific sense: it was the place where an intelligible unity of the empirical ends of everybody was to be brought about, where legality was to issue from morality" (115). Wharton chronicles the same decline in the public sphere that Habermas laments in the historical account offered in *The Structural Transformation of the Public Sphere*, and she observes consumerism and self-interest displacing concern for the maturation of democracy. Habermas articulates what is a fictional subject for Wharton, one that fulfills her wish to portray situations "in which some phase of our common plight stands forth dramatically and typically" (WF 29). In her introduction to *The House of Mirth* she writes that "when there is anything whatever below the surface in the novelist's art, that something can be only the social foundation on which his fable is built" (265). This thought is played out in *The Custom of the Country*'s confrontation of an ideology fostered by mass culture that dissolves the foundation "below the surface of her art," for undergirding the story of marriage and divorce as national sport there exists a portrait of transformations to the "social foundation" the novel combats. The association of mass culture with the new rich and the lower class, and tradition with an older, established elite, places the forms that are emblematic of each class-specific system of ideas at the center of the novel. Wharton examines the complicity of mass culture in building ideological consensus around the idea that laissez-faire capitalism erected on natural law, specifically in its overtaking and diminishment of the public sphere, is beneficial to individuals and institutions. Amy Kaplan writes that the novel subordinates clippings from *Town Talk* to a literary comprehensiveness capable of telling "the *real* truth behind the gossip" (*The Social Construction of American Realism* 85). Wharton thus asserts the primacy of fiction's ability to represent social processes. Interspersed with satiric passages on instantly forgettable "news" stories are portraits of complex business deals such as the Pure Water Move, the Ararat Trust deal, and the subsequent investigation of the latter by the authorities. These episodes show a different side of the ethics of business than is presented in the press, distinguishing the genre of the novel as one capable of exceeding the ability of other forms to portray more fully the social foundation.

As I have claimed, Undine's attitude toward the seemingly impenetrable "damask," "gilt," and "onyx" (CC 21–22) world she intrudes upon in the early chapters is a product of the press and literary forms that are just two aspects of mass culture. This influence creates in her consciousness "the key of the world she read about in the Sunday papers"[4] which she detects in the "masterly manner" of the society painter Claude Popple (37). She is a character given to saying, "I want the best" (38), who discovers standards of social prestige, fashion, and language in the pages of the newspapers, magazines, and sentimental novels she reads. In aligning Undine with such printed matter, the novel decries a mass culture unable to facilitate the "critical discussion of a reading public [. . .] [which] give[s] way to 'exchanges about tastes and preferences'" (Habermas 170) associated with the "instinctive" protagonist (CC 35). The joining of a superficial press to a shallow and primitive anti-heroine negates the capacity of much popular writing to contribute to the civilizing process Wharton seems to advocate.

The novel derides the absence of an effort to foster an "intelligible unity [. . .] of ends" in a public sphere supportive of Undine's notion that it is "the correct thing to be animated in society, and noise and restlessness were her only notion of vivacity" (36). Undine "had remained insensible to the touch of the heart" (210), and her insensibility prevents a connection to political life, which is only a haze in the deep distance of the plot's background. In making Undine subject to an early form of what Paul Virilio calls "industrial mediatization" (60), which is abundantly represented in the novel's references to widely read sub-journalistic newspapers and magazines, Wharton fashions her protagonist as stripped of rights by "communication technologies" that cause people to think "of themselves more as *contemporaries* than as *citizens*; they may in the process slip out of the contiguous space [. . .] of the old Nation-State (or City State), which harbored the *demos,* and into the atopic community of a 'planet state'" (Virilio 36). The *Radiator, Town Talk,* and tabloids equivalent to *People* magazine in the hands of grubby subway riders are signs of a mass culture "that, instead of doing justice to reality, has a tendency to present a substitute more palatable for consumption and more likely to give rise to an impersonal indulgence in stimulating relaxation than to a public use of reason" (Habermas 170).[5] Depictions of mass culture products lament a diminishment of the ability of the press to challenge the forms that structure assent.

That which Undine reads must be saleable. Such writing responds to public taste, but also helps to create it. What it also creates is Undine's representative and authorially devalued plasticity. Since her "novel-reading had

filled her mind [. . .] with pathetic allusions to women's frailty" (327), such a
sentiment is used by Undine to justify feeling wronged when her father orders
her to return the valuable pearls Peter Van Degen has given her. The protagonist, of course, is hardly frail. Rather, she is possessed of a "youthful flexibility"
(25) that gives the appearance of strength to her "incessant movements" (36).
To better fit her environment, Undine resolves, against her nature, "to trust
less to her impulses" (39). Her resolution, however, shows her determination
by mass culture, which possesses no message that would have Undine value
what is true of her. Determined by the fashionable values represented in the
papers, Undine's relativism becomes deeply engrained. The significance of her
use of a sentimental sensibility encountered in her "novel reading" is its
demonstration that she can adapt any stance within her view;[6] the mutability
of values evident in a fragile public sphere is fostered by the logic of a market-
driven mass culture that fosters Undine's transient personae.

Mining the tabloids for information, Undine initially takes their
representations as truthful. Marvell, on the other hand, "reads the fiction
number of a magazine" (113). He has no need of the facts she seeks.
Undine realizes that her attribution of factualness to the tabloids is mistaken. She finds this "confusing and exasperating. Apex ideals had been
based on the myth of 'old families' ruling New York from a throne of Rev-
olutionary tradition, with the new millionaires paying them feudal allegiance. But experience had long since proved the delusiveness of the
simile" (177). Undine is disoriented by her discovery, but her ability to
find a vantage where a better understanding would be possible is complicated by other forms of storytelling.

Novels such as "When The Kissing Had to Stop" and melodramas
called "Oolaloo" and "The Soda-Water Fountain" (CC 48) show market-oriented writers[7] issuing narratives that drown out socially useful tales which
create common ground for individual citizens, and which might educate
Undine.[8] Juxtaposed with these stories are the tastes of Undine's interlocutors at the Fairford dinner. They attend classical dramas that she hears incorrectly as "'Leg-long [. . .] Fade'" (48–49).[9] Upon leaving the dinner Undine,
realizing she is out of her depth, "faltered out stupidly from the depths of her
disillusionment: 'Oh—good-bye'" (50). Her disturbing discovery is a
moment when, for the consumer of the tale, "the contradictions inherent in
bourgeois society surface" (Porter qtd. in Anesko 84); the system of ideas
held by the gentry appears to Undine, and the reader, along with the fact
that mass culture does not present an accurate portrait of its subject. It is, of
course, the narrative that frames this, reading literature as a much-needed
guide, and goad, to cultural continuity.

After realizing that the idea of the elite she has assembled from the press is not true, Undine decides to "watch and listen without letting herself go" (46). The strategy of not "letting herself go" comes easily to so superficial a figure, one who possesses nothing interpretable save her ability to adapt and mimic the characteristics of others, as when "her attention was drawn to a lady in black who was examining the pictures through a tortoise-shell eye-glass. [. . .] It seemed suddenly plebian and promiscuous to look at the world with a naked eye" (57). Undine becomes a corollary of the popular papers.[10] Like them, she is attractive, but not cultured, and anticipates the needs of those who would consume her by adjusting the content of her persona. In her seeking for the "originals" of those images to which she relates so intensely, "unsuspected social gradations were thus revealed to the attentive Undine" (41). As a result, she discovers that her initial perceptions about the "golden aristocracy" are gross simplifications and eventually becomes able "to make distinctions unknown to her girlish categories" (176). This is a crucial moment in the novel, for as Undine discovers that representation and truth don't correspond in the press, so she understands that her beauty, her advertisement as it were, doesn't have to deliver the submissiveness exchanged for the "money, clothes, cars, the big bribe she's paid for keeping out of the man's way" (189).[11]

Wharton apparently took issue with what she saw as an American fetish for the new that blunted perception of the crucial distinctions handed down by tradition. She attributes this insensitivity to "[a] long course of cinema obviousness and of tabloid culture [that] has rendered the majority of readers insensible to allusiveness and irony" ("Permanent Values in Fiction" 179). Yet, Undine Spragg's "ear was too well attuned to the national note of irony" not to notice that her companions at the Fairford dinner are "making sport" of the society painter Claude Popple (47). She thinks highly of Popple and has seen him in the press. Undine's perceptiveness will eventually except her from the run of readers that take "tabloid culture" at face value. She comes to learn that the perceived correspondence between actual people and lives rendered by journalistic narrative or photograph is not to be trusted.

For a time, though, Undine mistakes the hackneyed plot and the time worn stereotype in the papers for valid portraits of the New York scene. She is thus shocked when she discovers, on coming into contact with actual members of the gentry, that the papers present a simplified portrait of the social network. Wharton's presentation of the press in general, especially in its effect on Undine, echoes Mott's observation about newspaper editorials of the period. He characterizes these pieces as "not long and never hard to read. Short words, sentences, paragraphs were the rule. Complex subjects reduced by symbol to the lowest common denominator" (581). Social progress is Undine's career, and she prepares by studying the "social potentates whose least doings Mrs. Spragg and Undine had followed from afar in the Apex papers" (27). The complexity of blue-blood social practices remains undetectable in the accounts Undine reads, however. Other forms of popular culture mislead her for a time as well. Sentimental novels supply a misleading notion regarding gentry values, as when the reader learns that "[h]er novel-reading had filled her mind with the vocabulary of outraged virtue" (327). But such unsubtle modes of expression are useless in a traditional social setting where "all Undine's perceptions bristle" (47) to ascertain the socially acceptable locution. What Wharton called "tabloid culture," Undine discovers, diminishes her perceptive powers.

Reversals and revelations are central aspects of Undine's experience. The limits of her mediated vision become ever clearer to her when the "camera obscura of New York society" turns her expectations upside down (94). When she discovers that Marvell's family will be involved in the couple's wedding plans she understands that in comparison to practices in her hometown of Apex, "New York reversed this rule" (91). In Paris she senses "[o]nce more that all the accepted values [of New York] were reversed" (254). After she terminates her marriage to Marvell, her "New York friends were at no pains to conceal from her the fact that in their opinion her divorce had been a blunder. Their logic was that of Apex reversed" (307). Even a princess does not conform to pattern. Undine expects a royal representative of the imperious Faubourg to be finely attired. Instead, Princess Estradina is "small, slight and brown" and is "dressed with a disregard of the fashion" (333). This "overthrew all Undine's hierarchies" (334). Some element of the society she moves in is clearly beyond the scope of the portrait offered by the press, and thus, for a time, beyond her own understanding.

As for revelations, all Undine "sought for was improvement: she honestly wanted the best" (60), but she learns about what is best by her continual pursuit of "something beyond" that is mirage-like and continually receding (62). At every new level of the fashionable, Undine finds another stratum above her. She first wants to "get away from Apex" (60). Later she meets girls "whose parents took them to the Great Lakes for August" and instantly wants to do the same (61). Her parents are "impelled" by Undine to a "Virginia 'resort'" and in another reference to the coloring of realities by mass-culture representations, "its atmosphere of Christmas-chromo sentimentality" (62). However, as soon as Undine hears from a Miss Wincher that the resort is a "hole" and that the Wincher family is "going to Europe for the Autumn" (63), the protagonist "loathed all the people about her" (63). A violent disappointment sweeps over her on these occasions when "everything was spoiled by a peep through another door" (62). Finally believing she has discovered *the* environment within which to achieve social and material progress, "Undine vowed to herself with set lips 'I'll never try anything again until I try New York'" (64).

"Undine's first steps in social enlightenment" (39), once she arrives in New York, find her seeking "in vain for the originals" she has encountered in the papers (41). She discovers that the tabloid portraits of the gentry lack important details. When Undine asks Mrs. Heeny about the social status of the Fairfords and another guest, Ralph Marvell, Undine is delighted to hear her reply: "if they ain't swell enough for you, Undine Spragg, you'd better go right over to the court of England" (38), for that is one trunk, another being Holland, from which the family tree of the American gentry has grown. She believes that Marvell's class is populated with the "originals" upon which are based the narratives in the "Boudoir Chat" column in the Sunday papers, which report on what "the smartest women" are doing (33). Finally, given the opportunity to realize her goal of moving into a better circle where she might find "the best" (38), she attends the dinner in a house that "was small and rather shabby. There was no gilding, no lavish diffusion of light [. . .]. The dinner too was disappointing. [. . .] With all the hints in the Sunday papers, she thought it dull of Mrs. Fairford not to have picked up something newer" (44). Such "hints" form Undine's definition of sophistication, but the variance she notes between portrait and experience indicates to her, and the reader, a competition between varied representations of social reality. Revelatory of a struggle in which media forms must adapt to the environment created by monopolistic capitalism, immigration, and the new demographic realities caused by the latter, Wharton illustrates the Darwinian selection of journalistic modes.

The narrative begins to draw the arc of Undine's changing perception of mass culture by recounting how, even before her family's move from Apex to New York, she takes representations of the elite found in the newspaper at face value: "She knew all of New York's golden aristocracy by name, and the lineaments of its most distinguished scions had been made familiar by passionate poring over the daily press" (41). She learns about "the smartest dinners in town" from the manicurist and hairdresser Mrs. Heeny's "newspaper cuttings" (25). Undine garners what she believes is knowledge about Marvell's class from poring over "the Society Column" (45). The young woman structures her mornings "after the manner described in the article 'On a Society Woman's Day'" (52).

Undine truly possesses "the instinct of adapting herself to whatever company she was in, of copying 'the others'" (150). Her identity, like the stories she reads in the tabloids, becomes "a product, generic and commercial, a roaming brand-name" (Preston 93), and she acquires a "press-agent" (CC 181). Undine interprets depictions of gentry behavior to constitute a standard that ought to be as easily realized as the act of buying the papers in which the Marvells and Dagonets figure so prominently. She sees no connection between the signs of class she notes and the traditions that underlie them.

Asserting an opinion on fictional methodology, Wharton writes that "[t]he subjective writer lacks the power of getting far enough away from his story to view it as a whole and relate it to its setting" (WF 78). In the context of Undine's first meeting with real members of Marvell's class, the novel warns that mass culture alienates its consumers from the essential, democracy-serving function of the press. Moreover, a "universal facility of communication" ("The Great American Novel" 154) that is a characteristic of Wharton's contemporary America displaces traditional narratives of continuity such as Raymond de Chelles's tale of his family's hereditary association with royalty, and Marvell's wish to merge "the personal with the general life" through "the releasing powers of language" (134). For Marvell, this experience would fulfill an aesthetic that seeks to present a fragmentary world in an artistically unified way. In its market-oriented ability to communicate quickly with the greatest number of people, the press obscures narratives which reiterate valued qualities of the social setting that stand against the instrumental use of people practiced by Undine. The novel presents the oppositional quality of artistic and mass culture narratives in the uses Marvell and Undine make of them. That the novel was serialized in the upmarket *Scribner's* magazine, certainly a cut above the periodicals depicted in *The Custom of the Country's* critical account of mass culture, indicates that Wharton's creative output was nevertheless subject to the tastes catered to and generated by the economic opportunities upon which the business of publishing capitalized.

Striking from the pages of a literary magazine in which the novel detailed the consequences for Undine of gaining her understanding of the public sphere from the popular press, *The Custom of the Country* parries mass culture's thrust at literature's authority. Wharton's incision into social reality reveals a mass culture ravenous for paying consumers that thrives on a feedback loop which conditions the self-perception of customers, and then validates the identities it molds. *The Custom of the Country* takes this object lesson to *Scribner's*, where readers like Marvell will find it. One imagines that Undine would not read this publication, for Mrs. Heeny responds to her pronouncement regarding her fear that Marvell's father will not approve of her by asking, "'Did you read the description of yourself in the *Radiator* this morning? I wish't I had time to cut it out. I guess I'll have to start a separate bag for *your* clippings soon" (89). With her likeness in circulation, Undine internalizes her own press. In the process, she ensures that a useful, though waning tradition in which even "graduations of tone were confusing" (48), will remain beyond her perception. Undine's fate is, in this respect, a cautionary tale issued to the consumers of this serialized novel who can glimpse whole ineffective cultural institutions that fail to inculcate the values Undine lacks.

Seemingly objective comparisons between Marvell's affiliation with tradition, and Undine's link to mass culture, can seem like the work of a social microscopist intent on dividing and analyzing. Yet Wharton's insights are those of an author who links her observations to a wider tradition of investigation that has as its key process "imagination," the same process Gillian Beer argues is key to the work of George Eliot. Of Eliot, whose influence on Wharton has been well documented,[12] Beer writes that she

> emphasises the congruity between all the various processes of the imagination: the novelist's and the scientist's enterprise is fired by the same prescience, the same willingness to explore the significance even of that which can be registered neither by instruments nor by the unaided senses. (*Darwin's Plots* 141)

Considered in light of this statement, Wharton's view that biological and social evolution are related bridges the "too deep an abyss of difference" (CC 337) separating the natural contingency represented by Undine and the project of supporting an intelligible, goal-directed public sphere that might be maintained by the narrative's more established leading class.

While with other characters, one might object to the suggestion that image and psychology could be viewed as identical, the text demonstrates that the surmise is appropriate in Undine's case, for she has a "delicious sense of being 'in all the papers'" (97) that satisfies her completely. This satisfaction does nothing to harness her primitive destructiveness because she finds no moral guidance in her reading. The story juxtaposes the fact that Undine's "mind was as destitute of beauty and mystery as the prairie schoolhouse where she had been educated" (139–40) with Marvell's and de Chelles's conviction that the "beauty and mystery" possessed by tradition is the source of social continuity. Her "education" by "the papers" is ultimately destructive to those two men's values, for she is both a subject, and agent, of mass culture.

The historian T. J. Jackson-Lears writes that "[w]hen antimodernists preserved higher loyalties outside the self they sustained a role of protest against a complacent faith in progress and a narrow positivist conception of reality" (xvi). *The Custom of the Country* is antimodern in this sense, then, in its negative depiction of Undine's notion of progress as social advancement at the price of common good. The novel also addresses a suspect "narrow positivist conception of reality" by using the ramifications of evolutionary thought to broaden it, for "Darwin consistently attempts to integrate man and animal, to make their actions, mental capacities, attitudes synonymous" (Kress 7–8). Wharton has little patience for positivist conceptions flavored with metaphysical assumptions, such as the idea that the survival of the fittest is a mechanism for the realization of a pre-ordained human destiny. In this she stands against a sentiment expressed by the one-time president of Yale University, Noah Porter, who in 1871 stated "we fear that soon it may be claimed that man has no rights which the student of nature is bound to respect" (18). From Wharton's perspective, the interrelatedness of humans and animals needs acknowledgement, not rebuttal.

Aside from a desire to consume and to rise within the social hierarchy there is little to Undine. But this is an effect of Wharton's representation and not a failure of characterization. Undine's narrow view of reality makes her irrelevant to the project of questioning faith in so-called progress, except as a negative example; Marvell "soon saw that she regarded intimacy as a pretext for escaping [. . .] into a total absence of expression" (143). What strikes one as the antimodernist orientation of *The Custom of the Country* may stem from its focus on the difficulty of forging mutually beneficial social bonds out of the material of Undine's callous, collectively useless individualism. The fictional rejection of the damaging trend Undine enacts is quite modern, though, in its attribution to unacknowledged and unregulated similarities between humans and animals of Undine's non-contributive "absence of expression."

A further example of the story's perspective on a "faith in progress" predicated on material gain and callousness exists in the fact that for Undine only the contractual is a suitable basis for hazarding one's assistance to another. This becomes apparent when she pleads with Moffatt, "Oh, Elmer, if you ever liked me, help me now, and I'll help you if I get the chance" (112). Even intimacy is a pretext for making smart arrangements, but this is unsurprising given the economic underpinning of the marital state Wharton details here and in *The House of Mirth*. Undine is strongly drawn to Moffatt. Her initial engagement to him in Apex and

their subsequent marriage presents no advantage socially in the view of
Marvell and his kind: "Undine felt that in the Marvell set Elmer Moffatt
would be stamped 'not a gentleman'" (112). Their attraction to each other
does represent, however, the operation of Undine's capacity for sexual selection, which works against mate selection based on exclusionary classism.

Physically, Moffatt is a powerful, "stoutish figure [. . .] thick yet com-
pact," who had "a look of jovial cunning" and a "brisk swaggering step"
(106–7). He bodily represents an unencumbered desire for material gain.
Moffatt cuts the figure of an animal. That Undine chooses him demonstrates that they are less governed by a moderation of sexuality that makes
Clare van Degen, who is in love with her cousin Marvell, "light and frivolous, without strength of will" (195). However, the fact that Undine's exer-
cising of her sexual selection seems to predict a problematic social and
genetic "renewal" through a union with Moffatt is inconsistent with the positive valuation of sexual selection present in *The House of Mirth* and *The Age
of Innocence*. This is explained by noting that Undine and Moffatt offer no
freshening of moribund gentry attitudes, such as Lily Bart and Lawrence
Selden, and Ellen Olenska and Newland Archer might in their respective
stories. Instead, Undine and Moffatt offer vigor without insight, except into
the weaknesses of those they dominate.

Undine's marriage to Ralph Marvell is a good one for her socially, but
she comes to understand that because of his relative lack of wealth, "money
was what chiefly stood between them" (204). Her perception can be traced
to the fact that she is "animated by her father's business instinct" (212). Furthermore, Undine is put forward in society on the premise of a calculation
that highlights how she differs from Marvell, and how the difference indicates class priorities: the Spraggs "had lived in New York for two years without any social benefit to their daughter; and it was of course for that purpose
they had come" (28). Undine grows impatient for the accrual of this "benefit." Finally marrying Marvell, she forms a union with one whose idea of
marriage bears little resemblance to her own. He had "preserved, through all
his minor adventures, his faith in the great adventure to come" and possessed
"the imaginative man's indestructible dream of a rounded passion" (85). His
imagination, affiliated with tradition and its pale of cultural stability, hinges
not on the contract, but on the human interaction the contract both formal-
izes and distances.

As a representative of an intrusive species, Undine imports her defining
moral blankness into the ranks of the elite. If Wharton is an antimodern social
critic who wishes to preserve her class loyalties, she does so with full knowledge
that simple denigration of modern social practices does little positive work, for

Marvell is unable to view Undine as a regression who also represents the future of a democracy aligned with commodities rather than conservatism. There is little authorial nostalgia for a past whose values cannot cope with the present. Undine adheres to no internalized code, save one that makes the evidence of her atavism invisible to others: "[h]er quickness in noting external differences had already taught her to modulate and lower her voice, and to replace 'The *i*-dea!' and 'I wouldn't wonder' by more polished locutions" (92). Like the papers she reads, her attractive form conceals an adaptive self-presentation addressed to the desires of her consumers. This key trait depends on an expertise at mimicry that makes it "instinctive with her to become, for the moment, the person her interlocutors expected her to be" (355). In this, she pointedly lacks any sign of being the product of social continuity.

The instinct that governs Undine is instantiated by mass-culture forms that project, in their status as throwaway objects, a world ephemeral and disposable, along with their message that change is progress whether it takes the form of new fashion or new identity. *The Custom of the Country* partially lays blame for Undine's harmful notions of progress on messages that propagate her tendency to emulate what she finds "in the glowing pages of fiction" (CC 68). She is a chameleon product of a world her aristocratic French husband is indignant about when he remarks of Americans, "You come from hotels as big as towns, and from towns as flimsy as paper, where the streets haven't had time to be named and the buildings are demolished before they're dry" (468).

In directing such blasts at America, Wharton would differentiate herself from a realist forerunner she greatly admired:

> For [. . .] W. D. Howells, literature ought to reflect and play a major role in encouraging the social and political progress that had received its fullest expression in the American effort to unite scientific inquiry and political democracy into a means for a better life for all men. [. . .] Howells [. . .] thus accepted wholeheartedly the central evolutionary premise of much nineteenth-century thought that loosely joined social, material, and intellectual life into a triumphant forward march. (Pizer "The House of Mirth" 66)

Wharton recalls in her memoir how "Howells was the first to feel the tragic potentialities of life in the drab American small town; but the incurable moral timidity which again and again checked him on the verge of a masterpiece drew him back" (BG 147–48). A degree of courage propels Wharton's anti-progressiveness, but she is too hard on Howells. The journalist Bartley

Hubbard's puff-piece interview of Silas Lapham shows that as early as the mid 1880s Howells addressed the role of the press in equating success within the American capitalist system with the suitability of one's ideals to the social environment.

Undine resembles Lapham, who is ignorant of a radical implication of Darwin's theory. He doesn't see that "evolution is not a process that was designed to produce us" (Dennett 56), but he is a figure to whose social-Darwinist logic Howells does not give free play. Wharton, on the other hand, traces out the consequences of the fact that Undine is "the perfect result of the system, the completest proof of its triumph" (190), in the words of Charles Bowen. It is a system, though, that does not grant credence to the importance of cooperation.

In Howells's novel, the journalist tells Lapham that he is "just one million times more interesting to the public than if you hadn't a dollar" (3). Here, Howells's realist narrative demonstrates that the papers' popular record of the noteworthy is responsive to the high value attached to material accumulation. It is a definition of progress he presents neutrally. Wharton's novels often reject such an association, and satirize this version of progress for its potential to commodify human relationships. An example of this occurs when Undine contrives for Marvell to pay her one hundred thousand dollars so that he might gain custody of their son. When Undine spots the boy, named Paul, on the railway platform, having forced Marvell to send him to her, she thinks "what an acquisition he would be" (414). With this statement Undine illustrates how her outlook on "progress" as accumulation objectifies the child, and presents Undine as unfeminine in her lack of maternal responsiveness. Judith Saunders zeroes in on the "bizarrely fragmented familial ties" (83) depicted in Wharton's *The Children* (1928), a novel related to *The Custom of the Country* not only in the former's interest in an "aberrant social environment" (Saunders 84) but also in its satire of "adults [that] devote their energies preponderantly to the search for new mating opportunities rather than to the nurture of existing children" (Saunders 86). Apposed to Undine's view of Paul as an object to sell is the outlook of the aristocratic de Chelles who, in accepting Paul into his household, asserts that progress is linked to acculturation by remarking that "he won't be a savage long with me" (414).

Undine's energy is wasted by an ethos that cannot turn her abilities away from "larger opportunities" and toward the project of controlled social renewal. Her inability to engage in practices that inhibit cultural fragmentation is a function of her training by mass culture, which can't educate her fully. "Fiction has been enlarged by making the background a part of the action," Wharton writes (qtd. in Wegener "Enthusiasm Guided by Acumen" 18), and Undine correlates with mass culture's effects in narrowing the perspective of the American citizen. This character's story articulates the interaction of the mass culture "background" and her advancement, which reads as logical in her ardently covetous world. But while the printed matter Undine reads cannot render subtle distinctions of class and status—one recalls her mistake in taking members of the newly moneyed class for the gentry—this is the very thing the novel does well.[13] *The Custom of the Country* asserts the ability of fiction to portray the state of the public sphere, which is not visible from the perspective offered by the hack writer of the society pieces Undine reads in The *Radiator*.

Fictional excavation of the social environment or "background" reveals that Undine's mediated idea of an undifferentiated elite persuades her, initially, to seek affiliation with a group that does not believe in linking material and social progress. She turns away from the provisional efforts of the gentry, and the small group making up the elite social pinnacle, to subdue the unpredictable results of immoderate individualism, realizing that she "had given herself to the exclusive and the dowdy when the future belonged to the showy and the promiscuous" (176–77). While waning social status is held by one subset of the elite represented in the papers she reads, waxing prestige and power belong to members of another group, such as "the wife of a Steel Magnet" (41), and to Peter Van Degen, who is "the hero of 'Sunday Supplements' [. . .] the supreme exponent, in short, of those crowning arts that made all life seem stale and unprofitable outside the magic ring of the Society Column" (58). Although it is true that Van Degen belongs to one of the first families of old New York, Wharton depicts him as leading the way toward the adoption of an outlook practiced by the *nouveaux riches*. His "odd physiognomy" (58) reminds one that unsuppressed sexuality is a worry of gentry tradition, for as Van Degen faces Undine, "his batrachian sallowness unpleasantly flushed," Wharton describes him as a "primitive man looking out of the eyes from which a frock-coated gentleman usually pined at her" (207). It is in their shared primitiveness, veneered with tradition in Van Degen's case, and gilded in Undine's, that Wharton finds a growing resemblance between "the exclusive and the dowdy" and "the showy and the promiscuous" that results from social evolution.

Undine learns from the angle of vision offered by mass-culture forms, though this learning limits her perception. She might see that the papers don't tell the whole truth, but she remains ignorant of their deterministic effect on her interaction with the broader aims of the social collective. She thus has "no clear perception of the forces that did not directly affect her" (97). As a representative of her type she is, like other Americans, "told every morning, by wireless and book jacket, by news item and picture-paper, who is in the day's spotlight, and must be admired (and if possible read) before the illumination shifts" ("Permanent Values in Fiction" 178). Wharton contains and represents Undine's attributes, particularly the fact that she is "passionately imitative" (34), and the novel therefore advertises its avoidance of the fallacy that adaptability, as exemplified by mass culture, can propel social evolution in a direction in keeping with the principles of equality and natural rights. Undine concludes, in what becomes "one of the guiding principles of her career," that "*It's better to watch than to ask questions*" (71). The italics are Wharton's, and the emphasis placed on this statement alerts the reader to the harmful consequences for all Americans of replacing political engagement with spectatorship learned from the "objectivity" of tabloids and how-to guides which normalize looking rather than participation.

Mass culture's influence on contemporary society in *The Custom of the Country* is analogous to the environmental influences on innumerable generations of species familiar to the Darwinist. As Undine finds fictions presented as facts in the newspapers, the novel presents such facts as creating new conditions in the broad social environment. A comparison with the long gestation of Marvell's class ideals is often implicit in the depiction of contemporary values uninfluenced by them. For example, a "Wall Street code" which creates "a world committed to swift adjustments" (233) shapes Undine's need for the immediate acquisition of "something still better beyond" (62). Marvell, though, reflects on an acting lesson he recalls observing as a young man, remembering the way a classic role was "dissolved into its component elements and built up again with a minuteness of elucidation and a range of references that made him feel as though he had been let into the secret of some age-long natural process" (233). The formation of one's identity has a history in Marvell's interpretation of the scene, despite the hint at the mediation of psychology offered by Wharton's contextualization in role creation of Marvell's musing. The process is both "natural" and intellectual in its reliance on "minuteness of elucidation" and "range of references." But he also understands this artifice to be a function of an "age-long [. . .] process" resulting from historical continuity and choice. The recording of Marvell's personal history, and the deeper social history he imagines shapes the self, contrasts with the immediacy of communication and the inconsequentiality of content that defines mass culture, Undine, and her contemporary society.

III. "THE STUDENT OF INHERITANCE MIGHT HAVE WONDERED"

In "The Great American Novel" (1927) Wharton comments on a failing of the criticism of fiction that echoes *The Custom of the Country*'s interest in popular culture's inability to value a refined tradition:

> The idea that genuineness is to be found only in the rudimentary, and that whatever is complex is inauthentic, is a favorite axiom of the modern American critic. To students of natural history such a theory is somewhat disconcerting. The tendency of all growth, animal, human, social, is towards an ever-increasing complexity. [. . .] Traditional society, with its old-established distinctions of class, its pass-words, exclusions, delicate shades of language and behavior, is one of man's oldest works of art, the least conscious and the most instinctive; yet the modern American novelist is told that the social and educated being is an unreality unworthy of his attention. (155)

This passage finds the perspective of a "student of natural history" to be a useful corrective to that of the "American critic." Its stance proposes the novelist's attention can be directed by science to forms of "human expression" a writer and natural historian such as Wharton can study, entailing the applicability of biology to manners, which signify the art of "traditional society."

But what within an instinctive traditional society is amenable to study through a scientifically minded fictional mode? Fusing particular architectural forms like the hothouse to a class stratum in *The House of Mirth* manifests tradition in Selden's grouping as invested in moderating the "tendency of all growth [. . .] towards an ever-increasing complexity." The mistake made by Selden and his type, though, is their idea that the social stasis represented by the hothouse is one that can be maintained with the weak force of manners. What Wharton suggests is that though social evolution converges on the wish to preserve "continuity and choice," such preservation is a rational goal. When Selden and Lily converse in the Brys' conservatory, the setting is emblematic of control over the natural by the novel's gentry, which is reflected in the bar against their romantic involvement—Lily can't stoop to marry Selden because she has been conditioned to "marry the first rich man she could get" (84) and Selden cannot afford her. The state of relations between them is one sign of "traditional society" set against social growth. The novel hybridizes "natural history" and "traditional society" in the figure of the hothouse.

Lawrence Selden, who is an "orchid basking in its artificially created atmosphere" (150), is like Marvell, who is preoccupied with "states of feeling" (194). Selden exemplifies "that little illuminated circle in which life reached its finest efflorescence, as the mud and sleet of a winter night enclose a hot-house filled with tropical flowers. All this was in the natural order of things" (HM 150). But Selden's order is not natural at all. The "little illuminated circle" is a product of nature, of course, to the extent that culture arises from a biological base, but the circle is alienated from natural processes by reason and tradition, which together attempt to forestall variation and class hybridization in the social realm by objecting to the kind of union one finds between Marvell and Undine in *The Custom of the Country.*

The novel's depicted social foundation comprised of economy, politics, and a primary tension between regulative moral and legal commands and raging want, projects multiple ideological stories. This is apparent in conflicting attitudes toward unregulated change displayed by a reactive gentry, and the socioeconomic elite's regressive ignorance of the hazard posed by chance to the underlying democracy that supports their business activities. The portrait of Undine's inhumane pursuit of wealth and power, and its harmful effect on Marvell and de Chelles, illustrates this. Relaxing standards that formerly connected wealth and social responsibility create her as "a creature of skin-deep reactions, a mote in the beam of pleasure" (202).

A primer standard is measured out for the reader in Marvell's condescending estimation of Undine, which signifies his class fable: "He was not blind to her crudity and her limitations, but they were a part of her grace and her persuasion. [. . .] her obvious lack of any sense of relative values, would make her an easy prey to the powers of folly" (85–86). Here, Wharton juxtaposes Undine's singular instinctive values against Marvell's recognition that "relative values" exist and compete with each other. The "skin-deep reactions" exhibited by Undine mark her as dangerously unaware of this fact, while Marvell's attraction to "her grace and her persuasion" is his weakness; he underestimates the vulnerability of "old-established distinctions of class."

In *The Custom of the Country* Undine's aggressive exploitation of what Bowen calls "the whole problem of American marriages" (187)—consensual divorce, the expectation of female passivity, and "[t]he fact that the average American looks down on his wife" (187)—goes unchecked within Marvell's class-bound enclave. Inside, the breakdown of an idealistic distancing of the uncivilized seen in *The House of Mirth* facilitates Undine's ability to act as she does. *The Custom of the Country* presents a hothouse damaged to such an extent that a native species epitomized by Undine and Elmer Moffatt over-grows the orchids of the gentry within it. Undine misidentifies the moderat-ing purpose of culture, seeing it instead as the source of a life ever "more luxurious, more exciting, more worthy of her" (62). The text confronts the effects of her erroneous distinction upon an organically based social entity which the protagonist sees as a mechanism that can satisfy "her usual busi-ness-like intentness on gaining her end," yet will not demand that she con-tribute (454).

In 1908, Wharton read Vernon Kellogg's *Darwinism Today* (*Letters* 146). "Variation [. . .] occurs according to the laws of chance," according to Kellogg (32), and Wharton extends his claim to her fiction by showing that from Undine's perspective the "best"—that is, the socioeconomic elite—hold their position through a coincidence of chance variation and receptive environment. Undine's ability to realize her intent, in other words, is the result of prevalent social conditions that favor her superficiality. Her varia-tion, as I have suggested, is also a regression that complicates the reader's understanding of the words "complexity" and "progress" in the Darwinian context, making difficult the task of interpreting the author's portrait of their class-centered definitions. Edward O. Wilson makes a distinction about these words that is useful in deciphering *The Custom of the Country*'s combi-nation of social evolution and natural selection:

> If we mean by progress the advance toward a preset goal, such as that composed by intention in the human mind, then evolution by natural selection, which has no preset goals, is not progress. But if we mean the production through time of increasingly complex controlling organisms and societies, in at least some lines of descent, with regression always a possibility, then evolutionary progress is an obvious reality. (98)

Accordingly, social evolution and regression are matters of increasing or decreasing complexity alone. Progress too consists only of increased com-plexity; teleology is problematic. Applied to *The Custom of the Country,* Undine's pursuit of "improvement" (CC 60) through the realization of her materialistic intentions is abject. The novel is dedicated to changing what lies within its field of vision, foregrounding the untapped capacity of a class intelligence able to observe "impartially from the heights of pure specula-tion" (187), but the work is morbidly satirical too. Rationalism cannot beat back the forces of chance.

The Spragg family's movement eastward and Undine's subsequent tri-umph exemplify the threat presented by uncontrolled natural competition.

Contained within this plot sequence is a Darwinian truism connected in the novel to the growing mobility of Americans in the nineteenth century. Yet the Spraggs are unaware of their conformity to anything but their own desire to see Undine advance, demonstrating again the novel's association of sudden material increase with a primitive attitude toward the social collective's purpose.

Geographical and class mobility are obvious characteristics of this new world. A passage from *On The Origin of Species* serves well to describe the family's journey from the unsophisticated, and thus ironically named Apex City, to the exploitable landscape of New York, and what happens to those with whom Undine mingles upon her arrival: "If the country were open on its borders, new forms would certainly immigrate, and this would seriously disturb the relations of some of the former inhabitants" (*Origin* 102). New York is opening up, something shown by the success of Elmer Moffatt. As if to prove the applicability of Darwin's statement in the social context, Undine's arrival in New York upsets the prevailing social equilibrium. Undine hears, for instance, "that Mrs. Marvell had other views for her son [than to marry Undine]," but "there had been no reprisals [. . .]. That was not her ideal of warfare" (92). No thought of fighting off the "intruder" enters Mrs. Marvell's mind (69). On the contrary, true to her ideals regarding cooperation, an adaptive trait no longer viable, Marvell's mother "seem[s] anxious to dispel any doubts of her good faith" once his decision to marry Undine has been made (92).

The portrait of class relations in the social environment of New York demonstrates how the values of the gentry and the socioeconomic elite posit a connection between nature and culture. Compare, for example, Undine's enactment of social life as a battle in which "she was going to get what she wanted" (42) by releasing "her blind desire to wound and destroy" (454), with Marvell's comment regarding the displacement of those who succumb to the invaders:

> Ralph sometimes called his mother and grandfather the Aborigines, and likened them to those vanishing denizens of the American continent doomed to rapid extinction with the advance of the invading race. He was fond of describing Washington Square as the "Reservation" and prophesying that before long its inhabitants would be exhibited at ethnological shows, pathetically engaged in the exercise of their primitive industries. (77–78)

Marvell's eyes are open to the displacement of his class, but his response denotes passivity. His comparison of his grouping to the American aborigine made extinct by the same "blind desire" exhibited by Undine lacks insight into the actual extinction of individuals and entire races. While fluent in abstractions, Marvell is unable really to conceive of the avidity summed up in Undine and her colonial, and biological, antecedents.

Marvell's comparison of his family to aborigines recalls Bromfield Corey's comparison in *The Rise of Silas Lapham* of the Lapham family to the Sioux: "clever but uncivilized" (96). Corey and Marvell share key traits. Both are aesthetes. Corey, a painter, believes that civilization starts with literature, while Marvell is an aspiring author. But they are relics. Marvell, a "vanishing denizen" himself, acknowledges the fact of invasion allegorically when he refers to his family as "Aborigines" and thus distances its reality. Corey, commenting on a member of the new socioeconomic elite in referring to Lapham, disparages the class that will displace his own by brandishing a now irrelevant ideal civilization whose authority is crumbling before the new capitalism. For both characters, the connection between nature and culture is obscured by a fixation on the reflection of culture in art, as when Marvell goes to "the length of quoting poetry" (175) to a woman deaf to its tradition and to its representation of a culture built up slowly through time. For Undine Spragg, nature and "culture," instinct and its enactment, are of a piece.

Shades of difference emerge between members of the "invading race," while members of the gentry possess a homogeneous character, except those such as Van Degen who are drifting to the other side. *The Custom of the Country,* it is arguable, puts forward New York's socioeconomic elite as an example of evolutionists' observations of "thousands of gradations and variations between organisms" (Dennett 35). Charles Bowen observes "a seemingly endless perspective of plumed and jeweled heads, of shoulders bare or black-coated" (CC 242) that catalogues display by the new rich in a way that recalls Darwin's descriptions of variations within a species: "No one supposes that all the individuals of the same species are cast in the very same mould. These individual differences are highly important to us, as they offer materials for natural selection to accumulate" (*Origin* 102). In such transpositions of evolutionary writing into fiction, class and species become coequal. Because of this, variation from the social mean can be presented as natural, while conformity to it can be seen as a sign of insupportable artifice.

Attitudes toward consumer goods provide class-specific examples of the high value placed on variety and novelty by Undine. For instance, she takes to heart the principle that fashion evolves. Undine's "unworn" dresses look "old-fashioned" almost as soon as they are purchased (35). What is best and new are synonymous to her. She is thrilled when de Chelles gives her "glimpses of another, still more brilliant existence, that life of the inaccessible 'Faubourg'" (253), even though it is a class enclave more shuttered than Marvell's New York. Meanwhile, the old money lives in unchanging fustiness where esteemed women wear "dowdy black and antiquated ornaments" (45). What marks one as fashionable in the socioeconomic elite is the ability to express wealth as "incoherence" unrestricted by tradition (243). Wandering through the rooms of an art gallery, Undine senses that "the ladies and gentlemen wedged before the pictures had the 'look' which signified social consecration" (57). In conforming to this look, ultra-rich newcomers symbolize visibility and mutability as properties of their class, rejecting the visible manifestation of continuity denoted by wearing "dowdy black." Undine's "sparkling eyes" (392), her "high fluting tone" (95), and the fact that a "blotched looking glass [. . .] could not disfigure her" (219) bestow upon her beauty a primal quality that, in contrast to the "plain" women of the gentry (45), distinguishes her as an example of her type and a symbol of superficiality.

In *Darwiniana* (1897), a work that Claire Preston suggests Wharton read (196), Huxley writes that

> *Atavism* [. . .] is [. . .] one of the most marked and striking tendencies of organic beings; but side by side with this hereditary tendency there is an equally distinct and remarkable tendency to variation. The tendency to reproduce the original stock has, as it were, its limits, and side by side with it there is a tendency to vary in certain directions, as if there were two opposing powers working upon the organic being, one tending to take it in a straight line, and the other tending to make it diverge from that straight line, first to one side and then to the other. (398)

Huxley means atavism in the following sense: "Resemblance to [. . .] remote ancestors rather than to parents; tendency to reproduce the ancestral type in animals or plants. [. . .] Recurrence of the disease or constitutional symptoms of an ancestor after the intermission of one or more generations" (OED 742). Atavism is one of Undine's defining traits: "Mr. and Mrs. Spragg were both given to such long periods of ruminating apathy that the student of inheritance might have wondered whence Undine derived her overflowing activity" (116). Marvell wonders "from what source Undine's voracious ambitions had been drawn" (279). She is the chance regression that causes others to question the source of her "inherited prejudices" (282). Among these prejudices is her attitude that social progress is intertwined with material accumulation and destructiveness.

Undine is in this way cast as a historically primitive type that has reappeared to define the future.

Undine's regressive aspect repels what would acculturate her into the ideals of the established elite she twice marries into. Her previously documented habit of seeking improvement is one that relies on exploitation, making of progress an end with no ethical restriction on the means used to achieve it. Huxley accepted an interpretation of Darwinism that acknowledged the struggle for existence and the elimination of the unfit. However, Huxley qualifies this point, which centers on the notion that humans, as reasoning beings, can take moral action in the face of the struggle for existence. It is a qualification the novel reiterates frequently:

> There is another fallacy which appears to me to pervade the so-called 'ethics of evolution.' It is the notion that because, on the whole, animals and plants have advanced in perfection of organization by means of the struggle for existence and the consequent 'survival of the fittest'; therefore men in society, men as ethical beings, must look to the same process to help them towards perfection. I suspect that this fallacy has arisen out of the unfortunate ambiguity of the phrase 'survival of the fittest.' 'Fittest' has a connotation of 'best'; and about 'best' there hangs a moral flavour. In cosmic nature, however, what is 'fittest' depends upon the conditions. [. . .] if our hemisphere were to cool again, the survival of the fittest might bring about, in the vegetable kingdom, a population of more and more stunted and humbler and humbler organisms, until the 'fittest' that survived might be nothing but lichens [. . .]. They, as the fittest, the best adapted to the changed conditions, would survive. ("Evolution and Ethics" 327)

In Huxley's view, conditions are the key factor successful adaptation must answer to within nature. His criticism is reserved for interpretations of social evolution that deny human control over social conditions. Refuting the "survival of the fittest" in the terms one finds in Wharton's narrative, he provides a position from which to view Undine as a character who is a "stunted [. . .] lichen" well adapted to the changed conditions of a modern world that favor such a creature.

Because Marvell's class has not arrested the decay of "conditions" allegorized by Undine's thriving, the gentry falls within the scope of Wharton's critical eye. Undine's enactment of the idea, though she could not articulate it, that "[f]ittest has a connotation of best," damages the people and traditions she comes into contact with. This contributes to the erosion of the social order whose material privileges she enjoys. But Wharton's harshness toward the socioeconomic elite is balanced by her criticism of an aristocracy inattentive to the changed conditions on which Undine capitalizes. That which is extinguished by the forces Undine represents—namely, the cultural practices of Ralph Marvell and Raymond de Chelles—has no special claim to endure. The inability of tradition to intervene in its diminution by mass culture and the market has made the leading class vulnerable to the dynamics of a cultural form of natural selection. With the old system no longer viable, contingency makes the same short work of gentry mores and practices that try to moderate contingency, as the dialectic of science makes of "Mrs. Marvell's classification of the world [. . .] absolute as medieval cosmogony" (177). Ancient and outdated, Mrs. Marvell's outlook is as vulnerable as the complex of traditions and rites overgrown by the lichen-like Undine.

In a passage that echoes *The Custom of the Country's* reasoning about the purpose of tradition, and Undine's ignorance of the protections offered by it to the collective, Huxley writes:

> Laws and moral precepts are directed to the end of curbing the cosmic process and reminding the individual of his duty to the community, to the protection and influence of which he [or she] owes, if not existence itself, at least the life of something better than a brutal savage. It is from neglect of these plain considerations that the fanatical individualism of our time attempts to apply the analogy of cosmic nature to our society. ("Evolution and Ethics" 328)

Undine's application of this analogy displays her own role in a socially construed selection process within the confines of old New York. Marvell dimly recognizes her individualism during a disagreement with Undine over the company she keeps. He perceives her refusal of his commands as "the perfect functioning of her instinct of self-preservation" (152). Furthermore, her connection to "cosmic nature," like Moffatt's, resists linguistic codification, reinforcing the regressive aspect of both characters: "here was someone who spoke her language," Undine notes of Moffatt, someone "who knew her meanings, who understood instinctively all the deep-seated wants for which her acquired vocabulary had no terms" (460). She views society as a part of the natural world, not a mitigation of it. In this view Undine's relation to a moderating tradition is occluded by the violence of enacted desire present in "the sinister change" that "came over her when her will was crossed" (154).

Marvell rebukes her by saying: "You know nothing of this society you're in; of its antecedents, its rules, its conventions" (151). Yet Undine's is not a willful disparagement of the old rules, but an expression of instinct. She is more like Peter Van Degen, who instead of thoughtfully discharging his responsibility as a social leader is presented as a sexually aggressive amphibian with a frog-like "batrachian countenance" (72). The latter is an allusion to his sexual attraction to Undine comprehensible to one with a thoroughgoing knowledge of Darwin's *The Descent of Man,* for in that work one finds that in nature "the male seems much more eager than the female; and so it is with [. . .] Batrachians" (200). Cecelia Tichi sees in Wharton's description of Peter Van Degen as "batrachian" the possibility that Wharton "developed the frog-like countenance in recollection of passages early in William James's *The Principles of Psychology.* [. . .] [in which] she would have found basic lessons in neurology instanced by frogs" (104). Hence, the image was available to Wharton in at least two sources. Van Degen's drives, like Undine's, distinguish him from Marvell, who seems particularly bloodless when Popple "leaned over to give Marvell's hand the ironic grasp of celibacy" (99). Marvell might refer to "antecedents" and "rules," but he does nothing to perpetuate them when he brings Undine into the walled garden of the elite. For her part, Undine works from instinct that transmits no memory of the "conventions" championed by Marvell.

Other scientific works contributed to Wharton's fictional analysis of nature and culture in *The Custom of the Country.* Her corrective to individualistic enactments of false but influential interpretations of natural selection was founded on sources that shed new light on heredity in nature. Familiarity with R. H. Lock's *Variation, Heredity and Evolution* (1906)[14] gave her insights into a contemporary interpretation of Darwin's work on natural selection and variation that, along with Kellogg's *Darwinism Today,* presented current thinking on the then inadequately understood medium of heredity. In *The Age of Innocence,* as I show in the next chapter, rituals of the elite "tribe" are one medium by which regulative cultural practices are perpetuated. In the novel under consideration here, though, factors outside the control of Marvell and his breed jam their mechanisms of cultural inheritance.

Lock's work is rich with passages descriptive of the changes wrought by the process of heredity. Many of these passages are expressed, moreover, in non-technical language that invites the application of biological principles to the analysis of social characteristics:

> the features of every part [of an organism] are aimed at some useful purpose; or if they are not, then they have been useful in former times and under different circumstances, and are now undergoing a process of gradual removal, because the individuals in which the useless structure is least developed will have the best chance of surviving. (Lock 51)

In the sociobiological framework of the novel, Marvell and his kind are undergoing "gradual removal" from the larger social structure that is Wharton's subject. Whereas Marvell appreciates the old world as the foundry of his traditions, Undine thinks of the European towns she visits with him as "places [that] seem as if they were dead. It's like some awful cemetery" (144). His suicide is the most extreme form of disengagement from a social organism to which he is not useful. It is an act attributable to the workings of the market, which dissolves his capital when he risks it to regain his son. Wharton's knowledge of Lock's work, like her knowledge of Huxley's, is another aspect of her literary view of a "process of gradual removal" in nature that persists across a perceived gap between human and animal nature.

The presence of such processes mandates others inherent in the traditions of the aristocratic collective (which are, of course, also exclusionary) to arrest the unjust removal of individuals like Marvell. In contrast to the notion of individual rights suggested by this position, Undine's assumption regarding her success recalls the reasoning of the nineteenth-century sociologist William Graham Sumner, who views natural selection as having escaped the effects of social modification. Sumner writes that

> [t]he millionaires are a product of natural selection, acting on the whole body of men to pick out those who can meet the requirements of certain work to be done. [. . .] They may fairly be regarded as the naturally selected agents of society for certain work. They get high wages and live in luxury, but the bargain is a good one for society. (qtd. in Hofstadter 58)

Undine's actions play out Sumner's assumption that natural selection acts freely on all people.

Her self-exemption from social regulation is founded on the belief that adhering to tradition would subject her to a spurious dilution of her will. The novel suggests that the period it chronicles witnesses the fruition of Sumner's statement. It is the effect of Undine's actions on others that is thus given significance: "[i]n all her struggles for authority her sense of the rightfulness of her cause had been measured by her power of making people do as she pleased" (454). Moreover, if Undine is a "naturally selected agent" deserving of the material gains she accumulates as she passes from marriage to marriage,[15] the fact remains that what "the whole body of men" receives in Undine and Sumner's "bargain" is nought.

The effects of ascribing a cultural role to natural selection in the way seen in Sumner's statement poses the question of how social Darwinism affects the continuity of tradition, social stewardship, and artistic achievement Marvell's class would carry on. As was the case with Huxley's, Kellogg's, and Lock's work, Wharton's familiarity with the German physician and biologist Ernst Haeckel's thinking presented her with a biological theory suggestive of forms with which to depict the regressive aspect of Undine's combative ideology of natural and social selection. One now discredited theory advanced by Haeckel, when examined alongside the novel, reveals another dimension of *The Custom of the Country*'s portrait of the reappearance in culture of primitive traits.

The question of whether Wharton was familiar with Haeckel's influential theory of recapitulation is resolved by turning to Kellogg's *Darwinism Today*. Wharton wrote that she was "deep in Kellogg's" book, in a letter to Sara Norton dated May 29, 1908 (*Letters* 146). This occurred during one of the periods in which Wharton wrote *The Custom of the Country* (Lewis 228). In *Darwinism Today* Kellogg summarizes Haeckel's theory[16] as follows: "The species recapitulates in the ontogeny (development) of each of its individuals the course or history of its phylogeny (descent or evolution). Hence the child corresponds in different periods of its development to the phyletic stages in the descent of man" (Kellogg 21). Recapitulation, in the sense outlined by Haeckel, deals with the relation between ontogeny, which is the science of the development of the individual human organism, and phylogeny. Phylogeny is "the science of the evolution of the various animal forms from which the human organism has developed" (Haeckel 255). Paralleling Kellogg's description, Undine is frozen in her childlike state. She is impulsive, "remote and Ariel like" (143), and she "wanted [. . .] amusement [. . .] despite her surface-sophistication her notion of amusement was hardly less innocent than when she had hung on the plumber's fence" (308). The presentation of her innocence finds her impervious simplicity of purpose and arrested moral development to be related; from Marvell's perspective, "she was completely unconscious of states of feeling on which so much of his inner life depended" (194). Represented as being "unconscious," Undine has no "inner life" except for those moments of insight into what must be emulated in order to gain an advantage. In this she represents an American character unsuited by its atavistic appetites to refashioning the incoherence of its history into a social ideal able to contain these energies.

To illustrate this, the narrative describes Undine as having come from "a ragged outskirt" (36) of a western town. Marvell wonders of the Spraggs "how long would their virgin innocence last" (84), not realizing that what he interprets as innocence is a regressive primitivism destabilizing to the Byzantine construction of "old-established distinctions of class, its pass-words, exclusions, delicate shades of language and behavior" ("The Great American Novel" 155). In the garden of New York's elite, Undine represents the ethical blankness of the new world asserting itself over old world standards. Her lack of a moral center leaves only instinct. Thus, Undine's wariness of Van Degen is presented as an ability to "go on eluding and doubling, watching him as he watched her" (201). This resonates with her perception in him of "a hint of the masterful way that had once subdued her in Elmer Moffatt" (258). Undine's attraction, in Moffatt's case, is an attraction to force unmediated by the cultural forms represented by Marvell.

I have noted that Wharton's *A Backward Glance* relates her excitement at reading Haeckel's work (94). Turning to the original passage in Haeckel that Kellogg discusses, one finds the former's account to be equally suggestive for Wharton's biologically informed interpretation of social history:

> the series of forms through which the individual organism passes during its development from the ovum to the complete bodily structure is a brief, condensed repetition of the long series of forms which the animal ancestors of the said organism, or the ancestral forms of the species, have passed through from the earliest period of organic life down to the present day. (255)

Wharton knew of Mendelism, and she evidently understood its premise that "discrete bodies (now called genes) control the inheritance of any particular character and that these are inherited in accordance with certain simple laws" (OED 662). Allusions to heredity that recall Haeckel's and Mendel's work surface in the narrative's account of how markers of class are passed on from one generation to the next.

Charles Bowen admires de Chelles as "a charming specimen of the Frenchman of his class" (245); Marvell thinks Moffatt a "good specimen of the one of the few picturesque types we've got" (195). The traits that define these "specimens" arise from a Whartonian mix of biological and social origins. Class specimens conform to a particular ideology. Yet the fact that the novel frames individuals as specimens invokes biological allegory as a potential factor in such descriptions. In bringing together ideology and biology to describe class species between which there is an "abyss of difference" (337) too deep for reconciliation,[17] the novel tenders two ways in which the individual is defined by his or her environment. However, as is the case elsewhere in the novel, these registers of influence run together in the name of the novel's broader aim of showing that nature and culture should not be thought of as separate phenomena.[18]

Wharton's portrait of Undine's regressive nature capitalizes on the theory of recapitulation to represent in her progress the historical development of a country. In drawing Undine thus, Wharton attributes to the evolution of the society that has spawned Undine the development of her moral characteristics. Gillian Beer demonstrates the interest in ontogeny and phylogeny during the nineteenth century, offering a way to link Haeckel's theories and *The Custom of the Country:*

> The new question formulated [. . .] by the contemplation of transformation and metamorphosis was this: can transformations within the individual life cycle (ontogeny) act as a valid model for species mutation (phylogeny)? And as a subsidiary question, do we see the phases of evolutionary process *recapitulated* in the individual organism. [. . .] The embryo was held to recapitulate (or condense) the development of the species to which it belonged. It seemingly offered, therefore, visual and experimental evidence for earlier phases of evolutionary development. (*Darwin's Plots* 98)

The novel reframes these questions in the context of social evolution distinguished by ideological shifts. Wharton's plotting of Undine's career, particularly her character's transformation from eager ingénue to savvy aggressor, charts America's progress toward empire by articulating how Undine's primitive energies drive the brand of "progress" valued by her. The novel illustrates, too, that "the phases of evolutionary process *recapitulated* in the individual organism," as Undine undergoes her formative experiences, "condense the development" of the new species of American and in this way visibly stage the social transformation that results.

Much textual evidence supports this conjecture. Undine begins the novel as a young woman convinced that the socioeconomic elite is corrupt: "[a]s her imagination developed the details of the Van Degen dining room it became clear to her that fashionable society was horribly immoral" (69). While she rebukes "fashionable society" for a time, she soon becomes its exemplar, and finds herself competing with, and ultimately weakening, Marvell's "inherited notion of 'straightness'" (273). In the depiction of this transition, Undine illustrates a dialectical process of social evolution. This suggests to the reader that Undine's optimistic definition of progress is not the linear fulfillment of attaining "the best" (60), nor the promise of something "still better beyond" (62) she believes it to be.

Undine's stunted social self is a manifestation of an earlier state of the social evolutionary process experienced by American culture. It is a regression that is predicted for the whole species by Undine's success, one that exhibits again the narrative's skepticism toward the kind of progress Undine embraces. Her immaturity is a trait prominent in the representation of her arrested evolutionary state. She is bewildered by the "eliminations and abbreviations" in conversation at the Fairfords (48). But despite this, Undine's striving, emulative tendency, evident in the fact that "all she sought for was improvement" (60), indicates her own sense that "ampler vistas" await her (64). In sensing a wider horizon that will mean "improvement" for her, Undine echoes an optimistic turn-of-the-century American attitude to the frontier, as well as a social-Darwinist habit of viewing dominance as progress. But rather than push westward with migration and expanding civilization, she moves east against the grain of Manifest Destiny to devour the decadent gentry efflorescence of Puritan colonization. In doing so, Undine embodies an authorial refutation of a narrow and optimistic progressivism, apparent in Wharton's comment that "the conditions of modern life in America, so far from being productive of great arguments, seem almost purposely contrived to eliminate them" ("The Great American Novel" 153).

The push westward strains the capacity of an already diminished cultural heritage to impart itself to the distant Undine in Apex City. Mass culture, however, and its ability to shrink distance through modern methods of distribution, fills the vacuum. This new form of acculturation contributes to Undine's replacement of Marvell as "Homo Sapiens Americanus" by making her its agent. She is a reiteration of a past phase in the social evolution of her country characterized by rapacious expansionism. "[T]he pioneer blood in Undine would not let her rest" (64), and her pioneering spirit lays waste to the social ground she settles.

One element of the value system held by Marvell and de Chelles that is pressured by the regressive Undine is the conceit of cultural continuity. While tradition *is* passed down through the generations of Dagonets, Rays and Fairfords, and de Chelles, its mutability is downplayed. Marvell's denial of the triumph of money over taste exemplifies this; he wants to save Undine from "Van Degen and Van Degenism" (85) without realizing that she is its prime exponent. He also hopes to "implant in Paul [his son] some of the reserves and discriminations which divided that tradition from the new spirit of limitless concession" (269), despite the fact that the new spirit has already dissipated the traditional symbol of continuity, the family, by permitting divorce. De Chelles uses arguments "drawn from accumulations of hereditary experience" (428) in his attempt to counter Undine's wish that they live a more regal life. His "plea," however, is "unintelligible to her" (428). A model for living that defers to the goals of community rather than the individual is to Undine unintelligible.

Wharton's synthesis of the cultural and the natural is a foundation for her valuation of a social ideal of interdependence neither class fulfills in *The Custom of the Country.* This approach foreshadows the premise of "gene-culture coevolution" that posits the existence of a "basic unit of culture—now called meme" (Wilson 136), related in its function in the social context to the role of the gene in biology. Representations of ideology in the novel intersect with the concept of memes, which Daniel Dennett describes as "units of cultural transmission analogous to the genes of biological evolution. [. . .] Like genes, memes are supposed to be replicators, in a different medium, but subject to much the same principles of evolution as genes" (143).[19] Systems of thought from which particular classes derive their values are never entirely stable in this group of novels, but they are instantiated in each generation, so are analogous to the genetic transmission of traits. However, there is no pure ideology; ideas are never as stable in individual psychology as their allegorical genetic equivalent. Stability exists only in the Platonic sense revealed in Newland Archer's notion in *The Age of Innocence* that "'Taste' [. . .] [is] that far-off divinity of whom 'Form' was the mere visible representative and viceregent" (14). Ideological miscegenation is unavoidable, as *The Custom of the Country* maintains through its portraits of gentry characters, like Van Degen, unmoored from a class-based system of ideas, and intermarriage between members of different strata.[20] Wharton does represent ideological "units of cultural transmission" in her fiction, and she depicts the applicability to them of "the principles of evolution." In being set against social evolution, moreover, tradition, as Marvell understands it, is overmatched by the absence of preordination.

Tradition has mystic beginnings to Marvell and de Chelles. Undine notes it too, finding it to be concentrated in the "spell [that] seemed to emanate from the old house which had so long been the custodian of an unbroken tradition" (445). But Marvell finds that tradition, irrevocably altered by Undine, conceals the same randomness it is set against. Despite its seeming immutability, that unnamable "spell" is a conceit placed in opposition to natural law's bedrock algorithms.[21] Indeed, social evolution is the process that brought provisional order to the classes—though never real or lasting order—but this is a fact that has not been appreciated by either Marvell or de Chelles, or Charles Bowen. Undine successfully dissipates the spell of the gentry's interpretation of tradition that imagines it as an unchanging and stabilizing force. Moreover, she illustrates that the main characteristic of social evolution is flux. Ideology is friable, as the custodians of old New York are beginning to comprehend when they sight "the social disintegration

expressed by widely-different architectural physiognomies at the other end of
Fifth Avenue" where the new money lives (77).

The self-involvement of both the gentry and the socioeconomic elite
projects no authoritative sphere of cultural protection against chance; mitigation of nature is despoiled by variability and regression. Cultural movement toward a complexity that seems like progress is countered by the
unforeseeable result in *The Custom of the Country*: Marvell's intoxication
with Undine results in his suicide; her own distaste for the socioeconomic
elite is reversed and she arrives at the pinnacle of new money "culture"
through her ultimate union with Moffatt. In a novel that the author considered a "chronicle" (BG 182), and a "magnum opus" (*Letters* 240), the effect
on Marvell of this reversal to accepted thinking documents the erosion of
continuity rooted in architecture, refined self-consciousness, and a separation of public and private selves by an alien ideology. In particular, Marvell
suffers the closing of a perceived gap between public and private by Undine's
"divorce-suit," which is "a vulgar and unnecessary way of taking the public
into one's confidence" (282).

IV. "SWEPT FROM THE ZENITH LIKE A PINCH OF DUST"

In *The Decoration of Houses* (1897) Wharton observes how "[t]he survival of
obsolete customs which makes the study of sociology so interesting, has its par-
allel in the history of architecture" (5). In comparing European and American
society, Ralph Marvell engages in social commentary using architectural terms
that contrast the single-minded pursuit of financial gain he finds in New York
with a code of conduct that "the very lines of the furniture in the old Dagonet
house expressed" (77). Marvell goes on to define previously unseen building
styles emerging from the mix of new tycoons and old ideals:

> what Popple called society was really just like the houses it lived in: a
> muddle of misapplied ornament over a thin steel shell of utility. The
> steel shell was built up in Wall Street, the social trimmings were hastily
> added in Fifth Avenue; and the union between them was as monstrous
> and factitious, as unlike the gradual homogenous growth which flowers
> into what other countries know as society, as that between the Blois gar-
> goyles on Peter Van Degen's [New York] roof and the skeleton walls sup-
> porting them. (77)

The appropriation of forms by the new rich results in an incoherent assemblage
of symbols gathered from other classes and countries. In being "monstrous,"

Van Degen's "misapplied ornament" recalls the random combination of traits familiar from Darwin's comment on the presence of variation within species. But the narrative tonally criticizes the forms "Van Degenism" creates. Described from Marvell's perspective, the union between Wall Street and Fifth Avenue bears deformed architectural offspring.

Historically shortsighted in its ignorance of the value of continuity, the socioeconomic elite sunders the "intrinsic rightness" (CC 77) of gentry architecture through the creation of new combinations of its parts. Marvell sees "his mother and Mr. Urban Dagonet [. . .] so closely identified with the old house in Washington Square that they might have passed for its inner consciousness as it might have stood for their outward form" (77). No distance exists between the ideas intrinsic to the graduated development of their society and the forms that express them in Marvell's mind. A new money attitude toward tradition is manifest too in borrowings of "locution" (92) or "vocabulary" (46) from the gentry, which Undine has yet to master when she exclaims, "I don't care if I do" and "I wouldn't wonder" (46) at Mrs. Fairford's dinner party. But Marvell, who might be more guarded in his attraction to a woman with such obvious "inherited prejudices," recalls ruefully that he "had thought Undine's speech fresh and natural" (282). What seems appealing to Marvell is certainly natural, but the newness of her speech, its capacity to reconfigure gentry language through appropriation, recombination, and ultimately authority (because of the power and position she accumulates) parallels in the linguistic realm "monstrous and factitious" hybridizations of architectural forms.

From Herbert Spencer, Wharton absorbed the lesson that nature and culture were not divisible, and found a theory of the ends of nature she would resist in her work.

> Progress, therefore, is not an accident, but a necessity. Instead of civilization being artificial, it is a part of nature; all of a piece with the development of the embryo or the unfolding of a flower. The modifications mankind have undergone, and are still undergoing, result from a law underlying the whole organic creation; and provided the human race continues, and the constitution of things remains the same, those modifications must end in completeness. [. . .] as surely as there is any meaning in such terms as habit, custom, practice;—so surely must the human faculties be moulded into complete fitness for the social state. (*Social Statics* 31)

However, Elmer Moffatt's "weapons of aggression" (180), unsheathed signs of the "new spirit of limitless concession" (269), assault the building blocks of literature, painting, and architecture that symbolize a cultural bulwark against unpredictable nature. In the monstrous combinations of old and new world architectural styles used to build their garish mansions, the titans reassemble elements of culture. Doing so breaks the "spell [. . .] [that] seemed to emanate from the old house which had long been the custodian of an unbroken tradition" (445); this "spell," of course, is a spectral gentry system of "habit, custom" that provides a façade of order and control. And while Moffatt becomes a culturally sophisticated collector, his acquisitiveness is not based on a desire to locate artistic representations of the way of life he represents. Instead, what is noteworthy about his collecting is his performance of acquisition as valuable in itself; in a predatory way, he gathers the symbols of a now splintered "tradition."

Fragmentation of the established symbolic order occurs when Undine shows Moffatt the art treasures secreted in the private collections to which she has gained access; he purchases a key symbol of Raymond de Chelles's familial association with royalty when he acquires a valuable Boucher tapestry, and Moffatt eventually corners the art market, putting these symbols beyond the reach of the penurious aristocracy. But he has, as Elaine Showalter demonstrates, taste and "a sensual as well as a financial response to art" ("Spragg: The Art of the Deal" 94). The success of Undine and Moffatt is destructive to those around them, and to the fabric of gentry ideology the tapestry could stand for. These two ungovernable characters embody energies disruptive to the symbolic order of both the aesthetically inclined American gentry and the French aristocracy. Charles Bowen thinks that "the surest sign of human permanence" is the impulse to create an illusion of volition (243), which exists in, for example, de Chelles's maintenance of class standards as political action. New projections of class power compete with his standards by making collages of old symbols, dispersing the illusion to which Bowen refers. Undine's set constructs its own "outward form" by reordering the symbolic system of establishment New York. Moffatt and company appropriate signifiers such as the "Blois gargoyles" and the "old lines" of the Dagonet furniture, and they reuse the resources of their prey. A new force on the social Serengeti intersects with Marvell's life when he becomes extricated in mass culture and the market. These are the very forces that model the recombination of forms for those, like Van Degen, resigning their hereditary membership in an old elite and eschewing "obsolete customs."[22]

"Inheriting an old social order," Wharton writes, "which provided for nicely shaded degrees of culture and conduct, modern America has simplified and Taylorized it out of existence" ("The Great American Novel" 154). Mass culture and industry have regularized a life of efficiencies. This violates an old ideal of interdependent classes, undone by the industrialist's dehumanizing emphasis on productivity, and the newspaper's selective, profit-driven pastiche of the significant. Despite the nostalgia that tinges Wharton's statement about "shaded degrees of culture and conduct," though, *The Custom of the Country* judges harshly the contemporary exemplars of the "old social order" because Ralph Marvell's class has lost in a haze of leisure its ability to lead.

Wharton wrote that leisure, "itself the creation of wealth, is incessantly engaged in transmuting wealth into beauty by secreting the surplus energy which flowers in great architecture, great painting, and great literature" ("The Great American Novel" 156). But Marvell is a failure as an artist, despite his freedom. He is an aesthete who mistakes Undine for a maiden. Although *she* exploits him, he "seemed to see her like a lovely rock-bound Andromeda" (86). He is artistically impotent, finding a question about his writing "distasteful to him" (283), and is irrelevant as a social actor in the new order.[23] He can ponder "the thought of his projected book" (146), but cannot overcome his creative inertia, thus symbolizing a class that has lost sight of a responsibility to convert surplus wealth into socially beneficial art useful in accommodating cultural complexity and change.

To understand the effects on Marvell of the appropriation of cultural forms it is necessary to define the romantic system of ideas that guides him. Marvell is named after the metaphysical poet Andrew Marvell (1621–1678), and his perspective on Undine is controlled by a system of ideas that resembles aspects of Wordsworth's initial "Preface" to *Lyrical Ballads.* This system of ideas focuses Marvell's attention on his feelings, causes him to look for artistic inspiration outside his environment, and facilitates an impressionistic viewpoint that makes little distinction between the reality of what he observes, and how his imagination transforms reality. Class ideology has become a class poetic in his mind. The artistic result of leisure, one that can bind the collective together, is now the end purpose of those like Marvell, forgetful of the responsibility attached to privilege—in Wharton's view. Exhibiting his place in society by engaging in work that fulfills only a class-defined role that demands idleness, Marvell looks for mundane subject matter to elevate poetically. He sees himself as an artist—"I'll write, I'll write" (142), but for him, artists don't weave experience into cash.

His unfinished critical and literary efforts—"'The Rhythmical Structures of Walt Whitman' [. . .] 'The Banished God'" (81)[24] possess titles contrived with avoidance of the marketplace in mind, and signify in the former case his interest in form, and not those underlying truths that Whitman's poetry—in the way his poetic line references the vital, bodily present, speaking person—might represent.[25] Wharton's preparatory comments for her own study of Whitman suggest what Marvell might have learned from the poet: "his characterization of natural objects is extraordinarily suggestive; he sees through the layers of the conventional point of view and of the conventional adjective straight to the thing itself, and not only to the thing itself, but to the endless thread connecting it to the universe" (qtd. in Janet Beer, *Edith Wharton* 82–83). On his honeymoon with Undine in Italy, though, Marvell can only look at Undine's hands and think that he "had never felt more convinced of his power to write a poem" (135), though he never does so. With Marvell, latency is artistry. Although alert to such situations in which a "spontaneous overflow of powerful feelings" (Wordsworth 163–64) might occur, he remains powerless to articulate them in a public way.

In commenting on the line "She neither hears nor sees" in Wordworth's "Lucy" poem "A Slumber Did My Spirit Seal," Wharton wrote that it is "the result of a great deal of writing, of a long & expert process of elimination, selection, concentration of idea and expression" (*Letters* 106). Marvell does not possess such a critical faculty, and his aesthetic, though it may be Wordsworthian, blurs his artistic subjects, rather than focuses them. Whereas he is "not blind to her [Undine's] crudity and limitations," he views these attributes as "part of her grace and her persuasion" (85), demonstrating that his powers of "elimination, selection, concentration of idea" are insufficient to discern and represent Undine's defining traits. His concentration on her "grace" is evidence of his wish to "throw over [Undine] [. . .] a certain coloring of imagination" (Wordsworth 162) that in the hands of Wordsworth might present a unified portrait of the "nereid-like" (137)[26] protagonist.

The aridity of the life bestowed upon Marvell by his class, a life in which he is expected to "go to Columbia or Harvard, read law, and then lapse into more or less cultivated inaction" (79), forces him to seek, under cover of literary interests, the "low and rustic" in which the "essential passions of [his] heart [. . .] are under less restraint" (Wordsworth 162–63). And while Undine is "low and rustic" in the sense of her class and geographical origins, the "coloring of imagination" required to perceive her as Marvell does reinterprets Undine's hard clarity, which is hyper-real in its defiance of his impressionism: "she paused before the blotched looking-glass [. . .]. Even that defective surface could not disfigure her" (219). Marvell's romantic ideas guide his perception of Undine, but unconstrained forces in the guise of Wall Street's unpredictable cycles of boom and bust soon singe his ties to the books that mediate his vision of Undine. As a result, "the whole archaic structure of his rites and sanctions tumbled down about him" (405).

Marvell's feelings toward Undine are guided by an aestheticism characterized by a broken connection between art and the wider social causes that,
according to the novel, it should serve. His concern is with the immediate
impression that fulfills his valuation of surface beauty, one divorced from
politically engaged art that might at least comment on the "structure of rites
and sanctions," for better or worse. This outlook prompts him to see in
Undine's physicality "mystic depths whence his passion sprang, [where]
earthly dimensions were ignored and the curve of beauty was boundless
enough to hold whatever the imagination could pour into it" (135). To rein-
force the need for an informed artistic consciousness able to connect aesthetics and ideology, the narrative depicts Undine's reaction to one of Marvell's
frequent comparisons between her and an unnamed mythological beauty.
During this sequence, she lets one of his obscure remarks "drop into the store
of unexplained references which had once stimulated her curiosity but now
merely gave her leisure to think of other things" (137), demonstrating that
his "allusions to pictures and books" (46) do not carry forward a social order
worth the label. The cost of Marvell's failure is, as a member of his vanishing
breed puts it, that Undine is "marrying into our aristocracy" (86). Her subsequent penetration of Marvell's cultural genome finds her "astray in a new
labyrinth of social distinction" (94) that she will wreck rather than refine.

Of course, Marvell's remoteness from the political task of fostering positive social change has a personal cost as well. After Undine leaves Marvell to
pursue Peter Van Degen, Marvell travels alone to the Adirondacks for a vaca-
tion. Leisure may be his, but he has a dawning sense that his structured existence is but a meadow of order in a forest of chaos: "[n]ow and then he got
into the canoe and paddled himself through a winding chain of ponds [. . .]
and watched the great clouds form and dissolve themselves above his head"
(294). The random permutations of the clouds mark an end to his uncon-
sciousness of nature's contingent state, in a moment when "[a]ll his past
seemed to be symbolized by the building up and breaking down of those
fluctuating shapes, which incalculable wind-currents perpetually shifted and
remodeled or swept from the zenith like a pinch of dust" (294). Marvell's
pastoral meditation foreshadows his encounter with mass culture and the
market, which force-feeds him a lesson on social evolution.

Mass culture intersects with Marvell's settled opinions when the
tabloids take an interest in his divorce. For a man whose romantic idealism
has previously caused him to take pleasure in elevating the low, "nothing that
had gone before seemed as humiliating as this [the newspaper's] trivial comment on his tragedy" (300). He finds being read by the press distressing.
Ironically, what the imagination of the press does with Marvell's divorce

approximates Marvell's own impressionistic rendering of Undine. His elevation of her through marriage, and an education in the ways of his class, had
been acts indicative of his attitude toward tradition as something that can be
benignly spread, for the "task of opening new windows in her mind was
inspiring enough to give him infinite patience" (139–40). Similarly, Newland Archer in *The Age of Innocence* feels, when contemplating May Welland,
that it "would presently be his task to take the bandage from this young
woman's eyes" (81). It is, however, the blindness of both Marvell and Archer
to what has defined them that is at issue in their respective narratives.

Marvell imagines that "the devouring monster Society careering up to
make a mouthful of her" warrants his intervention; to this end he pictures
"himself wheeling down on his winged horse [. . .] to cut her bonds, snatch
her up, and whirl her back into the blue" (86). But it is he who will be
devoured. Elevating Undine, whether by raising her into the sky in his day-
dream, idealizing her in poetry, or lifting her up to his class, is an action that
addresses a sense of class responsibility rendered irrelevant by her modernity
and its association with the press and the market. Rather than being a potential victim of society, Undine approaches differences between herself and Marvell and his kind in the spirit of competition. She knows that "[t]heir ideas are
all different from ours" (215). When Marvell becomes the subject of mass culture's imagination it is as if Undine's aggressiveness is externalized in its forms.

Marvell's tradition competes with the economically unpredictable,
market-driven actions of buying and renewing espoused in the Sunday
papers. The genetic material of ideology that will reproduce itself in the consciousness of mass culture's consumers is at odds with the principles of his
type. These are, as I have shown, configured by Wharton as "inherited obligations" that create a "sense of solidarity between classes." The presentation
of the scene in which Marvell discovers that his divorce has become a news
item is insightful about the novel's view of the way mass culture erodes existing standards regarding the subordination of public persona to "the slow
strong current [of tradition] already fed by so many tributary lives" (445).

Upon seeing the story of Undine's divorce suit against him, "the blood
rushed to Ralph's forehead as he looked over the man's arm and read: 'Society
Leader Gets Decree,' and beneath it the clause: 'Says Husband Too Absorbed
In Business To Make Home Happy'" (300). The irony is that Marvell is a
failure in business; Abner Spragg wonders, "wasn't he ever taught to work?"
(118). The headline cites the standard reason of abandonment given for
divorce, preserving a measure of his dignity, even though it is untrue in Marvell's case. In fact, Undine has left him and their son to take advantage of the
"Dakota divorce-court" and its lenient residency requirement (318).

When his eye is caught "by his own name on the first page of this heavily headlined paper, which the unshaved occupant of the next seat held between grimy fists" (300), the novel associates a belief in the validity of mass culture as an objective representation of social reality with this working-class reader. He represents the wider populace to whom Marvell's stratum, according to Wharton's statements, has leadership obligations. But proximity to this man magnifies Marvell's unease, for the poet has lost contact with the lower depths and the responsibilities that would connect their situations. His condescension toward this lost ideal is clear enough when he selfishly thinks the story a "trivial comment on his tragedy" (300). Marvell's reaction indicates the uniqueness he assigns to his divorce, despite the ready-made attitudes toward this activity in the newspaper, which indicate how common divorce has become. The aspiring literary artist sees his private failure transmuted into the gold of a saleable narrative by the tabloids. He suffers the dispersal of his previously stable association of private literary "work" with heightened sensitivity to his innermost thoughts. The marketplace has a use for his experience, even if he can only engage in unfocused attempts to create literature. As a result of his discomfort, he blushes as he feels "the coarse fingering of public curiosity" fumbling at "the secret places of his soul" (300).

No longer in control of self-representation, Marvell begins to understand that his desire to be an artist is an aspiration mediated by his class membership. The perennial lack of fulfillment of his literary goals indicates that what he takes to be his vocation is a fulfillment of ideological suggestion patterning his artistic pursuits. Even though Marvell is a member of the gentry, not the leisure class, Thorstein Veblen supplies a description applicable to the kind of "work" Marvell performs. That "work" consists of "quasi-scholarly or quasi-artistic accomplishments and a knowledge of processes and incidents which do not conduce directly to the furtherance of human life" (34–35). Veblen's statement shares Wharton's interest in defining class traits. The novelist, though, also looks to the effects on the communal project of the "Veblenesque socioeconomics" that in part anchors the "primitivism of Undine's character" (Ammons 105) and shrinks a barely efficacious public sphere. Fiction emerges as a potent discourse that can array these related subjects, showing that the significance of Marvell's desire to be a writer lies in the way this desire is alienated by "the performance of leisure" he mistakes for the writer's life, and which is nebulously expressed in his attachment to a romantic idea of poetry. His wish to make art, while once a real possibility for people with his freedom, is not contributive. Meanwhile, the tabloids will not make the finer observations a discerning sensibility would fashion into literature.

He should have negotiated royalties for the use of his story, but Marvell is no Undine. Wharton describes the way news of his divorce circulates: "[t]he paragraph continued on its way through the press, and whenever he took up a newspaper he seemed to come upon it, slightly modified, variously developed, but always reverting with a kind of unctuous irony to his financial preoccupations and his wife's consequent loneliness" (300). The falsehood that Marvell has driven Undine to divorce him is also used in a magazine contest. Marvell discovers a story that reports that he has isolated Undine by being engrossed in business, a possibility that is unlikely, for he has "an inability to get a mental grasp on large financial problems" (231). He finds his story "in a Family Weekly, as one of the 'Heart Problems' propounded to subscribers, with a Gramophone, a straight-front corset and a Vanity-Box among the prizes offered for its solution" (300). Such misinterpretation connects his plight with the anxiety in Wharton's story "The Descent of Man" over the way the marketplace distorts facts. Marvell's tale, by being printed in a mass-market magazine, recasts his sanctified private world in terms of a commodity. The misleading story is "served as a text for pulpit denunciations of the growing craze for wealth" (300). Fiction in the guise of fact elicits an institutional response addressed to a phantom generated by the tabloids. As social authority is distracted by a non-reality, the unchecked problem of tabloid distortions elides the predicament of a culture unguided by its declining leadership.

Marvell personifies Huxley's description of a society in which "[t]he stimulation of the senses, the pampering of the emotions, endlessly multiplied the sources of pleasure" ("Evolution and Ethics" 313). Until the events that lead to his suicide, Marvell is a remnant of an old world unaware that beyond the misted opacity of his hothouse lurk the conditions that required its creation. His conceptualization of self is in lock step with a class training whose faithfulness to an original ideological form is degraded by mutation. When he realizes he cannot reckon with the events of his life, particularly his divorce, in any frame other than that handed down to him, the flaw of his tradition as a medium of cultural heredity appears to him:

> He had been eloquent enough, in his free youth, against the conventions of his class; yet when the moment came [. . .] deflecting his course like some hidden hereditary failing. [. . .] his great disaster had been conventionalized and sentimentalized by this inherited attitude: that the thoughts he had about it were only those of generations of Dagonets, and that there had been nothing real and his own in his life but the foolish passion he had been trying so hard to think out of existence. (378–79)

Marvell sees nature in the guise of "passion" as both genuine and "foolish," again suggesting his inculcation into a code that distances unmanageable instinct. The real eludes Marvell at the same time the gossip columns strike down his ready-made identity.

Another aspect of Marvell's encounter with contingency focuses on his dealings with the stock market. As a member of a class destined for extinction, he is shown, within the novel's network of evolutionary metaphor, to be a "survival, and destined, as such, to go down in any conflict with the rising forces" (249). The market dissolves boundaries between the gentry and the socioeconomic elite, obliterating the class-consciousness that forms the foundation of Marvell's viewpoint. He sees the signs, reflecting thus on the modern version of marriage: "[t]he daughters of his own race sold themselves to the invaders; [. . .] it all ought to have been transacted on the stock exchange" (81). He has traded on his status to gain Undine's hand, marrying a woman who will, ironically, cause the final act of their union to play out on Wall Street.

The market is a primary feature of men's lives in the novel, even for those like Marvell previously insulated from its demands by a steady income that required no labor save for an appreciation of beauty: "he should live 'like a gentleman'—that is, with a tranquil disdain for mere money-getting, a passive openness to the finer sensations" (78). Still, the ability of the market to pull social mechanisms into its sphere is well illustrated by Marvell's experience. His perception that his fine feelings are insulated from economic matters is undone when he discovers that the free-spending Undine requires capital. Her sole custody of their son Paul provides her with an avenue by which to raise it, as has been noted. Marvell's experience with the market comes to a crisis point when he is faced with the task of raising enough money to pay Undine "to admit that it was for her son's advantage to remain with his father" (388). Undine's act further distances her from the tradition of close-knit bonds between family members because she has wanted, in fact, nothing to do with her son. Marvell needs to make the required sum through a "quick turn" on the stock market so he consults the "speculator" Elmer Moffatt (389).

Marvell has trouble focusing on Moffatt's "intricate concert of facts and figures" (391), for he is only able to think of his son: "when I pick him up to-night he'll be mine for good!" (391). Perhaps no other scene in the novel so succinctly juxtaposes the calculating rationality of the market and its chaotic effects with the traits of cooperation and familial bonds that Wharton sees such objectivity as diminishing. Ironically, Marvell's humane sensibility here seeks shelter in the shadow of what has been represented in the

novel as a dangerous form of capitalism free from modulation by social constraints. After learning from Moffatt that the investment has failed, Ralph
Marvell sees the market with a gritty realism at odds with his usual languid
and self-centered habits of perception. He stands "at the corner of Wall
Street, looking up and down its hot summer perspective. He noticed the
swirls of dust in the cracks of the pavement, the rubbish in the gutters" (406)
for the first time. His loss makes him see the world beyond the garden of his
class, from a fresh perspective. Having chanced his capital in an attempt to
gain custody of his son, he becomes a pauper. But he ultimately realizes that
what he has viewed as his authentic self relies on capital that must work in
the marketplace. This makes his way of life complicit with the institution he
had thought at arm's length. It is an insight that leaves him, as his work does
when he is forced to seek employment, "possessed of a leisure as bare and as
blank as an unfurnished house" (368). Deprived now of the illusions prof-
fered by a justificatory gentry ideology, he recognizes that his artistic pursuits
have no redeeming social purpose.

Marvell is ultimately destroyed by Undine's actions. She is a regressive
flashback to a remote point in the cultural history of the United States representative of a violent stage in the social evolution of a country marked by rev-
olution, and by colonial savagery directed against Native Americans; in this
she is quintessentially of the United States. The novel uses the variegating
tendency of biological evolution to illustrate the inevitability of unpredictable social change, which includes the recurrence of what is viewed by
the gentry as primitive. Undine succeeds in the avaricious environment of
New York because she possesses variations such as aggressiveness, beauty, and
superficiality that suit her to a social world where the "inner life" (194) is valued less than "the forces of business" (195), and she excels in the business of
marriage. Wharton's application to New York culture of a Darwinian interpretation of change in nature illustrates how chance variations personified by
Undine undermine the idea that social development occurs in a logical and
linear way. Rather, random mutations in the systems of ideas that guide
classes steer social change in unforeseeable directions. In depicting evolutionary laws in *The Custom of the Country* as applying to culture, Wharton delineates the specter of contingency at the center of Darwin's work on natural
selection, and finds no predetermined goal or direction for social change.
The novel, then, like *The House of Mirth,* confronts a pervasive ideal that
views humankind, and the nation, as perfectible.

Chapter Four

Newland Archer's "Hieroglyphic World"

I. "TWICE REMOVED FROM REALITY"

The previous two chapters have considered the ramifications of the claim that "Wharton's sociobiological frame of reference predicts modern social analysis, which has made [a] useful analogy between evolution/selection theory and social development, treating the macro-social structure as 'a selection environment'" (Preston 54–55).[1] Illustrating how this analogy contributes to Wharton's Darwinian allegory in *The House of Mirth,* by investigating Lily Bart's poor fit with the "selection environment" presented in that novel, I subsequently demonstrated how mass culture and a strengthening capitalism figure in a contest between systems of ideas that support subspecies of New York's elite in *The Custom of the Country.* In *The Age of Innocence,* set in the 1870s, decades before the period chronicled in those novels, Newland Archer attempts to make sense of his social selection environment, which is only just starting to be reshaped by the oppositional ideologies portrayed in *The Custom of the Country.* Archer's tale is marked by his ambivalence toward the ideological creation of identity. The limits marked off for him by the surveillance that members of his class subject him to mediate the novel's engagement with "successful ideologies [that] must be more than imposed illusions" (Eagleton 15).

Archer's ambivalence is evidenced by a questioning of "the elaborate futility of his life" (125) that causes him to feel that he is "being buried alive under his future" (139), and by his interrogation of a "traditional" world that causes him to wonder at "what age 'nice' women [like his fiancé May Welland] began to speak for themselves" (81). Despite his insights, and his mixed feelings, Archer's consciousness is, nevertheless, severely limited by his class identity, which stands in contrast to the more comprehensive vision of links between the social and the natural articulated by the framing narrative.[2] These two issues are the main concern of this chapter.

    This section examines Newland Archer's ideologically facilitated redi-
rection of his sexual and competitive drives toward social cohesion. Section
two relates a failure to understand the texturing of psychological experience
by one's status as an organism to Archer's aesthetic perspective, which is
formed by the artistic and scientific works he comes into contact with. These
works disrupt his capacity, for example, to react to Ellen Olenska's "bodily
presence" (AI 243). Disruption of this sort, I argue, is one symptom of a
mannered distancing of nature that fosters stability at the expense of feeling.
Further investigating links between Wharton's scientifically influenced fictional method and her socially critical engagement with old New York, I
focus on gradations of objectivity personified in the novel's characters, and
displayed in the omniscient register of the novel. This attribute of *The Age of
Innocence* is noteworthy because differences in perceptiveness between Newland Archer and the wider field of vision, in which the problematically invisible ideology of Archer's class is embedded,[3] indicate the presence of multiple
and authorially qualified perspectives.

    To cite one example, Wharton's analogy "between evolution/selection
theory and social development" facilitates her depiction of language as the
carrier wave of ideology, the former of which appears as a genetic means of
cultural reproduction. I examine this subject in section three. This is one area
of fictional analysis that distinguishes the narrator's frame of reference from
the point-of-view of Newland Archer, who, while suspecting that rites, rituals, manners, and language narrow his experience, cannot create anew his
consciousness, which they have molded. In section four, I look further at
how social form structures Archer's habits of thought; in doing so, I discuss
his superficial learning to argue that class doctrine makes it difficult for
Archer first to perceive—then later to act on—the real conditions of his life.
Section five applies this claim to the final sequence of the novel.

*   *   *

Newland Archer's sense that there exists something beyond his lawyerly existence is confirmed at many points. In one episode he meets at Ellen Olenska's house "Dr. Agathon Carver, founder of the Valley of Love community"
(157). Carver, whose strange garments inspire Archer's "curiosity" (155), gestures in a way that makes him appear to Archer as if he "were distributing lay
blessings to a kneeling multitude" (156). Indeed, Carver does have something to say, but Archer won't hear the message. Ned Winsett asks Carver if
there is time to explain to Archer the "illuminating discovery of the Direct
Contact" (158), but the visionary must rush to deliver a lecture. Carver's

phrase, and his philosophy, somewhat satirically invokes Whitman, of whom Wharton wrote, "[h]e has the direct vision" (qtd. in Janet Beer, *Edith Wharton* 82–83). Wondering whether "this young gentleman is interested in my experiences" (AI 158), the leader of the Valley of Love presents an opportunity to Archer to experience that which exists beyond the boundaries of the "life-in-death" (52) Archer and his tribe lead.

Direct contact with the real, or "direct vision" of it, is mediated by manners for Archer. His behavior is distanced from biological instinct. Formulated in the realm of social practices, what guides his perception of the available courses of action are "the conventions on which his life was moulded" (5). Archer is a man cognizant of the power of class-based rules and rituals, yet he is unable to free himself from their effects. Despite his frustration at this prospect, opulent signs of wealth charge his sense of identity, and compensate partially for his resentment of the system:

> There was something about the luxury of the Welland house and the density of the Welland atmosphere, so charged with minute observances and exactions, that always stole into his system like a narcotic. The heavy carpets, the watchful servants, the perpetually reminding tick of the disciplined clocks, [. . .] the whole chain of tyrannical trifles binding one hour to the next, and each member of the household to all the others, made any less systematized and affluent existence seem unreal and precarious. (218)

Archer's frequent disavowals of the anesthetizing effect of this atmospheric "narcotic" point out that the social surface is an elaborate fiction.

It is a fiction, though, that is taken to be the whole of reality by Archer's wife May Welland. Although his father-in-law's house may have the effect of quieting his perceptions, Archer at his most sensitive responds to "tyrannical trifles" with dread: "'Darling!' Archer said [to May]—and suddenly the same black abyss yawned before him and he was sinking into it [. . .] while his voice rambled on smoothly and cheerfully" (187). In his chilled heart, Archer harbors hope that his marriage to May might skirt convention, but "[t]here was no use in trying to emancipate a wife who had not the dimmest notion that she was not free" (195). Because Archer is the primary reflecting consciousness, it is easy to take his negative evaluation of May unflinchingly. Wharton, however, shows May's wisdom to be the intelligence of a collective that perpetuates social cohesion.

That Archer's previously blinkered perceptions are changing is clear from his ability to discern that May, in "making the answers that instinct and tradition had taught her to make" might, if she were to see things as they were, "only look out blankly at blankness" (82). His musing supposes that May's faculties are defined by "instinct" and her socialization, but it is Archer's understanding of the former term that is at issue. Although his dilettantish study of anthropology (67) obscures the biological essence of himself and others, Archer's interest in the discipline at least prods him out of a paradigm that he has taken for granted. The study of anthropology alerts him to the significance of social forms that repel alternatives to convention such as the ideas presented by Dr. Carver. Archer notes this, thinking that "we all are [. . .] old maids" when so much as "brushed by the wing-tip of reality" (85). Perceiving in his own marriage ceremony a ritualistic codification of some deeper reality to which he is not attuned—mating and propagation—he notes "the imitation stone vaulting" of the church in which he and May are married (180). Much else that only seems real attracts Archer's attention, but he can do little with his perception until he becomes, late in the novel, more aware of the confinement of his psychology by a mannered unreality. At another point, ossified codes of conduct and feeling demonstrate their inflexibility, and like the "archaic French" Archer reads (84), become progressively more irrelevant and restrictive as his involvement with Ellen Olenska deepens.

Wharton's interest in what is "felt in the blood" (*Letters* 433) takes the form in *The Age of Innocence* of tensions between instinct and tradition, the latter of which disunites a biological conceptualization of self from sociality; it is a state in which unmarried women are "not allowed the same freedom of [sexual] experience" as men (AI 46). Archer might seem to understand that "untrained human nature [. . .] was full of the twists and defences of an instinctive guile" (45), but trained human nature fosters a collective guile— one possibly created as a response to the hazards of environment—which demands individual deference to the needs of the group: "if the family had ceased to consult him it was because some deep tribal instinct warned them that he was no longer on their side" (252). The sublimation of biological imperatives into social forms—which are themselves adaptive social traits and therefore more natural than the elites believe—is a subject in *The Age of Innocence*. Manners and rites form Archer's framework for a standard view of "tribal instinct" as an extra-biological product of culture. "[U]ntrained human nature" must be subdued, ironically, into social forms that have a biological foundation. The infusion of new blood offered by exogamy, wherein desire and not social suitability would guide mate selection, is dangerous. This is visible in the conspiracy to eliminate Ellen Olenska, whom Archer loves, from the "tribe" (14). Yet the silent but mutually understood effort to expel Ellen targets the knowing Archer too:

He guessed himself to have been, for months, the centre of countless silently observing eyes and patiently listening ears, he understood that, by means as yet unknown to him, the separation between himself and the partner of his guilt had been achieved, and that now the whole tribe had rallied about his wife. (335)

Archer's tale is not a tragedy, for he finds compensation for his losses within his class privilege, but it is a story that relates the difficulty of transcending his training, and coercive manners. As the passage just quoted suggests, Archer's insight into the system that separates him from Ellen only liberates his perception of how securely he is chained to an ideology that in translating instinct makes a cage of privilege.

The analogy between evolution/selection theory and social development in *The Age of Innocence* identifies natural selection as a motor of cultural change, yet it is an analogy that can seem buried by a strategy of authorial concealment. As in the other novels examined in this study, the analogy potentially helps convince the reader of an explanation for the fact, as Archer's mother puts it, that "you couldn't expect the old traditions to last much longer" (48). Adopting the perspective that a narrative fusion of social and biological evolution denotes the superficiality of Archer's distinction between these elements foregrounds chance—which deflates teleological explanations of change—as the operative and inescapable phenomenon. Despite his awareness that it is impossible for him to inhabit "a world where action followed on emotion" (164), Archer's insights are only penetrating enough to dissatisfy him. Indicative of his affiliation with the traditions that encode spontaneous expressions of desire, and separate emotion and action, is his embrace of aesthetic achievement with an energy that is almost sexual. Representations of beauty and desire made by art, during a life of running to "the National Gallery [. . .] to catch a glimpse of the pictures" (194) are, like his memory of Ellen Olenska at the end of the novel, "more real" to Archer than other reference points in experience (362). His first sexual encounter with May Welland, which one imagines to have occurred on their honeymoon in London, is followed by Archer's odd comment that she resembles a virginal goddess, and "looked handsomer and more Diana-like than ever" (193).

Moreover, the validity of Wharton's fictional method as a way to analyze and diagnose Archer's problem, which is a wider problem affecting the capacity to address intense change, is one of the novel's subjects. This is tangible in the representation of Archer's grappling with the same analogy between evolution and selection theory and social change used omnisciently.[4] *The Age of Innocence* defines the specific qualities of Archer's thinking on this subject. Central to his interpretation are two elements. First, he idealistically views the social selection environment within which systems of thought compete as a ground for progress. In his view, being unsuited to one's environment does not necessarily imply extinction: "even after his most exciting talks with Ned Winsett he always came away with the feeling that if his world was so small, so was theirs, and that the only way to enlarge either was to reach a stage of manners where they would naturally merge" (102–3). For Archer, antinomies between social groups, or between groups and the social selection environment, are resolved under a progressive view that difference can be "naturally" accommodated. Archer's experience with the way bullying manners nullify his relationship with Ellen dashes this perspective.

The second element salient to Archer's view on evolution/selection theory and social development is his imagination, which consistently colors the real biological forces affecting him—for "thinking over a pleasure to come often gave him a subtler satisfaction than its realization" (4). This aspect of his character remains unchanged by his experience, and in fact ensures that this is the case. Archer and his class express the compelling ideas of evolutionary science only in terms of concern over social change, finding little in science to illuminate the problems presented by change. In fact, Archer imagines that a scientific instrument distances the novel's primary exponent of social form: "far down the inverted telescope he saw the faint white figure of May Welland" (77). This image of Archer using a scientific instrument incorrectly is clarified by noting that properly used, the telescope, and other scientific tools, might yield clues with which to construct an understanding of the physical universe and its relation to Archer's life.

The natural and the social exist on different planes for Archer. His association of ethnic difference with artificial hybridization helps illustrate this. Recalling a youthful trip to Italy, he remarks on how the Florentines he met "were too different from the people Archer had grown up among, too much like expensive and rather malodorous hot-house exotics" (197). Ethnicity, which he perceives as cross-breeding, is unnatural, as is a conception of sexuality uncontained by manners directed toward signifying class membership, and so one finds an "Archer-Newland-van-der-Luyden tribe" that "looked down on the grosser forms of pleasure" (32). As Archer distances pleasure, he also fails to recognize that sexuality is expressed in cultural forms such as fashion. This is evident, as Knights observes, when he notes Ellen's appearance in "a long robe of red velvet bordered about the chin and down the front with glossy black fur" (104).[5] However, his impression of Ellen fails to respond to her explicitly sexual appearance; she reminds Wharton's culturally inoculated art-lover only of a painting he has seen in London, limiting him to an aesthetic response to this thinly disguised presentation of Ellen's sexuality.

> [He] remembered, on his last visit to Paris, seeing a portrait by the new painter, Carolus Duran, whose pictures were the sensation of the salon, in which the lady wore one of these bold sheath-like robes with her chin nestled in fur. There was something perverse and provocative in the combination of fur worn in the evening in a heated drawing room, and in the combination of a muffled throat and bare arms; but the effect was undeniably pleasing. (105)

What is primary in Archer's perception is the way Ellen's outfit provocatively violates that "far off divinity" called "Taste" (14). Only as a second thought does he grant that Ellen is pleasing to the eye, but even then she is not positively sexual. This character trait is a function of Wharton's social criticism in the novel.

The apparent disjunction between omniscient voice and Archer's outlook is pointed. Wharton's engagement with evolutionary and sociological thought sweeps away hesitancy about the inapplicability of evolutionary theory to the changing texture of upper class life in the 1870s.[6] Nancy Bentley's consideration of Wharton's fictional method is thus valuable for its insight into the author's linkage of ethnography and culture. Bentley's approach reveals also that a formulation that does not consider the role of evolutionary theory in *The Age of Innocence* cannot accurately interpret Archer's assumptions, nor account for the novel's position that culture grows from a natural foundation:

> By splicing together the roles of novelist and ethnographer to create a figure she calls 'the drawing-room naturalist,' Wharton appears to blithely transcend the distinction between a humanist tradition, in which culture signifies a set of prized Western values that advance human perfectibility, and a sociological sense of culture as a web of institutions and lived relations that structure any community [. . .]. Within this expanded sense of culture, savage and civilized worlds can share, at long last, a common language of interpretation. (*The Ethnography of Manners* 3)

Bentley rightly views Wharton to be "splicing together the roles of novelist and ethnographer." The sociological focus on "institutions and lived relations" present in *The Age of Innocence* maintains evolution, bodies, and desire as touchstones for reality that the practices of rituals and manners contend with by distancing. This is apparently the case when May Welland, having returned from the "three months wedding-tour" during which her sexual initiation has taken place, "vaguely summarized [it] as 'blissful'" (AI 194).

An ideology of perfectibility inhibits Archer's deeper understanding of his culture's proximity to nature. He has, like Ralph Marvell, "the passionate man's indestructible dream of a rounded passion" (CC 85) that is optimistic in assuming its achievability. Bentley's formulation of Wharton's "smooth suturing [. . .] of antagonistic strains of the culture idea" helps define the interaction of *The Age of Innocence* with scientific and sociological currents, and posits the existence of a continuum between "savage and civilized" in the novel, even if Bentley's perspective does not include evolution. What is "rounded" for Archer is, indeed, a "dream," or rather, an imaginary view of a holistic passion more about beauty than sexuality, and, therefore, not as complete as he thinks. The story aligns this falsehood with Archer's appreciation of Western art and the values of "human perfectibility." He expresses an instinct denuded of its biological dimension in adherence to social form. Potential conflicts between instinct and class affiliation diminish in the intense ideological pull that guides Archer's reasoning. Pressuring his rational behavior, though, is the "sudden revulsion of mood" that causes him, "almost without knowing what he did" (AI 79), to send roses anonymously to Ellen.

That the novel's methodology is one of its subjects is a proposition strengthened by Wharton's pronouncement that "the mode of presentation to the reader, that central difficulty of the whole affair, must always be determined by the nature of the subject" (WF 72). When that subject is the difficulty of accessing what is "felt in the blood," Wharton's representation of Archer and his milieu, focused to the depth of the cultural background where social practices shape perception, depicts the substitution of taste and form for Eros. This seems a working out of her belief "that some new theory of form, as adequate to its new purpose as those preceding it, will be evolved from the present welter of experiment" in the novelistic genre ("The Criticism of Fiction" 124). Archer senses that he is being "shown off like a wild animal cunningly trapped. He supposed that his readings in anthropology caused him to take such a coarse view of what was after all a simple and natural demonstration of family feeling" (AI 67). In so thinking, he distances as uncivilized the scientific viewpoint he dallies with, bringing into conflict with the narrative's view the idea that he is both a "wild animal," or biological being, and capable of a finer "family feeling."

Wharton associates the implications for human society of evolutionary science with the kind of coarseness that Archer refuses to apply to himself. His anthropological learning, he understands, colors as "coarse" that which is interpreted through its framework. He assumes that the disciplinary lens of anthropology only focuses what is primitive, and he is mistaken. He should not use science to crudely classify human subjects as high or low, for natural selection dictates that simple organisms can be more successful than humans in the right environment. He does not realize that "family feeling" might exist in an instinctive form in non-human species. It is Wharton's point, and one aspect of a "new form" in literature that suppresses difference between the natural and the social through biological allegory, that Archer is wronged by his perspective. Furthermore, that Wharton may have been struggling toward a form capable of containing an evolutionary reading of social development, and finding it in biological allegory and scientific metaphor, helps explain her over-sensitivity to the perception that her social criticism was authoritative because of her membership in the social stratum she portrayed.[7]

II. "A CURIOUS INDIFFERENCE TO HER BODILY PRESENCE"

Despite her disinclination to be interpreted as authoritative solely because of her class affiliation, first-hand experience with elite manners and tastes certainly assisted Wharton's depiction of Archer's superficial appreciation of the opera he attends in the first scene of *The Age of Innocence*. This performance possesses edifying content that goes unnoticed by viewers not attuned to the ability of art to represent what is otherwise fragmentary. In the autobiographical fragment "Life and I," Wharton reveals the centrality of the literary work on which the opera she represents is based, pronouncing that her reading of "Faust was one of the 'epoch-making' encounters for me" (31).

The first sentence of the novel relates that "Christine Nilsson was singing in Faust at the Academy of Music in New York" (3). This performance is capable of demonstrating to Archer the error of viewing his world as explicable solely through the terms offered by his superficial study of "the books on Primitive Man that people of advanced culture were beginning to read" (44). He cannot find fulfillment through the quite limited knowledge of his primitive, or instinctive self, available through his dilettantism. Understanding the limits of knowledge might free Archer, but he is late for his lesson for the same reason he can't understand it once he arrives, for "it was 'not the thing' to arrive early at the opera" (4). His adherence to the standards of form, like Ralph Marvell's concentration on the rhythmical structures of Whitman's poetry at the expense of its content in *The Custom of the Country*, precludes the perception of vital ideas. Manners affect Archer's exposure to an argument about the limits of knowledge, and thus of the value of experience, that the primary narrative perspective illustrates on the spectacular scale of operatic performance.

In examining Goethe's *Faust*, which Gounod reworks for his opera, one finds that Archer's compulsion to be fashionably late causes the already feminized character to resemble the "Women of Crete" who "[n]ever listened when poetry/ Sang its sweet lesson" (Goethe 161). Under the sway of "what was or was not 'the thing'" (AI 4), his lateness is a function of a way of thinking that prefers the old "Academy of Music [. . .] to a new Opera House" because the Academy's small size keeps out "the 'new people' whom New York was beginning to dread" (3); this focus on adherence to the dictates of taste turns Archer's perception away from ideas on which to found an identity less dependent on his environment. Social ritual expresses the system of thought particular to his class, one crystallized in the centrality of "the thing" so full of power, yet so empty of expressible content. This system brings certain benefits to Archer.

One such benefit is his domestic arrangement, wherein "[a]n upper floor was dedicated to Newland while the women squeezed themselves into narrower quarters below" (33). The luxuriousness of Archer's surroundings compensates for the limits class membership places on him. But in being transfixed by manners he cannot elude, such as those dictating propriety in romantic relationships (even if he is aware of the "hypocrisy" [41] of these manners), he cannot progress intellectually and comprehend how he is controlled by class ideology. Although Archer makes a progressive assertion in "exclaiming [. . .] I hope she will" in reference to the possibility that Ellen Olenska will be divorced (41), he is beholden to "conventions" (5) that compel his interest in discovering who occupies the various family boxes at the Academy. Instead of discovering his entanglement in a thought system that is a "[f]able, more persuasive than truth" (Goethe 162), Archer "turned his eyes from the stage" (AI 5).

Even as *The Age of Innocence* defines the limits of Archer's perspective, it compromises its own objectivity. In recasting Darwinian theory Wharton creates a basis for the exchange of concepts related to natural law and manners. In *The Age of Innocence* this practice connects instinct and culture by depicting Archer's displacement of drives into a love of art and knowledge. Wharton makes this a function of his class when "the spoils of the ages" on display in the new Metropolitan Museum, created in 1870 by a mix of philanthropists, financiers, and artists, are reduced to "a series of scientifically catalogued treasures" (344) divorced from the individuals and histories that produced them. Archer's reflexive participation in the stripping of emotional and psychological contexts from cultural works is one product of the impulse to catalogue and classify. But in representing the countercurrents of training and impulse that affect Archer, Wharton slips out of her objective mode into representations of subjective human consciousness where her concern is no longer strictly with sociobiology, nor grounded on any explicitly scientific psychological model.

Wharton's scientific tone is often befogged by the focus of her narrative omniscience on the need to preserve stabilizing mores, and also the inevitability of their modification; her artistic struggle to render societal attitudes with clarity finds political judgment unavoidable. The maintenance of a smooth and untroubled social surface by Archer's class is insufficient to resist the impairment of values by the mutant individualism associated with membership in the socioeconomic elite. Aspirations of ascending to a place among the Four Hundred founded on the Struthers's shoe polish fortune, or on Julius Beaufort's wealth, rasp against class divisions annealed by the power of old rituals and the possession of old money. Although the sound of rustling silk dresses, the calling cards left in the front hall, and the predictable rhythms of the social season suggest a world of probity, Newland Archer's class must be atavistic in its repulsion of the new. The enactment of such power is linked to primitive rites in the novel; constant vigilance makes tradition impervious to changes in the social order that might follow on books being "out of place" in Ellen Olenska's drawing room (103), or from Ellen, "heedless of tradition" (104), wearing the wrong kind of dress in which to receive guests in the evening. Ellen, though, offers a potentially salutary perspective that finds tradition wanting.

Archer, whose dissatisfaction prods his attempt to span the two worlds that he and Ellen Olenska represent, would, if true to his type, prefer an undisturbed continuity of ritual that bars social miscegenation. But he becomes aware that this preference, the result of his training, limits his ability to experience Ellen's European ideas, which have the power "to brush away the conventions" (239) that smother him. Newland may be an Archer in the sense that he attempts to arc toward Ellen's way of life, but May is a "Diana-like" huntress (211) whose skills within her social context prove deadly to Archer's aspirations of freedom with Ellen. She proves in preserving her marriage how wrong Julius Beaufort is when he comments, within earshot of Archer, on May's skill with a bow and arrow: "that's the only target she'll ever hit" (211). This comment is notable because Beaufort is an outsider unable to see May's behavior as the perfectly modulated performance of encoded competitiveness in the arena of sexual selection, where her body can be displayed in athletic competition and all can see her "classic grace [. . .] nymph-like ease" (211) in a scene reminiscent of Lily Bart's arresting sexuality during her

staging of the portrait by Sir Joshua Reynolds in *The House of Mirth*. Biological imperatives exist within May's performance in the archery contest,
demonstrating the wrongness of Archer's assumption that sex and manners
are unrelated.

Despite his limitations, Archer does see May's actions as an exhibition of
cultural mores. This is apparent when he discerns in her "the factitious purity,
so cunningly manufactured by a conspiracy of mothers and aunts and grandmothers and long dead ancestresses" (45). His skepticism toward the naturalness of May's purity illustrates his deep suspicion of that set of rules which has
formed his judgment also, making Adorno's well-known statement, "[o]ne
must have tradition in oneself, to hate it properly" (52), as applicable to
Archer as it has always been to Wharton. His understanding, and wariness of
the socially constructed dimension of May's purity, inflects his role as the central consciousness of the novel with a detachment shaped by his contact with
"scientific books" (AI 82). However, Archer is capable only of a flawed objectivity, characterized by a belief that he might analyze the complexity of his
class from a perspective of a "sham" life (243) that has created within him an
impressionist's obsession with his perceptions. One finds this to be the case in
a passage where Archer's passion for Ellen is intense; he feels "a curious indifference to her bodily presence [. . .]. Now his imagination spun about [. . .]
[Ellen's] hand as about the edge of a vortex; [. . .] his one terror was to do
anything which might efface the sound and impression of her words"
(243–44). Archer's denatured desire is an intellectual experience that vacates
what is felt bodily at the point of incipient sexual contact with Ellen. His
hypothesized passion turns out to be mediated impotence.

The presence of a class-specific imperative to ensure order by arresting
Archer's desire is a requirement reinforced in everyday social practices. The
first line of defense against the erosion of social stasis is the intermarriage of
elect families. Archer is very pleased that he is "a New Yorker, and about to
ally himself with one of his own kind" through his impending marriage to
May (31). The gentry monitor potentially dangerous affiliations; Mrs.
Archer offers a prescient caution when she states that "grandfather Newland
always used to say to my mother: 'Whatever you do, don't let that fellow
Beaufort be introduced to the girls'" (35). Other methods of control lie in
the specifics of manners: rigid standards of dress, intricate rules governing
social calls, and the requirement of strict adherence to particular wording in
the refusal of invitations (47).

A reference to "the inscrutable totem terrors that had ruled the destinies of his [Newland Archer's] forefathers" (4) shows Wharton both utiliz-
ing and examining anthropology in her fiction. Archer muses on his

"readings in anthropology" (67). But his studies distance him from the ability to understand why it is that he feels that he has been "cunningly trapped" (67) by class values that arrest his passion for Ellen Olenska. Normal social relations blanket an understanding of sexuality for Archer. He evaluates his situation through his scientific readings, which allow him to analyze the "totem terrors" that ruled his ancestors, but this activity simultaneously distances him from the passions such terrors symbolize. Wharton uses an anthropologically inclined narrative omniscience for the negative valuation of such a perspective in Archer. In one instance, he skips a social evening because "a new volume of Herbert Spencer" has arrived from his London bookseller (138). This detail is significant because Spencer's teleological interpretation of Darwinism argued that only the fittest humans could, or should, survive. The ironic depiction of Archer's contact with Spencer shows that while the former "turned the pages with the sensuous joy of the book-lover, he did not know what he was reading" (138). Archer is not equipped to comprehend Spencer's biological interpretation of culture, which counters the separation of instinct and tradition valued by Archer's class.

Preston claims that "Spencer's blend of biology, sociology, ethics, and psychology are clear influences on much of her writing; the works was published in 1897" (196n.). The question of which of his works Wharton read (aside from *First Principles,* which was discussed in Chapter One) is best approached by juxtaposing their writing. One section of Spencer's *Principles of Sociology* (1876) theorizes how it is that an instinctive suspicion of unfamiliar individuals becomes a common characteristic in a social group. Finding this subject addressed by Wharton in the wariness of Rosedale in *The House of Mirth* and the expulsion of Ellen in *The Age of Innocence,* one feels justified in arguing that she extends Spencer's idea to cover the suspicion of unfamiliar practices and beliefs exhibited by members of Archer's class. Spencer suggests, in the following passage, that an acquired suspicion is partly organic and partly cultural. *The Age of Innocence* achieves its synthesis of organic and cultural elements through metaphorical combinations, such as the idea that the highly cultured Archer is an animal:

> To the evolutionist, it is clear that constant experiences received by men during tens of thousands of years of savage life, must have produced organic modifications; and he will not be surprised to see indications of them given by the child in arms. In *The Principles of Psychology* [. . .] I have shown that whereas on islands never before visited, voyagers find the sea-birds so tame that they will not get out of the way, birds of kinds which, through unmeasured ages, have been in contact with mankind,

have acquired an instinctive dread of them [. . .]. Similarly through
countless generations of men the mental association between stranger
and enemy, has, by perpetual repetition, been rendered partially
organic; so that an unfamiliar face causes the infant gradually to contract its features [. . .] [and] an unformed cloud of painful feelings is
raised by this presentation of an unknown appearance which, in the history of the race, has constantly preceded the reception of injuries. (*Principles of Sociology* 693)

This example of evolutionary psychology in Spencer might rely on the
Lamarckian heresy that acquired characteristics can be passed down to offspring, but it has the virtue of fusing organic processes to a socially reinforced "instinctive dread" of difference that is part of the point *The Age of
Innocence* makes about the biological foundation of society.

As a reader of scientific books, Archer seeks and supports a framework
that orders chaotic nature. If he were to understand the theories he reads,
though, he would discover the centrality of contingent processes in nature.
The rites and signs of learnedness exemplified by Archer's love of his library,
and the periodic shipments from his London bookseller, demonstrate his fulfillment of the forms that identify a man of his social position. Despite his
efforts, real knowledge eludes Archer; his habits of reading and perpetuating
the legible normality of his world are consonant with his wish "to keep the
surface [forms of his wedding ceremony] pure" (AI 23). For Archer, reading
and marrying cause instinctive imperatives, such as his latent desire to have a
sexual affair with Ellen, to dissolve in conversation with her and recede from
view. His learning does little to demystify the unknown.

The overarching narrative in *The Age of Innocence* frequently undermines Archer's sense of intellectual control by contrasting his belief in the
possibility of "pure" unchanging forms with the basic facts of evolution.
When Wharton represents Archer's scientism, its qualities appear flawed to
the reader. There is little difference between Archer and the aging leaders of
his class, "gruesomely preserved in an airless atmosphere" in an expansive
mansion (52), despite Archer's stated interest in a life with Ellen. These figures stand against a breakdown of values. Resistance to change exists in
Archer's inherited wish to keep forms stable, even as he seems clinically to
analyze them. Yet, his attraction to Ellen illustrates the difficulty posed to his
wish by the conflicting impulses of his reasoning, policing intellect, and
desire. Archer illustrates, in his wish to flee with Ellen, one way instinctive
energies and unpredictable evolutionary mutations in a cultural sphere—
such as the appearance of Ellen in her European uniqueness—are linked in

the fiction to cultural change, for his regard and desire for Ellen force Archer into an oppositional perspective on his world. Along with this portrait of what weakens Archer's affiliation with his class is Wharton's skepticism toward the idea that "Americans [. . .] regard the fact that a man has made money as something intrinsically meritorious" (FW 107). Members of the developing socioeconomic elite in the novel view the buildup of material wealth through aggressive means to be a form of progress. Yet, what would be "meritorious" in terms of the values assessed positively by the omniscient voice is an effort to resolve the conflicts produced by the forces of order and contingency the novel confronts. What seems like the control over exogamy evident in the expulsion of Ellen Olenska illustrates the complexity of Wharton's subject here, for Ellen has a blood connection with Archer's tribe and is, in this sense, not an outsider. The resistance to their union is, primarily, a result of the fact that Archer and May are married, and of Ellen's temperamental and ideological difference. The primacy of "surface forms" over sexual selection outlines the divide between biology and Archer's class mentality.

These manners are so deeply inculcated in Archer that "[f]ew things seemed to [him] more awful than an offence against 'Taste,' that far off divinity of whom 'Form' was the mere visible representative and viceregent" (14). The depiction of Archer's insight that there exists some irreducible foundation for the behavior he notes, beyond its manifestation in form, again demonstrates his interpretive tendency; the passage also shows, however, that his concern, indicated by his formulation that taste is the Platonic essence of which form is a manifestation, is fixated on the signs or effects of such foundations and not the patterning of chance, variation, and instinct which "taste" and "form" also signify. This preoccupation with signs is a distinguishing characteristic of Archer's thoroughly aesthetic orientation, which is signaled to the reader by the fact that his "boyhood had been saturated with Ruskin, and he had read all the latest books: John Addington Symonds, Vernon Lee's 'Euphorion,' the essays of P .G. Hamerton, and a wonderful new volume called 'The Renaissance' by Walter Pater" (69).[8]

These writers color Archer's evaluative habits, suggesting to the reader that the aesthetic values of his class modulate his perception. The pictures hanging in Ellen Olenska's room, in contrast, "bewildered him, for they were like nothing that he was accustomed to look at (and therefore able to see) when he traveled in Italy" (294). Spanning the ethical aesthetics of Ruskin and the art for art's sake detachment of aesthetics from moral teaching found in the work of Ruskin's student Pater, Archer's reading has exposed him to a variety of authoritative Victorian opinions on art. Immersion in the works of the writers Wharton names impresses upon Archer a general concept articulated by one critic, who writes that the "goal of the positive Victorian aesthetics [. . .] was not to objectify others as art, but to provide the conditions that would allow oneself and others to live with the freedom of art" (Gagnier 271). That Archer strives to realize this formulation is clear when May tells Archer that "[w]e can't behave like people in novels" and he replies by saying "[w]hy not—why not—why not?" (82). Archer's artistic interests demonstrate one way his connoisseurship sublimates instinct to aesthetics.

His struggle with the limits posed by his artistic understanding of self and society intensifies when his internal conflicts seem to him represented by paintings. When Archer visits the Louvre before he and his son Dallas are to see Ellen Olenska, "the pictures [. . .] fill his soul with the long echoes of beauty. After all, his life had been too starved" (358). When Archer "stands before an effulgent Titian" his old passion for Ellen is recalled, but "[f]or such summer dreams it was too late" (358).[9] Near the end of the novel, Renaissance painters like Titian proffer to Archer a more truthful representation of pre-Christian instinct than does the static primitivism of Italian painting before the Renaissance from which the Victorian pre-Raphaelite aesthetic was partially derived. Archer is sympathetic to this sensibility, and at odds with pre-Raphaelitism, for he speaks with "condescension" (69) of Fra Angelico, one of the group's touchstones. Moreover, the writers mentioned above are significant to the analysis of Archer's powers of appreciation because Pater, Symonds, and Vernon Lee are referred to in the Wharton manuscript "Italy Again" as examples of the "cultivated amateur," with whom Wharton contrasts the "trained specialist" (*The Uncollected Critical Writings* 292). The interpretations of painting, sculpture, and architecture Archer reads allow him to differentiate between the cultural values expressed in a Fra Angelico and a Titian, but Archer's dilettantism in matters of art gives him only a superficial appreciation of beauty and sexuality. He recognizes his "sense of inadequacy and inexpressiveness" (358) in the static forms or pre-Renaissance painting he dislikes, but he cannot experience the effulgence of feeling that would radiate toward Ellen had his capacity to express himself not been "starved" by the imposition of form on his feelings.

Differences between the authorial specialist and her amateur protagonist appear frequently. Early in the novel, upon seeing Ellen's "swarthy foreign looking maid [. . .] whom he vaguely fancied to be Sicilian," Archer reacts by deploying the classificatory method of his anthropological reading: "[h]e knew that the southern races communicated with each other in the language of pantomime, and was mortified to find her shrugs and smiles so unintelligible" (69). His inability to comprehend the maid illustrates that

Archer is indeed an amateur in anthropological matters. Although the maid is a visual pun, a real-life embodiment of the "Italian primitive" he dislikes in the work of Fra Angelico, she is, in Archer's characterization of her, a narrative expression of the difficulties he encounters in applying his partial scientific knowledge to people such as May. Though perceived as weak and unaware by Archer, his wife trumps him. Archer views with condescension a human being he encounters outside the representative capacity of art, and she is "unintelligible." His inattentiveness to the significance of *Faust* cost him a lesson on the limits of knowledge, and his aesthetic and scientific amateurism places a dehumanizing frame around Ellen's maid.

Wharton's presentation of Archer's feeble objectivity charts the framing of his perspective by the artistic, literary, and scientific works he consumes. While works of art history and aesthetic interpretation that depict a positive Renaissance revaluation of pre-Christian instinct also seem to Archer authoritative in their call for "a life as free as art," they both enlighten and lead to disappointment. Geometrical compositional principles and the perfectly smooth surface of a painted canvas can represent instinct, as the Titian that Archer is so moved by demonstrates. The ordered forms of the painting convey the naturalness of expressing the animality from which Archer is alienated. But the value to Archer of such works has been obscured by the aesthetic terms of his appreciation. What the Titian can teach Archer eludes him in practice. By the end of the novel, then, Archer understands—as he realizes it is "too late" for him—that "the new generation [. . .] had swept away all the old landmarks, and with them the signposts and danger signals" (358). This leaves him to question the principles by which he has lived, and confirms the presence of dynamic social evolution illustrated by shifts in the history of art.

When Archer unpacks the latest shipment from his London bookseller, finding "a new volume of Herbert Spencer, another collection of the prolific Alphonse Daudet's brilliant tales, and a new novel called 'Middlemarch' [. . .] he had declined three dinner invitations in favour of this feast" (138), it is a prelude to the dispersal of his assumption that he is leading a life that utilizes these works. In her 1902 *Bookman* review of Leslie Stephens's biography of George Eliot, Wharton defended Eliot against charges that she "was too scientific" ("George Eliot" 71), demonstrating her allegiance to the author of a work to which Henry James referred by writing, "*Middlemarch* is too often an echo of Messrs. Darwin and Huxley" (qtd. in Gillian Beer 139). Archer's reading of *Middlemarch* is a fictionalized encounter with a writer whose scientific frame of reference Wharton found appealing. Throwing over his social persona for the evening to immerse himself in these works, he demonstrates that he is quite ready to enjoy "possibly forbidden pleasures of the mind" (Preston 42)[10] that are capable of rubbing through the patina of a leisured life. Yet he is not prepared for the complexity of the new vision that he finds.

The dispersal of a fantasy generated by his immersion in a book of verse entitled "The House of Life," which "gave a new and haunting beauty to the most elementary of passions" (AI 138), comes the following morning when he looks out on the brownstone houses of the street. Again, Archer can't break down the binary of passion, or Eros, and "beauty" so characteristic of his perspective. His conception of "elementary passions" in terms of "warm [. . .] rich [. . .] ineffably tender [. . .] haunting beauty" (138) shows once more that for Archer sexuality is signified by aesthetic taste. He has pursued in "those enchanted pages the vision of a woman who had the face of Ellen Olenska," but making of this fantasy an actuality is "far outside the pale of probability" (138). His training disrupts his instincts. What completely dissipates his vision of Ellen is the "thought of his desk in Mr. Letterblair's office, and the family pew in Grace Church" (138). The social institutions of law and religion overmaster Archer's fantasies, and the expression of their authority as "desk" and "pew" is a metonymical illustration of his subordinate position to the system of ideas governing his class.

The novel's presentation of the forms taken by "rituals of exclusion" (Bauer *Brave New Politics* 12) is one of its primary concerns. Julius Beaufort is considered dangerous because he is "a 'foreigner' of doubtful origin" (44). In the case of Ellen's expulsion there "were certain things that had to be done, and if done at all, done handsomely and thoroughly; and one of these, in the old New York code, was the tribal rally around a kinswoman who was about to be eliminated from the tribe" (334). Ellen is to be expelled because the "individual, in such cases, is nearly always sacrificed to what is supposed to be the collective interest" (111). But "rituals of exclusion" are also the manacles of inclusion.

May does not possess Archer's consciousness of the harm potentially done by the "collective interest." Archer sees it though, reflecting upon how, after marrying May, "[i]t would presently be his task to take the bandage from this young woman's eyes" (81). But the inability to transcend expected thoughts and actions that Archer notes in May he also sees in himself, causing him to resent the extent to which his life is choreographed: "'[s]ameness—sameness!' he muttered, the word running through his head like a persecuting tune" (83). Archer reacts to the experiential narrowing caused by manners, providing an example of how, as Knights has argued potently, "the text makes it hard to sustain readings that dismiss cultural furnishings as 'background' (whether picturesque or oppressive) or that see characters as discrete beings, with an independent 'selfhood' separate and intact from any social inscriptions" (20). Archer is all too aware of inscription as a process that contorts his body and being. This tradition envisions marriage as a duty that if not considered as such, lapses into "a mere battle of ugly appetites" (AI 347). The difficulty of remaining coherent to oneself outside that tradition keeps Archer from smelling "the flower of life [. . .] a thing so unattainable and improbable" (347).

Standing at the center of the establishment, Archer becomes alienated from habits and customs that are transparent to his future wife. He is not afraid to remedy May's unawareness of the fact that she is the product of social determinism: "We're all as like each other as those dolls cut out of the same folded paper. We're like patterns stencilled on a wall," he cries (82). Despite the fact that he feels a responsibility to teach her, his sense that "she simply echoed what was said for her" (81) elicits foreboding: "[h]e shivered a little, remembering some of the new ideas in his scientific books, and the much-cited instance of the Kentucky cave-fish, which had ceased to develop eyes because they had no use for them" (82). This allusion to Archer's knowledge of natural selection figures social evolution in Darwinian terms, making of class ideology a component of the social selection environment that over the course of generations "blinds" May and those like her.

Another passage from Wharton's 1905 review of Howard Sturgis's *Belchamber* addresses the topic of representation in a way useful to understanding why Wharton constructs Archer's perspective in her novel as she does. In the essay, Wharton suggests that following the rules of taste by adhering to form in the creation of art denies an element of the real. She writes of form that "when it is a mere lifeless reproduction of another's design, the dreary 'drawing from a plaster cast,' twice removed from reality, it is of no more artistic value than any other clever reproduction; whereas [. . .] the thing personally felt and directly rendered, asserts itself through all accidental difficulties of expression" (107). In *The Age of Innocence* this artistic dilemma mirrors Archer's situation, for his is a position "removed from reality" by his training, which elevates "form," as has been shown, to a primary position that makes of his passion a thing that cannot be felt directly. This claim, which will be dealt with in the next section, finds support in the presentation of a class-specific lexicon that substantially affects what Archer can and cannot say.

One might object to the suggestion that Wharton creates Archer's compromised objectivity in order to articulate the dangers of a superficial scientific basis for social analysis, on the grounds that she seeks only to depict a tragic story of thwarted love. In fact, such an objection could rely on

Wharton's own words: "I did so want 'The Age' to be taken not so much as a 'costume piece' but as 'a simple and grave' story of two people trying to live up to something that was still 'felt in the blood' at that time" (*Letters* 433). But it is exactly what Archer and Ellen feel "in the blood" that their social environment forbids them to express, and it is those moments during which mutual understanding is elusive when the barriers to their expression become a subject.

One could object too that the novel's concern with "tribes" and ritual employs an anthropological point of view that responds to the fact that "[t]he subject of manners [. . .] had been newly discovered in this era by social scientists, anthropologists, social theorists, and psychologists [who] increasingly located the source of all social praxis and regulation in cultural habits and customs" (Bentley 69). Such an objection would imply that Wharton is not interested in the sources of Archer's viewpoint, but wishes only to represent it. Evidence to the contrary exists in the specific qualities of the contrasting perspectives of Archer, and the narrative within which his viewpoint is contained; in particular, such evidence is visible in the novel's representation of how linguistic norms modulate the way Archer views his world.

III. "WORD-DUST"

In *French Ways and Their Meaning*,[11] a treatise "[i]ntended to instruct American military men about French mores" (Benstock 348), Wharton characterizes an aspect of American language that in *The Age of Innocence* affects Archer's ability to express himself. Composed while she wrote the novel, *French Ways* bemoans the "deplorable loss of shades of difference in our blunted speech" (FW 83). Wharton attributes this loss of the means to make fine distinctions to the fact that in America one finds "a race that has had a recent beginning" (FW 83). Due to "the sudden uprooting of our American ancestors and their violent cutting off from all their past" (FW 82), Americans live in linguistic poverty in comparison to the French. This claim is evident in Archer's difficulty discussing with May his involvement with Ellen Olenska:

> '[T]here's something I want to say; [. . .] the slight distance between them [. . .] an unbridgeable abyss. The sound of his voice echoed uncannily through the homelike hush, and he repeated: 'There is something I've got to tell you [. . .]. Archer checked the conventional phrases of self-accusal that were crowding to his lips. He was determined to put the case baldly [. . .]. 'Madame Olenska—' he said; but at the same time his wife raised her hand as if to silence him. (323)

Archer's involvement with Ellen is a reality that cannot be represented by their class dialect. Linguistic means are reduced to signifiers of concepts and behavior appropriate to the drawing room.

In 1925 Wharton articulated a problem for the fiction writer that bears on her representation of language in *The Age of Innocence,* and my interest in the limitations to what Archer can represent linguistically:

> The novelist works in the very material out of which the object he is try-
> ing to render is made. [. . .] It is relatively easy to separate the artistic
> vision of an object from its complex and tangled actuality if one has to
> re-see it in paint or marble and bronze; it is infinitely difficult to render
> a human mind when one is employing the very word-dust with which
> thought is formulated. (WF 16–17)

The difficulty Archer has in recognizing why he cannot transcend his train-ing is a variation on the artistic dilemma Wharton outlines; his cultural analysis is limited by the breadth of a system of signification specific to his class, not just his intellectual amateurism. His shallow scientism is partly to blame for the inability of scientific knowledge to impassion him, and it con-ceals that what he wishes to learn through books can be understood only experientially. Furthermore, Wharton's depiction of the linguistic forms of old New York is an aspect of her controlling objective mode, one that subor-dinates Archer's perspective, and attempts to position the narrative's objectiv-ity outside the reach of the effects it describes.

Archer's limited ability to grapple with "hard facts" (AI 198) shines through the novel's reflection on the linguistic habits of his tribe:

> In reality they all lived in a kind of hieroglyphic world, where the real
> thing was never said or done or even thought, but only represented by
> an arbitrary sign; as when Mrs. Welland, who knew exactly why Archer
> had pressed her to announce her daughter's engagement at the Beaufort
> ball (and had indeed expected him to do no less), yet felt obliged to sim-
> ulate reluctance, and the air of having her hand forced. (44)

Beneath the glitter of the chandelier occurs the articulation of a mating rite in ritualistic forms. Mrs. Welland perceives the "arbitrary sign" as encoding or sig-nifying something she will not directly state. Although "she knew exactly why" Newland wanted a hasty marriage—he wants to take the focus off Ellen, and he senses that his increasing interest in Ellen threatens the order of his life—her knowledge cannot be expressed through the available language of the tribe.

Social "form" defines a system of referents available for Archer's objective inquiry, but this system depends not just on dress and gesture as media for signification, but on language. Doing the unspeakable consists in behavior that has no corresponding entry in the language of Archer's circle, one in which the fashionable is possessed of a gravity whose source is a historical past singular in its influence, for "[w]hat was or was not 'the thing' played a part as important in Newland Archer's New York as the inscrutable totem terrors that had ruled the destinies of his forefathers" (4). In linking habits with the "totem terrors" that guided the "destinies of his forefathers," Archer is similar to his law partner, who is seen by the protagonist as "the Pharisaic voice of a society wholly absorbed in barricading itself against the unpleasant" (98). This is not to say that Archer isn't skeptical of the appearance of absolute verity that gilds surfaces, ideas, and thoughts he finds in his class environment. In fact, while he stands at his wedding he thinks that "real people were living somewhere, and real things happening to them" (182). In this two-fold fictional world in which Archer's perspective is nested within that of the narrative, he is anchored in the unreal by a system of signification unequipped to represent the "real" to which he alludes.

Language is the transmission medium for cultural traits that in Wharton's genetic theory of inherited values is shown to convert into linguistic matter what is "felt in the blood." In Wharton's era, "Mendel's laws, and with them the concept of the gene as a unit of heredity, was the salvation of Darwinian thinking" (Dennett 220). Salvation though it was, these were daunting ideas, even for Wharton's discipline-crashing intellect. She recognized the significance of "the allelomorphs & heterozygotes" explained in Lock's book (*Letters* 151); but she portrays the transmission of values in terms that equate genes and language. Hers is not only a metaphorical representation of social reproduction in which language carries cultural information that manifests itself as a class-bound angle of vision. Rather, it is an argumentative strategy that demonstrates the inseparability of social expression, including language, from biological foundations.

In Wharton's implicit theory of cultural reproduction, mistakes in information transmission are inevitable, and drive change. Archer's statement that "[w]e've no character, no colour, no variety" (241), is thus a marker of a species running out of time. Errors in transmission result in Julius Beaufort and his mutative, variant type, whose presence hints at the reality of alternate classes and other ways of articulating passion in the social context. It is the resistance to mutation and variation that distinguishes Archer's class as being engaged in a maladroit attempt to preserve their social artifice under the rotting umbrella of so-called "natural [. . .] conventions"

(5) that are anything but. This effort, moreover, fixes linguistic borders of representation in such a way as to incite May's "blushing circumlocution" (344) and the other instances of inarticulateness, as when Archer's "arms were yearning up to her [Ellen]; but she drew away, and they remained facing each other, divided by the distance that their words [about the end of their relationship] had created" (172).

Knights recalls Ian Burkitt's work to show that Wharton pursued the effects of ideological inscription through language on individual psychology: "'[p]ersonality develops within discourse,' that is [. . .] 'self' and 'mind' are formed within the 'communicative activity of the group'" (21). The evidence necessary to grant that this exists in *The Age of Innocence* falls into two related categories; first, the novel depicts the use of language to be regulated by ideological interpellations regarding what can and cannot be said, and second, such communication affects the ability of individuals to conceive of ideas outside the "pale of probability" (AI 138). These aspects of language use in the novel exist within the hierarchy of character and narrative perspectives already discussed. For example, shortly before Archer is to leave for Washington, D.C., where he hopes to meet privately with Ellen, an omniscient narrative interjection follows an exchange between Archer and May, that differentiates Wharton's analytical mode from her protagonist's:

> 'The change will do you good,' she said simply [. . .]. It was the only word that passed between them on the subject; but in the code in which they had both been trained it meant: 'Of course you understand that I know all that people have been saying about Ellen, and heartily sympathise with my family in their effort to get her to return to her husband. I also know that, for some reason you have chosen not to tell me, you have advised her against this course, which all the older men of the family, as well as our grandmother, agree in approving; and that it is owing to your encouragement that Ellen defies us all, and exposes herself to the kind of criticism of which Mr. Sillerton Jackson probably gave you, this evening, the hint that has made you so irritable. . . . Hints have indeed not been wanting; but since you appear unwilling to take them from others, I offer you this one myself, in the only form in which well-bred people of our kind can communicate unpleasant things to each other: by letting you understand that I know you mean to see Ellen when you are in Washington, and are perhaps going there expressly for that purpose; and that, since you are sure to see her, I wish you to do so with my full and explicit approval—and to take the opportunity of letting her know what the course of conduct you have encouraged her in is likely to lead to. (267–68)

It is a "mute message" that they share (268), but as the narrator makes clear, much is communicated that is not verbalized.

Here one might object that Archer and May have transcended the linguistic code that only seems to limit their ability to conceptualize alternatives to scripted behavior. However, what is encoded is a not-said that is signified by oblique reference and gesture: "'and you must be sure to go and see Ellen,' [. . .]. Her hand was still on the key of the lamp when the last word of this mute message reached him. She turned the wick down, lifted off the globe, and breathed on the sulky flame" (267–68); thus is Ellen extinguished. The taboo subject of sexual infidelity can be signified within a class-specific system of meaning, but it is a sign at the margin that references forbidden ideas without entries in Archer's lexicon. In this unsaid is the potential for linguistic evolution that opens pathways for change along the lines of new concepts. This does happen, leaving Archer to regret the "stifled memories of an inarticulate lifetime" (357).

Such passages are an ironic manifestation of Wharton's edict governing "[t]he use of dialogue in fiction [. . .] [which] should be reserved for the culminating moments" (WF 73), for this key exchange passes in silence. At the level of what *is* enunciated, one finds that May, at the end of the scene, does not state directly her desire that Ellen's threat to the marriage be ended. Rather, May again refers to Ellen metaphorically when upon snuffing the flame of the lamp she remarks: "[t]hey smell less if one blows them out" (268). Although May's reference is to the imminent social extinction of Ellen, Wharton represents a felt need to avoid direct statement by depicting a system of signification that assiduously disperses the question of why such obscurantism exists.

The issue of *why* these characters can't speak plainly is advanced, in the portrayal of May's stifled thoughts, as a code that is "the only form in which well-bred people of our kind can communicate" (267). One could contend, as Wharton herself did, that "[w]hen, in real life, two or more people are talking together, all that is understood between them is left out of their talk" (WF 74). But in the quoted passages, Wharton's subject is an involuntary self-censorship evidenced by her insistent reiteration that meaning—such as it is—emerges in such exchanges from the context of straitjacketed communication that May and Archer's son Dallas refers to as a sign of the "deaf-and-dumb asylum" (357) that is their social context. That the requirement to encode is in full effect is also evident in the frequency with which Archer catches himself in ingrained habits and thoughts, as when he becomes "conscious in himself of the same instinctive recoil that he had so often criticized in his mother" (108).

Further evidence of Wharton's interest in identifying connections between language, social practices, and individual psychology exists in her statement that in "[i]nheriting an old social organization, modern America has [. . .] reduced the English language to a mere instrument of utility [. . .] so she has reduced relations between human beings to a dead level of vapid benevolence" ("The Great American Novel" 154). The vapidity of the smooth social surface that Archer both loves and loathes belies a deeper reality that Wharton represents. The announcement of Archer's engagement to May prompts him to reflect that "[h]is joy was so deep that this blurring of the surface [the public announcement of the engagement] left its essence untouched; but he would like to keep the surface pure too" (23). His preference, in other words, is to avoid social intercourse where the topic of his marriage is concerned, and to not see his affections interpreted in the language of the tribe: "it was not thus that he would have wished to have his happiness known. To proclaim it in the heat and noise of a crowded ballroom was to rob it of the fine bloom of privacy which should belong to things nearest the heart" (23). Archer doesn't want the private "essence" of his feeling toward May articulated in stock phrases.

In so thinking, he shuns the use of English as an "instrument of utility," preferring to avoid the discursive fray altogether. "Now we shan't have to talk," he whispers to May at the beginning of a dance as they ritualistically float "away on the soft waves of the Blue Danube" (23). May follows Archer into silence. He observes how "she made no answer [. . .] as if bent on some ineffable vision. What a new life it was going to be, with this whiteness, radiance. Goodness at one's side" (23). But May's "whiteness" is blankness, and her "Goodness," like her "niceness," nearly empty except for its signification of stock language affiliated with the power of "admonitory" manners (65) to narrow experience. The veneer of normalcy that makes of ideological effects an objective reality for May has been rubbed off in Archer's perception, giving him "an awkward way of suddenly not seeming to take the most fundamental things for granted" (252). However, Archer's joy at the imminence of his marriage to May does not survive his first meeting with the adult Ellen (with whom he once played as a boy).

Ellen is a woman who can satisfy Newland's yearning for "transcendent experience" (Wolff 319) both sexually and intellectually. Late in the novel, as Archer and Ellen travel by steamboat to Point Arley, Ellen's effect on Archer is cast in terms that allude to the value placed on the unblemished surface by his world, and also the potential for movement toward an alternate reality Ellen represents: "As the boat left the harbour and turned seaward a breeze stirred up about them [. . .]. The fog of sultriness still hung over the city, but ahead lay a fresh world of ruffled waters, and distant promontories with light-houses in the sun" (238). This vision, distinguished by the visual clarity bestowed by multiple sources of illumination, is related to a sensual image in which "Madame Olenska, leaning back against the boat-rail, drank in the coolness between parted lips" (238). The inexpressible truth (to Archer) of sex, its association in the scene with nature, and the knowledge of the world beyond New York that Ellen possesses, draw Archer away from his love of surface. Wishing to evade the social order, he feels solidarity with yet another phantom—that imaginary place he longs to escape to with Ellen.

Ellen, for her part, sees the matter clearly and articulates the situation using words that sound alien to Archer's ears:

> 'Is it your idea then that I should live with you as your mistress—since I can't be your wife?' The crudeness of the question startled him: the word was one that women of his class fought shy of, even when their talk flitted closest about the topic. He noticed that Madame Olenska pronounced it as if it had a recognized place in her vocabulary [. . .]. Her question pulled him up with a jerk, and he floundered. 'I want—I want to get away with you into a world where words like that—categories like that—won't exist. Where we shall be simply two human beings who love each other, who are the whole of life to each other; and nothing else on earth will matter.' She drew a deep sigh that ended in another laugh. 'Oh, my dear—where is that country? Have you ever been there?' (290)

Archer, in fact, need not look past his own world to find a place where such words and categories "won't exist."

In conceiving of ideal conditions in which he and Ellen can live, he imagines a place where limitations on vocabulary and concepts are in full force. This describes the very world he seeks to flee. Finding himself within an alien signifying system, he flounders and proposes a return to the sphere he knows. Alternative frameworks in which they might be together would be contexts in which he, as a socially construed subject, would not exist—so tightly integrated with his milieu does Wharton conceive of his psychology. The only context in which contact between them can continue, Ellen observes, is that of kinship relations; however, this framework does not allow for the expression of desire either:

> 'Then what exactly is your plan for us?' he asked. 'For *us*? But there's no *us* in that sense! We're near each other only if we stay far from each

other. Then we can be ourselves. Otherwise we're only Newland Archer, the husband of Ellen Olenska's cousin, and Ellen Olenska, the cousin of Newland Archer's wife, trying to be happy behind the backs of people who trust them.' 'Ah, I'm beyond that,' he groaned. 'No, you're not! You've never been beyond. And I have,' she said in a strange voice, 'and I know what it looks like there.' (291)

Ellen's "beyond" is a psychic, material, and sexual state outside of the linguistic and experiential boundary within which Archer interprets and analyzes his social stratum. It is also the state to which Lily Bart unsuccessfully aspires.

Particular limitations on the meaning of language, certain programmatic evacuations of meaning from key words and concepts, make it difficult for Archer to imagine Ellen's "beyond." His perceptions are directed by "the invisible deity of 'Good Form'" (182). For example, in Archer's set the concept of women's equality contains no arguments, suggests no thesis or antithesis, a fact made tangible in the way his exclamation that "'[w]omen should be free—as free as we are,' struck to the root of a problem that it was agreed in his world to regard as non-existent" (43). Additionally,

'Nice' women, however wronged, would never claim the kind of freedom he meant, and generous minded men like himself were therefore—in the heat of argument—the more chivalrously ready to concede it to them. Such verbal generosities were in fact only a humbugging disguise of the inexorable conventions that tied things together and bound people down to the old pattern. (43)

In contemplating May, he wonders: "What if 'niceness' carried to that supreme degree were only a negation, the curtain dropped before an emptiness?" (212); May's "niceness" is a socially generated aspect of "inexorable conventions" that in part explains how it is that in her, "such depths of feeling could coexist with such absence of imagination" (188).

May's deep feelings are expressed in conventional marriage-day statements. When Archer admits that "I thought I'd lost the ring. [. . .] I had time to think of every horror that might possibly happen" (187), May responds by "flinging her arms about his neck. 'But none ever *can* happen now, can it Newland, as long as we two are together?'" (187). Such wishful thinking does have depth insofar as their marriage will be vigorously defended by the same "conspiracy of mothers and aunts and grandmothers and long dead ancestresses" (45) responsible for May's attitudes, and in this sense nothing *can* happen to them. But May is not cognizant of the psychologically formative pressures she has been subjected to, and upon which her so-called happiness rests. Her statements are like her "clear eyes [which] revealed only the most tranquil unawareness" (188). May's physical characteristics mirror the fact that she speaks for a social order and its traditions: "[p]erhaps that faculty of unawareness is what gave her eyes their transparency, and her face the look of representing a type rather than a person; as if she might have been chosen to pose for a civic virtue or a Greek goddess" (189). Nothing as natural as the chance variation in the codes passed from generation to generation exists in this static environment, one in which the *ingenue* is, though an embodiment of ideal physical grace, a type rather than a person, and one seen as stone no less, for "her face wore the vacant serenity of a young marble athlete" (141).

Preston expresses a key critical response to the issue of May's "niceness" as a negation in terms that view the linguistic nullities of Archer's tribe as a sign that it avoids the "real":

> 'Not-niceness' is an odd litotes which seems to summarise an essential linguistic and behavioral demarcation in Wharton's fiction. It represents an impoverishment of vocabulary, in which the opposite of a thing is formulated merely as its own cancellation. It is the evasion of particularity (what is 'niceness,' *exactly,* and how far would one have to go not to be nice?). Non-logical and 'indeterminately evaluative,' it represents the linguistic atrophy of her fictional tribe. (1–2)

In contrast to May's conformity to a static class-world in which the opposite of "niceness" has no signifier, Ellen's fate in the selection environment, as Archer states, is "what we've all contrived to make it" (144). His group deflects change through limitations on what can be said. Ellen's ability to think for herself makes her an oddity in a world that favors May's adherence to a typology in which "nice women" never claim the kind of freedom Ellen has. Yet to call it "linguistic atrophy," as Preston does, underestimates the capacity of a supposedly weak linguistic system to quell unorthodox ideas through the exclusion of their signifiers.

In Archer's world, verbal utterances in the form of refusals of invitations, and linguistic gestures of opprobrium and obliquity, manage to direct the collusion that excludes Archer from discussions of Ellen's fate, and Ellen's eventual banishment. Archer sees that "to all of them he and Madame Olenska were lovers, lovers in the extreme sense peculiar to 'foreign vocabularies'" (335). Such otherness must be expelled. "[T]he silent organization which held his little world together" (339) harshly reacts to the pressure of foreign concepts, and is arguably an instinctive tribalism that holds Archer's "little world together." But it is a silently enacted bond belied by a fixation on form and refinement. In contrast to the inability to speak plainly that is character-istic of Archer's class, his initial conversations with Ellen contain "hard facts [. . .]. Their very vocabulary was unfamiliar to him, and seemed to belong to fiction and the stage" (108). Only in the language of the imaginary do "hard facts" have any substance. The strange vocabulary of the real which he encounters only in literature and drama causes him to feel "awkward and embarrassed" when it crosses the proscenium (108). Confronted with Ellen's frank discussion of her past, he does not verbalize a response to Ellen's ques-tion regarding her marriage to Count Olenski when she asks, "You know about my husband—my life with him?" (108). Instead, "[h]e made a sign of assent" (108) that avoids the bramble of locution. Archer cannot enter into such conversations.

IV. "THE KNOWLEDGE OF 'FORM' MUST BE CONGENITAL"

The opening sequence of *The Age of Innocence* at the old "Academy of Music" (3) blurs distinctions between the high art the audience takes its evening's entertainment to be, and the gatherings of "Primitive Man" (44) with which Archer compares it. The scene introduces the reader to Archer, to the way gentry manners create the group psychology affecting him, and his concomi-tant sense of apartness and superiority. Archer won't openly challenge "the carefully brushed, white-waistcoated, button-hole-flowered gentlemen who succeeded each other in the club box" (7) because doing so will impair his connection to the group. However,

> [i]n matters intellectual and artistic Newland Archer felt himself dis-tinctly the superior of these chosen specimens of old New York gentil-ity; he had probably read more, thought more, and even seen a good deal more of the world, than any other men of the number. Singly they betrayed their inferiority; but grouped together they represented 'New York,' and the habit of masculine solidarity made him accept their doc-trine on all the issues called moral. He instinctively felt that in this respect it would be troublesome—and also rather bad form—to strike out for himself. (7–8)

Archer feels unity with these men even as he distinguishes himself from them; his insight is acute in matters of habit and dress. As a "white-waist-coated" gentleman he conforms, in part because of a compulsive "masculine solidarity," and the potential violation of form likely caused by independent thought.

"Form" is primary in Archer's world; its violation leaves a mark of difference on the offender. In turning again to the language found in Wharton's characterization of men as "specimens" and Archer "instinctively" sensing a threat in the group, variation from which would be "troublesome," she figures black tie as attire expressive of tribal conformity. Yet, Archer does something similar to the author. In the posture of the concealed anthropologist as he stands in shadow at the back of his opera box, he is struck "by the religious reverence of even the most unworldly American women for the social advantages of dress [. . .] and he understood for the first time the earnestness with which May [. . .] had gone through the solemn rite of selecting and ordering her extensive wardrobe" (198). As his focus turns to Ellen Olenska's dated outfit, adherence to sumptuary codes becomes visible as a primary marker of membership in the tribe, and its violation an act that invites observation and sanction. Ellen appears in a "dark blue velvet gown rather theatrically caught up under her bosom by a girdle with a large old-fashioned clasp. The wearer of this unusual dress, who seemed quite unconscious of the attention it was attracting, stood a moment in the center of the box" (9). It is Lawrence Lefferts who spies Ellen across the auditorium. His surveillance of the audience, conducted through a "glass" (9), indicates sensitivity to matters of form. This sensitivity compels him to note nuances of dress and gesture. Lefferts is only one of many who "turned their opera-glasses critically on the circle of ladies who were the products of the system" (8).

Lefferts is a metonymical caricature. He monitors all who pass under his gaze and stands for the watchfulness of the audience as a whole. He is "the foremost authority on 'form' in New York" who can only stammer "My God!" (8) when he sees Ellen Olenska attired archaically. Lefferts had, Archer notes, "probably devoted more time than any one else to the study of this intricate and fascinating question; but study alone could not account for his complete and easy competence. One had only to look at him [. . .] to feel that the knowledge of 'form' must be congenital" (8). In this way Archer suggests that Lefferts was born with this trait, and that it is common to the stratum Lefferts represents. Archer's statement is biologically inflected in calling Lefferts's knowledge "congenital," and inductive in drawing its conclusion through an accumulation of facts.

The terms of Archer's quasi-scientific commentary reflect the superficial learning acquired in his "Gothic library" (4) where he dallies before arriving late to the opera. Archer's mind earlier touched on works by Herbert Spencer and George Eliot when he occupied this special room (138), one decorated "with glazed black-walnut bookcases and finial-topped chairs" (4).

His appreciation of the decoration scheme of the library parallels his light skimming of "one book after another [that] dropped from his hand" (138). Once in his box at the opera, Archer surveys the scene alongside Lefferts, but as he "turned his eyes from the stage and scanned the opposite side of the house" he merely notices the "monstrous obesity" of Mrs. Manson Mingott (5), and does not police the scene as Lefferts does. The omniscient narrator here presents Archer's shallow knowledge as both hereditary and defective. His spurious objectivity enables his comment on Lefferts's knowledge of form, but comes from one "shocked and troubled" by the way Ellen's dress "(which had no tucker) sloped away from her thin shoulders. [. . .] He hated to think of May Welland's being exposed to the influence of a young woman so careless of the dictates of Taste" (15). Wharton's amateur anthropologist cannot grasp how form limits his analysis of its effects by deflecting deeper considerations. Present in the scene are varieties of false objectivity represented by Lefferts, who observes Ellen, but is watched by Archer, and the authoritative scope of the narrative that depicts both viewpoints.

Following the sighting of Ellen Olenska at the opera, audience members in Lefferts's box look to Sillerton Jackson for an interpretation of her unexpected presence: "the whole of the club turned instinctively to hear what the old man had to say; for old Mr. Jackson was as great an authority on 'family' as Lawrence Lefferts was on 'form'" (8). A tribal elder possessed of vital knowledge regarding kinship ties, Jackson

> knew all the ramifications of New York's cousinships; and could not only elucidate such complicated questions as that of the connection between the Mingotts (through the Thorleys) with the Dallases of South Carolina, and that of the relationship of the elder branch of Philadelphia Thorleys to the Albany Chiverses [. . .], but could also enumerate the leading characteristics of each family. (9)

The depiction of this thicket of intertwining family trees emphasizes the importance of knowing each person's place in a social hierarchy where ambiguity over whether one belongs or not, as is the case with Ellen, can provoke a certain and devastating response.

That Wharton was intent on representing such intolerance of difference through a narrative lens shaped by current trends in anthropology and sociology is an argument made by Bauer, who observes that Wharton had,

> in *The Age of Innocence* only a few years before Margaret Mead's *Coming of Age in Samoa* and Branislaw Malinowski's *Sex and Repression in Savage*

Society, already dismantled the binary opposition between primitive and civilized cultures, by showing that civilized New York is as dependent upon rituals of exclusion and scapegoating as any other pattern of culture. (*Brave New Politics* 11–12)

The "binary opposition" Bauer refers to, moreover, is exploded in *The Age of Innocence* by the depiction of Archer's flawed scientific angle of vision, which is a devalued point-of-view.

One consequence of Archer's reading of culture is the maintenance of a perceived gap between the primitive and civilized. He therefore sublimates instinct, or what is "felt in the blood," to the requirements of a group whose "masculine solidarity," symptomatic of its power of exclusion and inclusion, controls Archer's urge to "strike out for himself." In this way social evolution is potentially arrested. But the tactic of "exclusion and scapegoating," while successful at keeping Archer within the fold, will fail to mold the next generation, one represented by Archer's son, who finds his father's attitudes "prehistoric" (356) and so stands as evidence of irresistible change; Dallas does not subscribe to the doctrine held by Archer that deviation from the group is dangerous. His son, Archer thinks, looks "at fate not as a master but as an equal" (358). The pairing of Archer and May has produced a child who expresses Archer's oppositional—yet contained—difference in a way free of the conventions that have hindered the father. Dallas "belonged body and soul to the new generation" (356) and Wharton's characterization of the young man expresses the unity of physical and social transformation.

In the novel's opening scene, the potential joining of Archer and Ellen is foreshadowed by a depiction of botanical hybridization. In observing the stage scenery, Archer notes how "a daisy grafted on a rose-branch flowered with a luxuriance prophetic of Mr. Luther Burbank's far-off prodigies" (6).[12] Considered in terms of the novel's advocacy of the notion that new ideas and new blood are needed to reinvigorate a desiccated class, this passage presents the possibility of renewal to be inherent in fresh combinations of social and genetic pairings. Archer's demonstration that he knows Burbank's work, however, is spurred not by real flowers, but by stage dressing for which "[n]o expense had been spared" (6), reinforcing the fact that this costly portrayal of hybridization is safely confined to the stage, where it can be seen from a distance and controlled for viewers like Archer, who has previously associated "hard facts [. . .] with fiction and the stage" (108). He comments on mere representations of flowers. His difficulty in transcending manners that encourage him not to look deeply into scientific matters is confirmed by his hesitance at invigorating timeworn form and inbred genetic stock.

In shifting focus from Archer's quasi-scientific viewpoint to Wharton's sociobiological conception of the relation of individuals to their collectives, it is important to consider Garlepp-Burns's discussion of *The Custom of the Country*, which argues that the novel's scientifically informed narrative contains significant contradictions. Her argument allows one to view the political dimension of *The Age of Innocence* as compromising the apparent objectivity of Wharton's method. Objectivity, Garlepp-Burns writes,

> may seem to exclude the subject, but since its very definition requires a subject to observe the object, the apparently alien element of *subjectivity* complicates the picture; its connotation of impersonality and impartiality may suggest a neutral purpose, but it often masks the desire and acts as the very mechanism for *control* in narratives; and it may appear totally subservient to outward facts, but it is frequently used as a form of moral and intellectual *authority* derived from its source, the revered discipline of science. (29–30)

Wharton's representation of New York's elite as a "clan" or "tribe" (AI 32) whose qualities are presented in a framework cobbled from the author's evolutionary, biological, and anthropological sources, controls the narrative intermittently. The disparity between apparent neutrality and didactic social criticism is too great for Wharton's method to bear without its constituent parts being revealed.

Wharton's is not a mode of literary realism that unselfconsciously aligns her narrative method with the conventional view Archer represents. Instead, she distances her story from the conventions it portrays by highlighting Archer's manqué-scientist judgments. These judgments reveal a socially generated and problematic objectivity that transforms Ellen, for example, from a potential source of positive cultural change into "a young woman [. . .] careless of the dictates of taste" (15). It is in these juxtapositions between a scientifically influenced "moral and intellectual *authority*" provided by the narrator, and Archer's mediated conclusions, that one finds Wharton's tendency to place an always troubled objectivity in the service of social renewal.

This strategy supplies one possible reason why Wharton does not suppress omniscience in the way practiced by her modernist contemporaries during the period of the novel's composition. Phrases that originate with the controlling voice, such as "beyond that his imagination could not travel" (71), and the abandonment of Archer as a reflecting consciousness in the novel's final chapter, indicate that a single narrative register would be insufficient for Wharton's analysis of Archer's psychology, and her representation of the cultural elements that shape it.[13] Wharton writes that "the modern American novelist is told that the social and educated being is an unreality unworthy of his attention" ("The Great America Novel" 155). This statement is related to her abjuration of modernist narrative practices, for the fact that Archer is such a being, one that cannot disentangle himself from mediation by manners, requires a narrative position from which to assess and value socialization and education without handing over the task to the reader, who is presumably compromised by the same forces affecting Archer.

In "The Great American Novel" Wharton writes, surely including herself, that "students of natural history" might assume they can evade the complex ideological pressures exerted by "society [. . .] one of man's oldest works of art" (155). Such an evasion seems possible to a writer representing the collective through a scientifically inflected omniscience. However, Wharton's narrative objectivity produces a problem that in her critical writing she both describes and distances herself from. She finds fault with

> the early French 'realists,' that group of brilliant writers who invented the once-famous *tranche de vie,* the exact photographic reproduction of a situation or an episode, with all its sounds, smells, aspects realistically rendered, but with its deeper relevance and its suggestions of a larger whole either unconsciously missed or purposely left out. (WF 10)

Wharton's articulation of what is "left out" by this literary form accurately describes Archer's dilemma, wherein the conventional social surface made up of manners and speech he observes and analyzes "tended to draw him back into his old habits of mind" (195) and away from the "deeper relevance" of the coerciveness of these habits.

For Archer, as for the early French realists (in Wharton's estimation), form is all. But her commentary describes a literary problem she faces in attempting to depict a social self troublingly inattentive to the deeper meanings of manners: how to represent superficiality as a feature of a character and an ideology. Her politically sensitive objectivity avoids a superficial naturalism "totally subservient to outward facts" by employing an omniscience that colors in what is "unconsciously missed" by her main character. Again, in Archer's case what is averted is "naked instinct" (*Letters* 159), or desire. This is clear when the narrator relates that Archer sent flowers to Ellen "almost without knowing what he did" (AI 79). The representation of the "deeper relevance" and "larger whole" unperceived by Archer causes his shallow consciousness to resemble a supposedly exact literary mode Wharton disparages. *The Age of Innocence* transcends this mode because it maintains a politically invested projection of neutral observation, the maintenance of which is itself an elaborate fictive strategy.

I have argued to this point that *The Age of Innocence* relies on a polemical sociobiology that advances the genre of the novel as a form capable of critical acuity beyond that possessed by the frame through which Archer, a cataloguer of social habit himself, analyzes his class. But within the narrative is a representation of the protagonist's disquiet at the limitations imposed on him by the habits and standards he notes. Such clouds of disillusionment indicate the presence of social evolution, which is manifest in the attitudes of the next generation, as I have suggested, represented by Archer's son:

> Dallas belonged body and soul to the new generation. He was the first-born of Newland and May Archer, yet it had never been possible to inculcate in him even the rudiments of reserve. 'What's the use of making mysteries? It only makes people want to nose 'em out,' he always objected when enjoined to discretion. (356)

Archer's partial awakening to the narrowness of his world foregrounds the existence of alternatives to the paradigms of his class. It is too late for Archer, though, whose indoctrination has crippled his capacity to redefine himself. This impoverishment leads him to feel that the "things that had filled his days seemed now like a nursery parody of life, or like the wrangles of medieval schoolmen over metaphysical terms that no one had ever understood" (182). Although he feels dissatisfied, those who have moved outside the bounds of acceptable behavior and attitude disturb Archer.

While the novel contains characters who believe that "tolerating men of obscure origin and tainted wealth" such as Julius Beaufort can only end in the "total disintegration" of society (338), this representation, made by the hypocritical Lawrence Lefferts, ignores the fact that Beaufort is a variation that the enlightened know their closed system needs. Granny Mingott's intuition that "new blood" (30) can infuse a hermetic class with variations that will ensure its continued viability makes of Beaufort, who is heedless of straitening moral codes, a carrier of new values who shares traits with outcasts such as Ellen Olenska and Fanny Ring. Indicating the extent to which standards have changed, in speaking to his father Dallas refers to Ellen as "your Fanny" (356).

Archer earlier reacts to Beaufort with hostility; believing himself to be in competition with Beaufort for Ellen, he thinks that, "to have routed Beaufort [from Ellen's house] was something of a triumph" (108). Archer illustrates how the pall of linguistic convention settles over one's ability to discern any sensibility beyond that given by moral standards, limiting his sympathy with, and understanding of, Beaufort and Ellen's European sensibility. This is evident when Ellen, by uttering the phrase "my husband," causes Archer to wonder at her ability to say the words "as if no sinister associations were connected with them, [. . .] Archer looked at her perplexedly, wondering if it were lightness or dissimulation that enabled her to touch so easily on the past at the very moment when she was risking her reputation in order to break with it" (105–6). Beaufort's cordiality with Ellen models the possibility of codes of conduct other than those Archer knows. But blindness to the possibility that Beaufort represents an expansion of his narrow world causes Archer to rehearse class-based prejudices: "his business would be to make her see Beaufort as he really was, with all he represented—and abhor it" (77). For one who wishes to be free of convention, an abhorrence of the unusual indicates deep internal conflict.

Not only do Archer's mores inform his distaste for Beaufort, and Archer's ambivalence toward stepping out of his cage with Ellen, they descend upon him from external sources too. Counter-pressure to Archer's desire for Ellen surfaces in subtle expressions of reproach directed toward him mere moments after he becomes conscious that she stirs his interest. During their first conversation, Ellen touches Archer's knee with her "plumed fan." For Archer, "it was the lightest touch, but it thrilled him like a caress" (65). In the following seconds, however, the intimacy shared by the two characters is peremptorily terminated when Archer feels "his host's admonitory glance on him" (65). His innermost sensations are noted by an external authority, which seems to divine his silent desire, but can it be so? Rather, Archer, knowing it is wrong to feel the thrill he attributes to Ellen's touch, interprets the glance in a way consistent with his internalization of regulatory manners. Evidence that he is being watched, or that he is watching himself for others, exists also in the closing of ranks by his family, who, divining his feelings for Ellen, intervene to preserve the smooth social surface for which he frequently expresses a desire: "[h]e saw it in a flash that if the family had ceased to consult him it was because some deep tribal instinct warned them that he was no longer on their side" (252). Archer pursues a path that, as a student of kinship ties, he should foresee ending in intervention.

An equally serious impediment to his freedom is his subjugation by form. Wolff notes that "the danger that his life will be insignificant lies not so much in the probability that he will fail to fulfill these fantasies [of an unconventional life with Ellen] as in the more immediate possibility that, having failed to fulfill them, he will lack the capacity to give *any* aspect of his life authenticity" (318). This lack of capacity, though, results in part from the fact that even avenues for escape are predetermined, and lead back through that "narrow passage" to the "ball-room" in which "Form" dominates. This is clear from the account of Archer's affair with Mrs. Thorley Rushworth:

> He passed for a young man who had not been afraid of risks, and he knew that his secret love-affair with poor silly Mrs. Thorley Rushworth had not been too secret to invest him with a becoming air of adventure. But Mrs. Rushworth was 'that kind of woman'; foolish, vain, clandestine by nature, and far more attracted by the secrecy and peril of the affair than by such charms and qualities as he possessed. When the fact dawned on him it nearly broke his heart, but now it seemed the redeeming feature of the case. The affair, in short, had been of the kind that most of the young men of his age had been through. (95–96)

The path to authenticity, and a capacity for self-definition at least partially free from determination by form, lies in an unmediated passion represented by Ellen. In an earlier attempt to realize what he might find with her, Archer discovers that even his pre-marital affair is understood within his social context as conventional behavior.

Desirous of Ellen, her "words stole through him like a temptation, and to close his sense to it he moved away from the hearth and stood gazing at the black tree-boles against the snow. [. . .] Archer's heart was beating insubordinately" (133). As he moves in his mind away from the heat of sex represented in Ellen's words, and the blazing fireplace, toward the icy scene outside, the reader sees him crave Ellen and distance her simultaneously. But it is not solely self-regulation that halts him. He senses at this moment that the watchfulness of his class permeates even the architecture of "the house of the old Patroon" (132), which is empty save for the unhappy couple. As he feels observed, so he becomes again a watcher when their solitude is interrupted by the appearance of Beaufort, whose presence causes Archer to withdraw into his anthropological perspective. The real represented by sexuality grows dim in the presence of Beaufort's social otherness and its pressure on gentry mores, both of which Beaufort symbolizes. While "strolling back through the park" with the conversing Ellen and Beaufort, Archer feels "the ghostly advantage of observing unobserved" (135). His surveillance is central to maintaining order within himself, and within his class.

Despite his apparent powerlessness, Archer, at one level, knows that social institutions need to evolve to remain viable. This is the case when, seeking to correct an affront to Mrs. Mingott and Ellen (all the invitees to a dinner in the latter's honor have refused Mrs. Mingott), Archer visits the van der Luyden clan. Of all the leading families in New York, this family is "[one] of the three in it who can claim an aristocratic origin in the real sense of the word" (49). The van der Luydens are the touchstone of taste, the gold standard from which form arises. As the petitioners approach these deities, Mrs. van der Luyden seems emblematic of inscrutable powers of influence that, as far as Archer is concerned, more properly belong in a museum showcase: "She always, indeed, struck Newland Archer as having been rather gruesomely preserved in the airless atmosphere of a perfectly irreproachable existence, as bodies caught in glaciers keep for years a rosy life-in-death" (52). Archer—already feeling the pinch of what one review of the novel described as "artificial and false standards, the desperate monotony of trivial routine, the slow petrifaction of generous ardours, the paralysis of emotion, the accumulation of ice around the heart, the total loss of life in upholstered existence" (*Reviews* 285)—understands that his description of Mrs. Van der Luyden is equally applicable to himself.

Facing these totemic embodiments of the past, he recognizes that his social heritage is materialized in the stony pair before him: "Archer contemplated with awe the two slender faded figures, seated side by side in a kind of viceregal rigidity, mouthpieces of some remote ancestral authority" (54). The van der Luydens are venerated icons, statues imputed to have oracular abilities within a social religion predicated on genealogical mysticism. Their static form is notable because other sculptural forms exist in the novel: the stiff figurations of the Italian primitives, whose paintings and pre-Raphaelite followers Archer rejects, and even May's face, which "wore the vacant serenity of a young marble athlete" (141). May's eyes, moreover, are thought by Archer to "look out blankly at blankness," much like an ancient Greek *kouros*. Indeed, May has the look "of representing a type rather than a person" (188). That she represents, like a *kouros*, an ideal of youth, rather than the individualism Archer strives for, is suggested in the narrator's phrase that she is like other "ladies who were the product of the system" (8). Later, while looking upon May, Archer himself wonders at "[h]ow young she is! For what endless years this life will have to go on!" (266). Archer extends his perception that May is static to her personality. She possesses, he thinks, a "Diana-like aloofness [. . .] not a thought seemed to have passed behind her eyes or a feeling through her heart" (211) at the moment she strides out to take her turn in the archery competition. Those most strongly connected to tradition—May and the van der Luydens—are associated with a sexless rigidity, with virginal figures such as Diana, and with marble statues that are representations of people, but not the "real thing."

Wharton uses time as a symbol to place Archer in relation to, and at a distance from tradition. After relating the story of the wrong done to Mrs.

Lovell Mingott, Archer notes "a silence during which the tick of the monumental ormolu clock on the white marble mantle-piece grew as loud as the boom of a minute gun" (54). In the presence of New York's oracle, Archer interprets the van der Luydens' consideration of the matter before them in a way he ties to a particular temporal mood. Tradition, ritual, and the passage of time (the latter perceived to occur with military precision) encompass and define an ordered, inelastic chronometry. "[T]he perpetually reminding tick of the disciplined clocks [. . .] made any less systematized and affluent existence seem unreal and precarious" (218). In contrast to these scenes, while Archer is in Ellen's apartment and therefore outside the boundaries of his sphere he finds himself, as he notes that the clock has stopped, in "a room unlike any room he had known" (69). The pairing of the smooth passage of time with the flow of an undisturbed social surface—so evident in Archer's perception of the scene at the van der Luyden residence, and at the announcement of Archer's engagement to May—is disrupted by his passion for Ellen outside of time, and his sympathy toward her nonconforming perspective.

Archer's sense of fleeing a life ordered by "reminding" ticks is present during his trip to Boston to see Ellen. There he senses a weakening of his connection to the training that underwrites his identity. Having lied to May about his reason for the journey, despite her apparent knowledge of it, he finds himself outside a defining frame of reference. He nods in greeting to the men at his club in Boston, but having strayed out of context through his intent to enter into an unsanctioned relationship, he has compromised himself as a signifier of ritual act and utterance. What results is social vertigo: "the usual greetings were exchanged: it was the same world after all, though he had such a queer sense of having slipped through the meshes of space and time" (229). Physically absent from the New York environment, intent upon putting distance between himself and the "booming" minute-gun of an ordered existence, Archer feels dissociated from his native frame of reference. Through the representation of the van der Luydens and May, the reader comes to feel how the material richness of architectural surfaces, and a particular construal of temporality as mechanically measured and closely tied to ritualistic pattern, structures and constrains Archer's energies.

Archer finds in Ellen a woman who is not a two-dimensional representation of New York's aversion to social evolution; her European upbringing has allowed her to avoid indoctrination. The feelings that exist between her and the disillusioned Archer are complicated by the fact that each sees the other's world as an escape from that which they know. Archer's nascent belief that it is possible to evade the reach of society is at odds with Ellen's opinion that the growth of the individual within the context of the social is the only viable means of attaining selfhood. In this way, Ellen's attitudes resemble those implicit in the framing narrative's perspective, for she asks, "Does no one want to know the truth here Mr. Archer? The real loneliness is living among all these kind people who only ask one to pretend" (77). As a perspective by which Archer's views are countered, Ellen's viewpoint epitomizes the view put implicitly by the novel that instinct and social forms are related at a fundamental level.

That Wharton considered the ways in which "material forces and human instincts" affected each other is tangible in her statement that "real men, unequal, unmanageable, and unlike each other, [. . .] are all bound up with the effects of climate, soil, laws, religion, wealth—and above all, leisure" ("The Great American Novel" 155–56). Social and physical environments are inseparable in this view, and the social selection environment in *The Age of Innocence,* an allegory of Darwinian nature, makes just this point. Ellen recognizes what Archer does not: the "country" to which he hopes to flee, a place where they might, in his words, "be simply two human beings who love each other, who are the whole of life to each other" (290), would, if they found it, strip them of their identities.

V. "SAY I'M OLD FASHIONED"

The Age of Innocence depicts the material characteristics of the post-civil war era of Wharton's youth with the same detail she devotes to her flesh and blood characters. Of a planned dramatization of the novel she wrote that she was "very anxious about the staging and dressing. I could do every stick of furniture & every rag of clothing myself for every detail of that far-off scene was indelibly stamped on my infant brain" (*Letters* 439). This focus on accurately representing the material culture of the period is part of the novel's bestowal of an ideological aura upon furniture and fashion, architecture, art, and even the books Archer reads. The impressionistic psyches of subjects trained to locate their proper coordinates in the field of social meaning triangulate their position in relation to "the luxury of the Welland house and the density of the Welland atmosphere" (218). The luxury and atmosphere in which Archer lives, though, is one in which "superiorities and advantages [. . .] [are] the surest hindrance to success" (201), and conformity is valued.

Archer's story reproduces elements of a past less tangible than Parisian dresses or Fifth Avenue brownstones, but equally indicative of the flavor of the age. Wharton builds her observations into a vivid portrait of how class values resolve—if unhappily—Archer's experience of his own life. "He perceived with a flash of chilling insight that in future many problems would be [. . .] negatively solved for him" (204). The characterization here, which concentrates on displaying that class-based values insulate Archer from the new, demonstrates that the value of a detailed rendering in fiction of both individual consciousness and the broader social fabric lies in its ability to depict their interrelation. Fictionally analyzing the instilling of ideology in social beings by employing a sociobiological framework can also be read as Wharton's response to the early-twentieth-century sociologist Wesley Mitchell's statement that "[i]t is not lack of will that impedes progress, but lack of knowledge. We putter with philanthropy and coquette with reform. [. . .] What we need as a guide for all this expenditure of energy [in the study of society] is sure knowledge of the causal interconnections between social phenomena" (qtd. in Ross 305). In her exploration of causal connections between social form and class-specific systems of thought in the novel, Wharton outlines impediments created against social evolution. Moreover, she shows how the "bare and cool" reality of a desire for the new (AI 239) undermines gentry thought. The reader finds this in the place apart where Archer and Ellen meet, in a "room [. . .] with the sea coming in at the windows. [. . .] with a table covered by a coarse checkered cloth" (239). Here is a fresh atmosphere pointedly lacking in luxury, one in tune with Ellen's ability to "brush away the conventions and make him feel that to seek to be alone was the natural thing" (239). Deprived, though, of language and a system of thought wherein his inmost desires can be expressed, Archer finds that "[t]he taste of the usual was like cinders in his mouth" (139).

While what he discovers makes, for a time, a desert of his heart, Wharton ties his unhappiness to the matrix of class and politics in which his situation indicates to the reader that ideology operates. In doing so, Wharton articulates a thought similar to Lukács's pronouncement on an essential choice facing a man in Archer's position:

> [T]he veil drawn over the nature of bourgeois society is indispensable to the bourgeois itself. For the insoluble internal contradictions of the system become revealed with increasing starkness and so confront its supporters with a choice. Either they must consciously ignore insights which become increasingly urgent or else they must suppress their own moral instincts in order to be able to support with a good conscience an economic system that serves only their own interests. (66)

The version of "moral instincts" Archer's class practices denies natural law by attempting to throttle social evolution and individual instinct. Archer's indecisiveness, and his ultimate failure to achieve the escape velocity required to overcome the gravity of his class affiliation, demonstrates that the novel's view of his ability to transcend the "endless distance" (AI 230) he perceives between Ellen and himself is perhaps less optimistic than Lukács's attribution of actual agency to members of "bourgeois society" like Archer.

The novel of character, according to Wharton, provides a framework in which the literary artist "develops his tale through a succession of episodes, all in some way illustrative of the manners [. . .] out of which the situation is eventually to spring" (WF 137), and Archer's entanglement with Ellen is the mainspring of the story. Thus, Wharton at the end of the novel makes no explicit indication of whether Archer's desire to stay below and avoid the reality of the aged Ellen is a tragic moment, for this emotion, felt by an individual, is subsumed under the attention given to the reasons for the impasse. The concentration on what stands between them depicts Archer's particularly American attitude toward history, one which sees in sunset hues "[t]hat vision, faint and tenuous" of a past more real (AI 347). The novel's nuanced portrait of Archer's youthful encounter with Ellen makes of it the single transcendent experience of his life, but one from which he must return.

Like *The House of Mirth,* a novel focused on the effects of a hostile social environment on Lily Bart, the true antagonist of *The Age of Innocence* is the iron band of class-based rules, rituals, and linguistic practices which are regulative in their capacity to finally elevate the disenchanted Archer to his socially sanctioned roles of husband, father, and politician. This compensation has its own price. By the novel's conclusion, Archer is "the kind of man the public wants" (345); yet such a man, what "people were beginning to call 'a good citizen'" (346), represents not cowardice, but the narrow spectrum of choices available to him. Nostalgia for a lost romance causes Archer to recall Ellen, by the novel's end, as "the composite vision of all that he had missed" (347). His avoidance of her in the final pages is thus an indication that he never learns to conceptualize a path by which he might pass through the tangled hedgerow of tradition and the undergrowth of language that restricts understanding.

When Archer and his son Dallas stand in the square looking up at the "modern building, without distinctive character, but many windowed" in which Ellen lives (360), one encounters another illustration of Ellen's ability to see life from multiple perspectives. Archer tells Dallas to go up without him. The son, searching for an excuse to give Ellen for his father's absence, rejoins that he'll "say you're old-fashioned, and prefer walking up five flights because you don't like lifts" (361). Archer, though, wishes Ellen to understand; he instructs Dallas to "[s]ay I'm old fashioned: that's enough" (361).

To be "old fashioned" in the sense he means is to be unable to transcend the "fear lest that last shadow of reality [his memory of Ellen] should lose its edge; this kept him rooted to his seat" (362). His fear at having this image of Ellen replaced makes him reluctant to surrender the vision of a reality into which he could not travel. This figures the social world he has occupied as unreal, while confirming the hold of taste and form over his character, adding a note of resigned awareness to Archer's closing statement that "[i]t's more real here than if I went up" (362).

Conclusion
The Limits of Wharton's "Objective Faculty"

In making the arguments contained in the previous chapters, I have been conscious of the tenuousness of Wharton's Darwinian allegory, for she invokes Darwinism at a moment in its history when it was being reassessed in the light of Mendel's work on genetics.[1] The resultant fiction, indebted in part to ideas that were the subject of intense debate among evolutionists by 1900, bear witness to the great interest in science that existed during the period addressed in this study. Characters such as Lily Bart, Ralph Marvell, and Newland Archer are insufficiently aware of how contingent nature compels the codes by which they live, and how their enmeshment in class ideology, and, in Archer's case, scientific amateurism, has prevented them from seeing a dimension of their actual life conditions; natural laws exist in whatever social garden humans might create. Lawrence Selden's air of detachment in *The House of Mirth,* Charles Bowen's socially critical observations in *The Custom of the Country,* and Archer's dilettantish anthropological mode of social observation are, finally, insufficient to the task of preventing the gentry from succumbing to change.

The fractured objectivity of these characters keeps them from understanding what is at stake in the maintenance of an ideologically supported divide between nature and culture. But while the texts devalue the compromised objectivity of their characters, there are difficulties in Wharton's analogizing of ideology and the biological medium by which traits are inherited that may be the result of the provisional status of knowledge on the latter subject in her scientific sources. The analogy functions to illustrate the fact that individuals, in a qualified sense, inherit the systems of thought that govern their class. Yet the analogy is limited in that through her adoption of terminology from an evolutionary context, Wharton represents a connection between biological law and social change that is not provable in the fictional context. It is a connection, though, that she does hypothesize.

Because Wharton is concerned with the interaction of random variation and environment, and demonstrating her disbelief in the association of evolution with progress, natural selection functions well as an allegory of progress from which intentionality is absent, emphasizing the unpredictability of social transformation. One cannot evade, moreover, the suggestion that natural selection is more than a figurative presence in the novels because of the implication that it plays a formative role in the ideological competition of different sub-species of the elite in Wharton's fiction. As an allegorical referent, natural selection, which is textually evoked by evolutionary language and characters that fail or thrive in transformed environments, foregrounds the radical contingency concealed by the gentry thought system, which is subject to variation and intermixing with that of the socioeconomic elite. Darwinian allegory, in mediating between social forms and natural and sexual selection, is a significant dimension of Wharton's major novels, linking the social and the biological to confront a historically specific distinction between the two.

The sociobiological dimension of these works suggests that while the increasing complexity of culture in the United States might represent growth away from its biological foundation, though the new elite represents an atavistic devolution of culture, the organic is implicated in collective morality through adaptive cooperation and symbiosis. This is demonstrated by Lily Bart's revulsion at the prospect of marrying a man who is sexually and intellectually incompatible with her, by the example presented by Gerty Farish's establishment of a niche for herself, and by Ellen Olenska's poorly received European attitudes, which the *The Age of Innocence* ultimately values positively. The presence of "desire" that is aesthetically mediated details the way the ideology of form and taste—or manners—desexualizes sympathetically portrayed male characters.

In her attempts to depict the viewpoint evident in Archer's inability to reckon with the new elite's demotion of moral fitness to just another survival mechanism (one does what one must to survive), Wharton co-opts for her sociobiology a form of moral agency inflected, or infected, with humanism. The humanism contained within the texts discussed in this study defines the sphere of human thought and human variety that must be protected from the vagaries of natural competition. If Archer's standards of taste and form have become detached from a set of values inimical to creating "the real culture" ("The Great American Novel" 156), then they have also turned away from the challenge of countering the pressure on individual rights presented by biological imperatives. Good taste detached from reasoning over the maintenance of stabilizing traditions leaves only Archer's obliviousness to the antinomy between contingent natural change and goal-directed cultural transformation.

Wharton's formal refinement of the narrative means by which to object to the assertion that the survival of the fittest is a law that not only does obtain in human culture, but should, is evident in Darwinian allegories of ideological competition and selection that are clearer in *The Custom of the Country* and *The Age of Innocence* than they are in *The House of Mirth*. The conflict between old and new class worlds seems decided in Ralph Marvell's tale, and is stated in terms of the superior adaptation to a rapidly changing social environment of the socioeconomic elite. This is evident when Marvell likens his mother and grandfather "to those vanishing denizens of the American continent doomed to rapid extinction with the advance of the invading race" (77–78). In *The Age of Innocence,* the gentry still hold the advantage, but Beaufort and his type, whose daughter marries Archer's son, are already asserting their dominance. Furthermore, the latter two novels move beyond *The House of Mirth*'s isolated reference to a "cinematograph syndicate" (87) to present mass culture as a factor in ideological competition. When one finds that "the daily press had already learned to describe" the opera goers in *The Age of Innocence* as "'an exceptionally brilliant audience'" (3), it is clear that Wharton intends to show the way the press, by embracing the logic of the marketplace, responds to its customers, rather than enact its crucial role in an increasingly apolitical public sphere.

The investigation of my subject here is far from complete. The pathways for further study are numerous. For example, when *The Custom of the Country*'s Undine Spragg exercises her sexual selection, she seems to predict a problematically regressive social and genetic union with Moffatt that will assert a new and dismissive attitude toward social responsibility. This portrait is not consistent with the narrator's positive valuation of sexual selection in *The House of Mirth* and *The Age of Innocence,* which poses a challenge to existing mores; this inconsistency needs to be investigated for its potential to further the understanding of Wharton's implicitly genetic theory of cultural transmission, which works in a still undefined sense with the concept of memes.[2]

This study of evolutionary allegory in Wharton's major novels has argued that these texts are well furnished by the investigations of Darwin and other evolutionists. In building on the work of critics who have explored Wharton's engagement with science, I have demonstrated some of the ways natural selection, among other natural laws, is figured by Wharton to play a role in social change. By bringing nature and culture into proximity, she is able to depict how individuals "unequal, unmanageable, and unlike each other, [. . .] are all bound up with the effects of climate, soil, laws, religion, wealth—and above all, leisure" ("The Great American Novel" 155–56); indeed, from Wharton's perspective it is leisure that testifies to the opportunity open to privileged classes to address the effects of harmful interpretations of nature such as social Darwinism, and the reality of the material world of "climate, soil" and natural and sexual selection. In fictionally fusing biology, as she understood it, to the ideas by which classes, and societies, define themselves, Wharton inhabits a self-defined borderland between biological instinct and evolution, social institutions and practices. This narrative strategy challenges the absence of alternatives to rituals of exclusion, the codification of desire, and the propagation of inflexible ideology found in a world that refutes nature in the name of an evanescent order, and prevents equality for unequal individuals like Lily Bart.

Notes

NOTES TO CHAPTER ONE

1. The term refers to those who carried on Darwin's project with the knowledge of Mendel's work in genetics.

2. Useful to the delineation of Wharton's portraits of class-specific ideologies in the novels explored here is Eagleton's articulation of ideology as signifying "ideas and beliefs which help legitimate the interests of a ruling group or class specifically by distortion or dissimulation" (30). Wharton illustrates the element of distortion most forcefully in the depiction of mass culture in *The Custom of the Country.*

3. I owe a debt to Donald Pizer's extensive work on American literary realism and naturalism, which has shaped my understanding of Wharton's reaction to these movements.

4. For an illuminating discussion of American exceptionalism (the sense that America had a special destiny) see Ross 22–50.

5. Claire Preston insightfully discusses Wharton's recurring theme of an elite society that saw itself in terms of a walled garden or hothouse, without reference to Huxley's text.

6. Preston writes, "Of Huxley's many works it is difficult to guess which she might have read, but obvious ones would have been *The Advancement of Science in the last Half-Century* (1887); *American Addresses* (1877) (three lectures on evolution); and *Darwiniana* (1893)" (196n.). Bentley states that "Wharton was fascinated by biology and evolutionism, reading deeply in Darwin, Huxley, Ernst Haeckel, and in current studies of heredity and Mendelism" ("Hunting for the Real" 51). The appearance of George Ramsden's book *Edith Wharton's Library* will aid critical activity that seeks to connect the author's scientific interests to the formal properties of her fiction. Wharton owned Huxley's *Collected Essays,* which included "Evolution and Ethics," and *Darwiniana* (Ramsden 60).

7. See Jennie A. Kassanoff's "Extinction, Taxidermy, Tableaux Vivants: Staging Race and Class in *The House of Mirth*" for an incisive discussion of a

problem she finds to be present "in both [The] *Decoration* [of Houses] and *The House of Mirth* [which] is that of staging racial perfection without sacrificing the privileges of personal specificity. If America's elite was threatened by what Edwin Lawrence Godkin caustically called 'chromo-civilization,' a 'pseudo-culture' that 'diffused through the community a kind of smattering of all sorts of knowledge,' then blue-blooded Americans were urged to vigilance" (65).

8. For a learned account of Wharton's "imperial sensibility" (784) see Frederick Wegener's "'Rabid Imperialist': Edith Wharton and the Obligations of Empire in Modern American Fiction."

9. See William Macnaughton's "Edith Wharton's 'The Blond Beast' and Friedrich Nietzsche."

10. These words occur to Archer as he admires Ellen Olenska, who is resplendently sexual as she stands before him "in her long sealskin coat, her hands thrust in a small round muff" (AI 310). Seeming not to register the sexual display that the narrative symbolizes through Ellen's attire, Archer instead curses "change" for the purely aesthetic reason that it will alter the "pure harmony of line and colour" (310) presented to him by Ellen's appearance. This is another example of the way instinct is shown in the narrative to be patterned into terms of connoisseurship associated with Archer's class.

11. The New York diarist George Templeton Strong wrote in 1871 that *The Descent of Man* was making "a sensation" (348). Strong had read *On The Origin of Species* in 1860, a year after its publication in England. The references to Darwin's work in Strong's diary make clear that *On The Origin of Species* was of great interest to individuals of Wharton's class in New York society before the Civil War. Of note too is the mention made in the diary that D. Appleton and Company, later to publish Wharton's writing, was the original publisher of Darwin's work in the United States.

12. Of this same review, Amy Kaplan discusses Wharton's attribution of "[. . .] Eliot's waning reputation to the hostile reception of her scientific metaphors and vocabulary" (*The Social Construction of American Realism* 75). In addition to illustrating Wharton's sense of the danger to literary reputation of a feminine appropriation of masculine scientific language, Kaplan reports that "[s]cience conferred the authority to represent social reality in the late nineteenth century; such knowledge distinguished the expertise of the specialist from the common sense of the lay person" (*The Social Construction of American Realism* 75). Establishing this as one reason for Wharton's appeal to science, Kaplan leaves for others the task of examining the ways in which Wharton's "scientific metaphors" affect her representation of human subjects and their collectives.

13. In "Life and I," Wharton catalogues her youthful non-scientific reading: "Ford & Marlowe & Webster! [. . .] the Niebelungen in the original [. . .] my studies led me naturally to philology, & Skeat, Kemble, Morris [. . .]. I plunged with rapture in the great ocean of Goethe. At fifteen I had read every word of his plays & poems" (42).

14. Bauer *Edith Wharton's Brave New Politics* 164; Bentley "Hunting for the Real" 47–67, *The Ethnography of Manners* 160–211; Hoeller 144–45; Pizer "The House of Mirth" 242; Preston 49–91; Tichi 89–114.

15. Beer refers to the novellas *The Touchstone* (1900), *Sanctuary* (1903) and *Madames de Treymes* (1906). Short stories that draw imagery from scientific contexts exist as well. Notable among these is "The Descent of Man" (1904), which I discuss in chapter two.

16. Wharton depicts the way primal energies are patterned by social conventions, bringing her fiction into the proximity of Freud's statement in *Civilization and its Discontents* that "civilization is a process in the service of Eros. [...] man's natural aggressive instinct, the hostility of each against all and of all against each, opposes this programme of civilization" (81–82). A reactionary attitude to Freud's work has been attributed to Wharton as a result of her comment in a 1922 letter to Bernard Berenson, in which she directs Berenson's wife Mary "not to befuddle" a mutual friend "[...] with Freudianism & all its jargon. She'd take to it like a duck to sewerage. And what she wants is to develop the *conscious,* and not grub after the subconscious" (*Letters* 451). This hostility to Freud's theories of human psychology should not bar exploration of the fact that Wharton's work exhibits a sustained interest in representing how civilization patterns instinct along lines similar to Freud, who was, of course, also influenced by Darwin.

17. It is worth noting the similarity between the bond shared by the sailors in Crane's short story, and Wharton's modeling of sympathy as what Darwin called a "distinct emotion" (*The Descent of Man* 391) in Lily Bart's encounter with Nettie Struther in *The House of Mirth*. The fellowship of the men in "The Open Boat" provides comfort, even while their preconception about fate controlling destiny is undermined by the seeming randomness of events that happen "Willy-Nilly" (744). Nettie's chance discovery of Lily in Bryant Park is followed by Nettie's soothing unction toward the protagonist, which is clearly the focus of the scene.

18. In reference to *The House of Mirth* Lewis relates that "[t]en days after publication Brownell notified Edith Wharton gravely that 'so far we have not sold many over 30,000' [...]. Edith observed in her diary that 20,000 more copies were being printed by October 30, and 20,000 more on November 11" (Lewis 151).

19. In an essay on Nietzsche's importance to Wharton's short story "The Blond Beast," Macnaughton writes that the philosopher's "influence is also present in *The Custom of the Country,* not only in the way Wharton uses the idea of the will to power to explain character relationships, but also in her conception of individual characters" (17) such as Elmer Moffatt. Macnaughton characterizes the "will to power" as "the active drive to expand and dominate, rather than merely to survive by adapting, or to obtain pleasure—[this] is the principle that governs all organisms in the universe" (14). In

The Age of Innocence this "naked instinct" also exists, but is the subject of punitive "admonitory" glances (65) radiated by the stifling traditions Wharton portrays. I examine this in detail in chapter four.

20.   I am grateful to Claire Preston for pointing out that *French Ways and Their Meaning*, because it is primarily a work of propaganda, should be used carefully as a source for Wharton's views.

21.   Wharton's knowledge of biology was limited, obviously, by the state of the discipline itself, but also by her lack of formal scientific training. As a self-taught scientist she struggled, for example, with "Lock's 'simple' exposition of Mendelism" (*Letters* 151). Significantly though, her exposure to Mendelism through Lock meant she was familiar with the basic principles of genetics.

NOTES TO CHAPTER TWO

1.   In *The Social Construction of American Realism* Amy Kaplan states that "[a]ppeals to 'the scientific spirit' were commonplace among realists as diverse as Zola and Howells. Science conferred the authority to represent social reality in the late nineteenth century, much as portraiture had entailed the authority to represent the individual in an earlier period. In general, science became the major source of legitimation for most professions in the late nineteenth century" (75). Kaplan also notes that Wharton defended George Eliot's brand of scientific realism, a subject I addressed in chapter one, and it should be noted that this criticism of Eliot has the same thrust as a number of reviews of Wharton's novels in the first two decades of her career.

2.   In his biography, Lewis remarks that Wharton was "sketching out" the novel during 1900 (109).

3.   This theme appears again in Wharton's fiction as a tension between the methods of the amateur and the specialist in *The Age of Innocence,* where the "dilettante" (4) anthropologist Newland Archer's perspective is portrayed as flawed by the more informed narrator; a detailed discussion of this subject appears in chapter four.

4.   Yet Wharton could be enthusiastic about what she perceived to be sociobiological thought that struck her as not being strictly scientific. In an assessment of *Beyond Good and Evil* she writes in a letter to Sara Norton that Nietzsche "has no system, & not much logic, but wonderful flashes of insight, & a power of breaking through conventions that is most exhilarating" (*Letters* 159).

5.   My claim that Wharton hoped to produce popular books is based on her great interest in ensuring that her work was marketed to maximum effect. In 1899 she complained to William Crary Brownell at Charles Scribner's Sons about the firm's handling of her collection of short stories *The Greater*

Inclination: "I do not think I have been fairly treated as regards the advertising of 'The Greater Inclination.' [. . .] I have naturally watched with interest the advertising of the book, & have compared it with notices given by other prominent publishers of books appearing under the same conditions. I find that Messrs. McMillan, Dodd & Mead, McLure, Harper, etc., advertise almost continuously in the daily papers every new book they publish, for the first few weeks after publication [. . .]. Certainly in these days of energetic & emphatic advertising, Mr. Scribner's methods do not tempt one to offer him one's wares a second time" (*Letters* 37–38). In a 1902 letter to Brownell, Wharton took issue with "the lettering of the title" for *The Valley of Decision* (1902) and suggested that the book be sold "for a little less than $2. If it could be sold for $1.75 it seems to me that it would make a great difference" (*Letters* 47–48). Later that year, she urged Brownell to "add [to *The Valley of Decision*] that undefinable Wanamaker Touch that seems essential to the booming of fiction nowadays" (*Letters* 58), calling for the kind of commercialization of her novel familiar to shoppers at Wanamaker's, the first department store chain in the United States.

6. See *A Backward Glance* (95); Lewis (56–57); *Letters* (131, 136); Pizer "*House of Mirth*" (242).

7. See Desmond (267–91) for a concise discussion of the reaction that followed the publication of *On the Origin of Species.*

8. Rosedale distinguishes himself from Trenor near the end of the novel by not expecting anything back from Lily—she is of no possible use to him at this point—when he buys her tea.

9. See Desmond, Dennett, and Ridley for accounts of how different interpretations of Darwin's work, particularly Spencer's, linked evolution to social progress.

10. Ammons (25–55) offers a feminist approach to Wharton's handling of the "marriage question" in this novel and *The Fruit of the Tree.*

11. Although Darwin focuses on non-human animals, discussions of "organic beings" strongly suggest, obviously, the applicability of his argument to humans.

12. See Dimock for an authoritative discussion of the debasement implicit in exchanges of many types in the novel.

13. Lily's oneness with nature anticipates Wharton's association of Charity Royall's sexuality with the natural world in *Summer* (1917), in which the protagonist is

> blind and insensible to many things, and dimly knew it; but to all that was light and air, perfume and colour, every drop of blood in her responded. She loved the roughness of the dry mountain grass under her palms, the smell of the thyme into which she crushed

her face, the fingering of the wind in her hair and through her cotton blouse, and the creak of the larches as they swayed to it. (66)

14. Claire Preston identifies the hot-house as "[a]n important image in *The House of Mirth* [. . .] the romantic climax, when Lily and Selden kiss after her *tableau* performance as Reynolds's Mrs. Lloyd, takes place in the deserted Bry conservatory, a sort of *in vitro* simulacrum of the world outside its panes, an environment as delicate and improbable as Selden's 'republic of the spirit'" (49). In Chapter One I suggested that Wharton uses the image of the enclosed garden to represent society in a way similar to that present in T. H. Huxley's essay "Evolution and Ethics." The hothouse is obviously another, even more hermetic version of this enclosed garden.

15. A Claude glass is a "small mirror, slightly convex in shape, with its surface tinted a dark colour. Carried in the hand, it was used by artists, travellers and connoisseurs of landscape and landscape painting. It has the effect of abstracting the subject reflected in it from its surroundings, reducing and simplifying the colour and tonal range of scenes and scenery to give them a painterly quality, similar in appearance to the work of Claude Lorrain, hence its name. A larger variant, which could be fixed to the side of a carriage window to reflect the passing scenery, also appears to have existed" (*Grove Dictionary of Art* 387). Wharton felt an affinity with Lorrain's work. A passage from *Italian Backgrounds* praises his rendering of landscape. "With each bend in the road the views down the Vatelline toward Sondrio and Como grew wider and more beautiful. No one who has not looked out on such a prospect in the early light of an August morning can appreciate the poetic truth of Claude's interpretation of nature: we seemed to be moving through a gallery hung with his pictures" (32). Selden's harmful simplification of Lily is analogous to the abstraction of landscape by the Claude glass. An attempt to resolve these negative and positive examples of isolating a presumed essential reality, or "poetic truth," of a character (Lily by Selden, and both, of course, by Wharton) or a landscape may advance the understanding of Wharton's characterization, in which the authorial consciousness abstracts and intensifies a limited set of traits, avoiding the more expansive psychological realism Henry James practiced.

NOTES TO CHAPTER THREE

1. Initial reviews of *The Custom of the Country* were very favorable (see *Reviews* 201–18). However, *The House of Mirth* has attracted greater positive critical attention over the years. One explanation for this is suggested by Wolff's remarks on *The Custom of the Country*'s complexity. She argues that it is "a deliberate unsettling of every comfortable conviction: the Marvell-Dagonet

culture is beautiful and ugly [. . .]. Ralph is both admirable and pitiable; Undine both villain and victim. The fictional world of *The Custom of the Country* is a daring tour de force: view it head on, you will draw one set of inferences; shift your vantage to a slightly different angle, it will become something altogether different" (235).

2. Hofstadter's analysis (1955) of the conflict between social Darwinism and equality and natural rights remains useful because his views are consistent with Wharton's representation of the issue, and supported with abundant quotation from sources that are contemporary with the novel's setting.

3. As I noted in Chapter Two, Darwin writes of how "[t]he dependency of one organic being on another, as of a parasite on its prey, lies generally between beings remote in the scale of nature" (*Origin* 126). Importing this view into the sphere of human society might suggest a politically distasteful interpretation of the relationship between poor and rich as one of dependency that rationalizes paternalism. The selectivity with which Wharton metaphorically transforms certain aspects of evolutionary thought while leaving others untouched is potentially a rich area for further study.

4. Mott reports that an English observer of the period declared that "American journalism [. . .] has reached its highest development in the Sunday newspaper. [. . .] It is at once a newspaper and a miscellany, a society journal and a household magazine" (482). The papers presented news, society gossip, and standards of taste in a form requiring high circulation, and thus broad appeal. In *French Ways and Their Meaning* Wharton opined that "[a]s long as America believes in short-cuts to knowledge, in any possibility of buying taste in tabloids, she will never come into her real inheritance of English culture" (55).

5. Habermas finds this to be true of the "newer media" such as radio, film, and television. He finds "the rigorous distinction between fact and fiction is ever more frequently abandoned" in modern media, something which "only intimates itself in the daily press" (170). The intimation that such a crucial distinction is abandoned is a concern of *The Custom of the Country.*

6. In one sense, Wharton is similar to her protagonist in that she adapts other literary traditions within her view by recreating the tonal qualities and scenic traditions of sentimental texts. This is noticeable in the novel's staging of the Spraggs' attempts to help Undine realize the "social benefit" of marrying off Undine for which "they had come" to New York (28).

7. The irony, of course, lies in Wharton's status as a popular author and the serialization of *The Custom of the Country* in *Scribner's Magazine* alongside advertisements for various products similar to those consumed by Undine.

8. Near the end of the novel Mrs. Heeny takes out of her bag a fistful of newspaper clippings about Undine and shows them to Undine's son. "Paul listened, fascinated. He had the feeling that Mrs. Heeny's clippings, aside from their great intrinsic interest, might furnish him with a clue to many

things he didn't understand, and that nobody ever had time to explain to him" (500). Like his mother before him, Paul looks not to traditional institutions such as his now-defunct family for training, but to the media. However, as he listens to Mrs. Heeny read to him from one of her clippings about how his stepfather Elmer Moffatt has by continual purchases driven up the value of art by "at least seventy-five percent" (500), Wharton suggests the constancy of the need to connect when Paul states "I'd rather hear about my mother" (500).

9. Preston identifies these as Rostand's *L'Aiglon* and Racine's *Phèdre* (116).

10. I am grateful to Mary Chapman for pointing out that William Randolph Hearst and Joseph Pulitzer had, in the 1890s, realized that they could sell newspapers more cheaply if rising circulation numbers, buoyed by the influx of immigrants, increased advertising revenues. This is germane to my discussion of Habermas and the decline of the public sphere, since papers, in the period the novel chronicles, became more devoted to selling commodities than trafficking in ideas.

11. That an anti-heroine such as Undine should violate this contract, one vital to the perpetuation of gentry tradition, seems to suggest its positive valuation by the narrative. But there is a lack of sympathy toward the fact that the business of marriage compels Undine to seek the "choicer fare" of Elmer Moffatt (57).

12. Lewis 94; Wolff *A Feast of Words* 89–90; Waid 7. In her *Bookman* review of Leslie Stephens's biography of Eliot, Wharton writes that "[t]he great investigators have never wearied of repeating that all the forward steps in science have been made by an imaginative effort, by the deductive rather than the inductive method. Goethe the poet was nourished, not stunted, by the scientific inductions of Goethe the morphologist. [. . .] Is it because these were men, while George Eliot was a woman, that she is reproved for venturing on ground they did not fear to tread?" ("George Eliot" 71–72).

13. The American studies scholar Amy Kaplan makes the argument that "[t]he power of Wharton's social criticism stems not from the external perspective of a writer who resisted an incipient consumer culture, but from one whose identity as an author and whose narrative forms were shaped by her immersion in this very modern culture" ("Edith Wharton's Profession of Authorship" 453).

14. See *Letters* 146, 151.

15. This is not to suggest that the system of marriage Undine exploits is equitable or worthy of preservation. Obviously, consensual divorce facilitates her nuptial repetitions. The novel is clear about its position that Undine's instrumental attitude toward marriage, like Lily Bart's recalcitrance toward sacrificing her freedom for material comfort, is justified by the disparity in benefits assigned by the marriage contract.

16. Wharton owned Haeckel's *The History of Creation* (1868) (Ramsden 55) and notes Haeckel's influence on her intellectual development in *A Backward Glance* (94).

17. The episode from which this quotation is taken finds the princess Estradina puzzled over Undine's habit of leaving her son in the care of others. This habitual disregard for intimacy in family relations is a frequently illustrated characteristic of Undine.

18. Obviously, the nineteenth-century evolutionists Wharton read had no knowledge of genes. However, the neo-Darwinists had started to incorporate Mendel's work at the beginning of the twentieth century, and Wharton was almost certainly aware of this, having read Lock's book.

19. Dennett goes on to argue that "[i]f this is right, then all the achievements of human culture—language, art, religion, ethics, science itself—are themselves artifacts (of artifacts of artifacts . . .) of the same fundamental process that developed the bacteria, the mammals and *Homo sapiens*. There is no Special Creation of language, and neither art nor religion has a literally divine inspiration" (143–44).

20. This is evident in Undine's marriages to Marvell and de Chelles, and in the marriage of Newland Archer's son Dallas to Julius Beaufort's daughter in *The Age of Innocence*.

21. See Dennett 52–61.

22. Contrasts between the living spaces occupied by Clare and Peter Van Degen in their "palace" (280) illustrate a transition between the forms of Washington Square and the gaudy styles embraced by the new business elite: "The lowered awnings of her [Clare's] inner drawing-room cast a luminous shadow on old cabinets and consoles, and on the pale flowers scattered here and there in vases of bronze and porcelain. Clare's taste was as capricious as her mood, and the rest of the house was not in harmony with this room. There was, in particular, another drawing-room, which she now described as Peter's creation, but which Ralph knew to be partly hers: a heavily decorated apartment, where Popple's portrait of her throned over a waste of gilt furniture" (280).

23. Ironically, the only genuine social comment he contributes is his suicide. This act protests the way his private life has been made a commodity by the press, and the way the market insinuates itself into his familial relationships when he finds himself constantly short of the money Undine requires to live luxuriously, and when he is unable to ransom his son Paul from Undine.

24. The association of Marvell with Whitman is consistent with Wharton's implication that Marvell's class is capable, if not at this point able, to exhibit artistic and moral leadership. She writes that "being a Whitmanite, like being an agnostic, cultivates forbearance and humility" (qtd. in Lewis 193).

25. Janet Beer discusses "the outline of a study of Whitman's poetry Wharton had planned to write, and, indeed, had mapped out in some detail" (*Edith Wharton* 81). Further investigation of this planned study might help elucidate authorial attitudes toward artistic achievement in *The Custom of the Country*.

26. Notable in Wharton's choice of the word is that Nereid is a mythological figure (a daughter of Nereus), and also the name of a species of sea centipede. Undine is thus characterized in a way that is coherent both from Marvell's angle of vision and the novel's scientific perspective.

NOTES TO CHAPTER FOUR

1. The passage from Preston refers in a note to the philosopher of science Rom Harré's discussion of one lesson offered by Darwin. This lesson can be seen to underwrite the novel's method in portraying Archer's display of socially mediated instinct. Harré describes how

   > [t]he sciences have been at their most fruitful when they have exploited analogies and borrowed conceptual systems, modifying them in the process. [. . .] the social order is no exception. But if I borrow from organic evolutionary theory there must be some preliminary adjustments of that theory [. . .]. The lesson biology learned from Darwin, that adaptation need not require some form of teleological explanation, can also be taken to heart by social theorists. Part of the charm of mutation/selection systems is that they offer us the possibility of the explanation of adaptive change without positive causality for that change, and in particular they allow us to separate the processes by which mutant forms are created from those by which they are selected. (164)

   This statement describes a primary difference between the perspectives offered by the overarching narrative's application to social evolution of the Darwinian "explanation of adaptive change," and Archer's own point-of-view. Wharton implies a truth-value for change without "positive causality" in depicting the efforts of Archer's class to subdue "adaptive change" through the teleology of human perfectibility. The mutation of values, the reader finds, is a naturally occurring process not containable by manners.

2. The biological facts of the sexual act are transposed into an architectural register in an allusion to the lowering of barriers to entering the leisure class. Beaufort's house "had been boldly planned with a ball-room, so that, instead of squeezing through a narrow passage to get to it (as at the Chiverses') one marched solemnly down a vista of enfiladed drawing rooms" (21). Beaufort's type is thus made to seem promiscuous, and his house—a place that anyone can enter—a reflection of this fact.

3. Raymond Williams relates "the distinction suggested by Engels, in which ideology would end when men realized their real life-conditions and therefore their real motives, after which their consciousness would become genuinely *scientific*

because they would then be in contact with reality" (157). Demonstrating the difficulty of achieving "scientific consciousness" seems to be one goal of Wharton's characterization of Archer. He sees, in his amateurish scientific manner, partway into his "life conditions," but cannot achieve sustained contact with the reality Ellen represents.

4. Further work should be done on the fact that while these analogies are aspects of Wharton's literary texts, they exist also in the society the novel represents, where they do the cultural work of containing base energies and directing them toward social cohesion. Wharton's realism thus parallels a cultural practice wherein manners analogize and convert biological impulses.

5. Pamela Knights uses this passage to make the point that Ellen presents "herself as the image of sexuality" (33). Her insight facilitated my discernment of other instances in which Ellen's attire encodes her sexuality.

6. In this, Wharton's narrative may owe a debt to the methods of European social science, which were filtering into American universities during the period prior to the novel's composition. Ross relates how

> [t]he historic-political scientists set out to strengthen their science by using the critical historical method developed most fully in Germany. Grounded in philology and the historiographical program of Ranke, this conception of historical method as a science providing real access to the past had made its way to America through the influence of study abroad and American adaptations. [. . .] The gentry political scientists were not, as has long been thought, nominalistic historical positivists, believers that historians could discover 'facts alone, with no generalizations and with a renunciation of all philosophy.' Rather they believed that the facts, when contemplated, would yield those underlying principles that guided political progress. (71)

In its focus on underlying ideological principles that give rise to the view that taste and form represent all of reality one needs to know, Wharton's narrative method in excavating Archer's world pursues a historical account of the evolution of social forms.

7. One need only look to the way Charles Scribner's Sons advertised *The House of Mirth* to find that Wharton's class membership was seen to affect the reading public's perception of her authority to write about the rich. Her reaction to the efforts of her publisher illustrates that she wanted to downplay this perception, which might be seen to color her own objectivity. The novel was initially marketed as a realistic inside narrative of elite New York. Wharton duly complained about this, writing to her editor William Brownell to demand that he remove "that dreadful ad on the paper cover of

the H. of M.: 'for the first time the veil has been lifted from N. Y. society by one who etc. etc." (Aaronson 8).

8. Of this group, Renaissance scholars all, the least known today is likely Vernon Lee, the pseudonym of Violet Paget (1856–1935). R. W. B. Lewis describes her as "the author of many brilliant and scholarly studies of Italian history and art" (*Letters* 35n). Wharton states that her books *"Euphorion, Belcaro* etc.— were the delight of a generation initiated by Ruskin and Wallace into the beauties of the great Italian primitives [. . .] she was one of the last representatives of that world before the war, where one gathered with friends to talk about beautiful paintings and beautiful music, without suspecting under what mortal blows this peaceful society was soon to crumble" ("Memories of Bourget Overseas" 221).

9. Further research may make it possible to identify the Titian to which Archer refers on his visit to the Louvre. Doing so will no doubt result in a fuller understanding of what he feels he has missed in giving up Ellen, refining the existing sense that he sacrifices an opportunity for a passionate and emotionally fulfilling marriage. Two candidates are "Woman with a Mirror" (1512–1515) and "An Allegory, Perhaps of Marriage, with Vesta and Hymen as Protectors and Advisers of the Union of Venus and Mars" (1488–1490).

10. Preston discusses the role of libraries, and the reading habits of Selden and *The Custom of the Country*'s Ralph Marvell (40–48).

11. Lewis writes that *French Ways* is "a hurried, rambling book, though not lacking in the usual perceptive and delicate observations of the French reverence for life" (422). Wolff pronounces the work "a superficial study of French society" (*A Feast of Words* 296), while Benstock writes that it "revealed her commitment to its [France's] cultural and political values" (348). The book's importance to this study is, first, its method, which is implicit in its statement that "intellectual honesty" is comprised of "the courage to look at things as they are" (58), and second, its revelations about Wharton's own aesthetic values: "That a thing should be in scale—should be proportioned to its purpose—is one of the first requirements of beauty, in whatever order. No shouting where an undertone will do; and no gigantic statue of liberty in butter for a world's fair, when the little Wingless Victory, tying on her sandal on the Acropolis, holds the whole horizon in the curve of her slim arm" (41). This valuation of subtlety is illustrated in the deft portrait of the way class ideology in *The Age of Innocence* operates, through the relay of language, on the psychology of individual characters.

12. Luther Burbank was famous in Wharton's day for his experiments in hybridization.

13. Wharton seems to have thought that the exclusion of an omniscient perspective created difficulties in limiting the selectivity of a represented consciousness. The potential result of doing so, one surmises from her few statements on the

matter, would be the elimination of a lens to focus the welter of sense perception bearing in on the fictional subject, and in the case of her own work, the elimination of a textual space from which to contrast omniscient and character-centered perspectives on manners. Wharton's statement in her essay "The Criticism of Fiction" (1914) supports this claim:

> two principal perils seem, in fact, to lurk for the new novelist. One is consequent on the shock of his sudden release from the white-washed cell of conventions into the daylight and the outer air. To the poor Caspar Hauser of the pen everything in this grimy noisy rough-and-tumble outer world is so new and of such amazing interest that he is solicited with equal urgency by facts and instances that are not always of equal value. (127)

Her lack of enthusiasm for the work of Woolf and Joyce turned on her perception that, particularly in Joyce's case, "the raw material of sensation & thought can't make a work of art without the cook's intervention" (*Letters* 461).

NOTES TO THE CONCLUSION

1. See Bender (314–26) for a discussion of the difficulties Wharton must have encountered in creating correspondences between different aspects of evolutionary theory and their representation as themes in the novels.
2. As I reported in Chapter Three, memes are "units of cultural transmission analogous to the genes of biological evolution. [. . .] Like genes, memes are supposed to be replicators, in a different medium, but subject to much the same principles of evolution as genes" (Dennett 143).

Works Cited

Aaronson, Marc. "Wharton and the House of Scribner: The Novelist as Pain in the Neck." *New York Times* 2 Jan. 1994, sec. 7: 7–8.

Adorno, Theodor. *Minima Moralia*. Trans. E. F. N. Jephcott. 1951. London: Verso, 1996.

Ammons, Elizabeth. *Edith Wharton's Argument with America*. Athens: U of Georgia P, 1980.

Anesko, Michael. "Recent Critical Approaches." *The Cambridge Guide to Realism and Naturalism*. Ed. Donald Pizer. Cambridge: Cambridge UP, 1995. 77–94.

"Atavism." *Oxford English Dictionary*. 2nd ed. 1989.

Bannister, Robert. *Sociology and Scientism: The American Quest for Objectivity: 1880–1940*. Chapel Hill: U of North Carolina P, 1987.

Bauer, Dale. *Edith Wharton's Brave New Politics*. Madison: U of Wisconsin P, 1994.

———. "Wharton's 'Others': Addiction and Intimacy." *A Historical Guide to Edith Wharton*. Ed. Carol Singley. New York: Oxford UP, 2003. 115–45.

Beer, Gillian. *Darwin's Plots: Evolutionary Narrative in Darwin, George Eliot and Nineteenth Century Fiction*. 2nd ed. Cambridge: Cambridge UP, 2000.

———. *Open Fields: Science in Cultural Encounter*. Oxford: Clarendon, 1995.

Beer, Janet. *Kate Chopin, Edith Wharton, and Charlotte Perkins Gilman: Studies in Short Fiction*. London: MacMillan, 1997.

———. *Edith Wharton*. Hornden: Northcote, 2002.

Bender, Bert. *The Descent of Love: Darwin and the Theory of Sexual Selection in American Fiction, 1871–1926*. Philadelphia: U of Pennsylvania P, 1996.

Benstock, Shari. *No Gifts From Chance: A Biography of Edith Wharton*. New York: Scribner's, 1994.

Bentley, Nancy. "'Hunting for the Real': Wharton and the Science of Manners." *The Cambridge Companion to Edith Wharton*. Ed. Millicent Bell. Cambridge: Cambridge UP, 1995. 47–67.

———. *The Ethnography of Manners: Hawthorne, James, Wharton*. New York: Cambridge UP, 1995.

Borus, Daniel. *Writing Realism*. Chapel Hill: U of North Carolina P, 1989.

Bowlby, Rachel. *Just Looking: Consumer Culture in Dreiser, Gissing, and Zola.* New York: Methuen, 1985.

Bratton, Daniel. "Conspicuous Consumption and Conspicuous Leisure in the Novels of Edith Wharton." Diss. U of Toronto, 1983.

Carroll, Joseph. *Literary Darwinism: Evolution, Human Nature, and Literature.* New York: Routledge, 2004.

Chapman, Mary. "'Living Pictures': Women and Tableaux Vivants in Nineteenth-Century American Fiction and Culture." *Wide Angle* 18.3 (1996): 22–52.

"Contingency." *Oxford English Dictionary.* 2nd ed. 1989.

Cosmides, Leda, and John Tooby. "Evolutionary Psychology: A Primer." 13 Jan. 1997. Center for Evolutionary Psychology, U of California, Santa Barbara. 12 July 2005. <http://www.psych.ucsb.edu/research/cep/primer.html>.

Cowley, Malcolm. "'Not Men': A Natural History of American Naturalism." *Documents of American Realism and Naturalism.* Ed. Donald Pizer. Carbondale: Southern Illinois UP, 1998.

Crane, Stephen. "The Open Boat." 1897. *Norton Anthology of American Literature.* Shorter 6th ed. New York: Norton, 2003. 1721–38.

Darwin, Charles. *On The Origin of Species by Means of Natural Selection or the Preservation of Favoured Races in the Struggle for Life.* 1859. Ed. John Burrow. New York: Penguin, 1968.

———. *The Descent of Man, and Selection in Relation to Sex.* 1871. Princeton: Princeton UP, 1981.

Dennett, Daniel. *Darwin's Dangerous Idea.* New York: Touchstone, 1995.

Desmond, Adrian. *Huxley.* New York: Penguin, 1998.

Dimock, Wai-Chee. "Debasing Exchange: Edith Wharton's *The House of Mirth.*" *PMLA* 100 (Oct. 1985): 783–92.

Eagleton, Terry. *Ideology: An Introduction.* London: Verso, 1991.

Freud, Sigmund. *Civilization and its Discontents.* 1930. Trans. and ed. James Strachey. New York: Norton, 1961.

———. *Three Essays On The Theory of Sexuality.* 1905. Trans. and ed. James Strachey. New York: Norton, 1953.

Gagnier, Regenia. "A Critique of Practical Aesthetics." *Aesthetics and Ideology.* Ed. James Levine. New Brunswick, N.J.: Rutgers UP, 1994. 264–82.

Garlepp-Burns, Karin. "The Paradox of Objectivity in the Realist Fiction of Edith Wharton and Kate Chopin." *Journal of Narrative Theory* 29.1 (1999): 27–61.

Goethe, Johann Wolfgang. *Faust.* Trans. Martin Greenberg. New Haven: Yale UP, 1998.

Habermas, Jürgen. *The Structural Transformation of the Public Sphere.* Trans. Thomas Burger. Cambridge: MIT P, 1989.

Haeckel, Ernst. "The Fundamental Law of Organic Evolution." 1906. *Evolution.* Ed. Mark Ridley. Oxford: Oxford UP, 1997.

Harré, R. "The Evolutionary Analogy in Social Explanation." *The Philosophy of Evolution.* Ed. U. J. Jensen and R. Harré. Sussex: Harvester, 1981. 161–75.

Hartt, Frederick. *Art: A History of Painting, Sculpture, Architecture.* 4th ed. New York: Abrams, 1993.

Hoeller, Hildegard. *Edith Wharton's Dialogue with Realism and Sentimental Fiction.* Gainesville: UP of Florida, 2000.

Hofstadter, Richard. *Social Darwinism in American Thought.* 1944. Boston: Beacon, 1955.

Howard, Maureen. "The Bachelor and the Baby." *The Cambridge Companion to Edith Wharton.* Ed. Millicent Bell. Cambridge: Cambridge UP, 1995. 137–56.

Howells, W. D. *The Rise of Silas Lapham.* 1885. Boston: Houghton Mifflin, 1957.

Huxley, T. H. "Prolegomena" and "Evolution and Ethics." *The Major Prose of Thomas Henry Huxley.* Ed. Alan P. Barr. Athens: U of Georgia P, 1997. 283–308.

———. *Darwiniana.* New York: Appleton, 1897.

James, William. *The Principles of Psychology.* 1890. Cambridge: Harvard UP, 1981.

Kaplan, Amy. *The Social Construction of American Realism.* Chicago: U of Chicago P, 1988.

———. "Edith Wharton's Profession of Authorship." *ELH* 53:2 (1986): 433–57.

Kassanoff, Jennie A. "Extinction, Taxidermy, Tableaux Vivants: Staging Race and Class in *The House of Mirth.*" *PMLA* 115.1: 60–74.

Kellog, Vernon. *Darwinism Today.* New York: Holt, 1907.

Killoran, Helen. *The Critical Reception of Edith Wharton.* Rochester: Camden, 2001.

Knights, Pamela. "Forms of Disembodiment: The Social Subject in *The Age of Innocence.*" *The Cambridge Companion to Edith Wharton.* Ed. Millicent Bell. Cambridge: Cambridge UP, 1995. 20–46.

Kress, Jill M. *The Figures of Consciousness: William James, Henry James, and Edith Wharton.* New York: Routledge, 2002.

Kuhn, Thomas S. *The Structure of Scientific Revolutions.* 1962. 3rd ed. Chicago: U of Chicago P, 1996.

Lears, T. J. Jackson. *No Place of Grace: Antimodernism and the Transformation of American Culture, 1880–1920.* New York: Pantheon, 1981.

Lewis, R. W. B. *Edith Wharton: A Biography.* 1975. New York: Fromm, 1985.

Lock, R. H. *Variation, Heredity and Evolution.* 1906. London: John Murray, 1916.

Lukács, Georg. *History and Class Consciousness: Studies in Marxist Dialectics.* 1968. Trans. Rodney Livingstone. Cambridge: MIT P, 1999.

Macnaughton, William. "Edith Wharton's 'The Blond Beast' and Friedrich Nietzsche." *Edith Wharton Review* 15.2 (1999): 13–19.

Makaryk, Irena R., ed. and comp. *Encyclopedia of Literary Theory.* Toronto: U of Toronto P, 1993.

McCosh, D. D. "Herbert Spencer's 'Data of Ethics.'" *The Princeton Review* 2, 1879 (July-Dec. 1879), 607–36.

Menand, Louis. *The Metaphysical Club.* New York: Farrar, 2001.

"Mendelism." *Oxford English Dictionary.* 2nd ed. 1989.

Moddellmog, William E. "Disowning 'Personality': Privacy and Subjectivity in *The House of Mirth.*" *American Literature* 70.2 (June 1998): 337–64.

Montgomery, Maureen E. *Displaying Women: Spectacles of Leisure in Edith Wharton's New York*. New York: Routledge, 1998.

Morris, Edmund. *Theodore Rex*. New York: Random, 2001.

Mott, Frank Luther. *American Journalism: A History, 1690–1960*. New York: Macmillan, 1962.

Nevius, Blake. *Edith Wharton: A Study of Her Fiction*. Berkeley: U of California P, 1953.

Nowlin, Michael. "Edith Wharton and the Matter of Contexts." *Studies in the Novel* 33.2 (2001): 224–29

Orgel, Stephen. "Introduction." *The Tempest*. By William Shakespeare. Oxford: Oxford UP, 1987. 1–87.

Papke, Mary E. *Verging on the Abyss: The Social Fiction of Kate Chopin and Edith Wharton*. New York: Greenwood, 1990.

Pizer, Donald. "The Naturalism of Edith Wharton's *The House of Mirth*." *Twentieth Century Literature* 31 (1995): 241–48.

———. *Realism and Naturalism in Nineteenth-Century American Literature*. Carbondale: Southern Illinois UP, 1984.

———. *The Theory and Practice of American Literary Naturalism*. Carbondale: Southern Illinois UP, 1992.

Porter, Noah. *The Sciences of Nature Versus the Science of Man. A Plea for the Science of Man*. New York: Dodd, 1871.

Preston, Claire. *Edith Wharton's Social Register*. New York: St. Martin's, 2000.

Rakoff, David. "Questions for Steven Pinker." *New York Times Magazine* 22 Sept. 2002, national ed.: 27.

Ramsden, George. *Edith Wharton's Library*. Settrington: Stone Trough, 1999.

Ridley, Mark. "Introduction." *Evolution*. Ed. Mark Ridley. Oxford: Oxford UP, 1997. 3–8.

Ross, Dorothy. *The Origins of American Social Science*. Cambridge: Cambridge UP, 1991.

Saunders, Judith P. "Evolutionary Biological Issues in Edith Wharton's The Children." *College Literature* 32.2 (Spring 2005): 83–102.

Showalter, Elaine. "The Death of the Lady Novelist." *Edith Wharton: New Critical Essays*. Eds. Alfred Bendixon and Annette Zilversmit. New York: Garland, 1992. 3–26.

———. "Spragg: The Art of the Deal." *The Cambridge Companion to Edith Wharton*. Ed. Millicent Bell. Cambridge: Cambridge UP, 1995. 87–97.

Singley, Carol J., ed and introd. *A Historical Guide to Edith Wharton*. New York: Oxford UP, 2003.

———. *Matters of Mind and Spirit*. New York: Cambridge UP, 1995.

Spencer, Herbert. *First Principles*. 3rd ed. London: Williams & Norgate, 1875.

———. *Principles of Sociology*. 1876–1896. Hamden: Archon, 1969.

———. *Social Statics, or The Conditions essential to Happiness specified, and the First of them Developed*. 1851. New York: Appleton, 1872.

Strong, George Templeton. *The Diary of George Templeton Strong: Post War Years: 1865–1875*. New York: MacMillan, 1952.

Sumner, William Graham. "Sociological Fallacies." *North America Review* 138.331 (June 1884): 574–80.

Terukazu, Akiyama, et al. *The Dictionary of Art*. New York: Grove, 1996.

Tichi, Cecilia. "Emerson, Darwin, and *The Custom of the Country*." *A Historical Guide to Edith Wharton*. Ed. Carol Singley. New York: Oxford UP, 2003. 89–114.

Thomas, Brook. *American Literary Realism and the Failed Promise of Contract*. Berkeley: U of California P, 1997.

Tudge, Colin. "Monkey Business." *Times Literary Supplement* 23 Sept. 2005: 29.

Tuttleton, James, Kristin O. Lauer, and Margaret P. Murray, eds. *Edith Wharton: The Contemporary Reviews*. New York: Cambridge UP, 1992.

Tuttleton, James W. "*The Fruit of the Tree*: Justine and the Perils of Abstract Idealism." *The Cambridge Companion to Edith Wharton*. Ed. Millicent Bell. Cambridge: Cambridge UP, 1995. 157–68.

Veblen, Thorstein. *The Theory of the Leisure Class: An Economic Study of Institutions*. 1899. New York: Funk, 1967.

Virilio, Paul. *The Art of the Motor*. Trans. Julie Rose. Minneapolis: U of Minnesota P, 1995.

Waid, Candace. *Edith Wharton's Letters from the Underworld: Fictions of Women and Writing*. Chapel Hill: U of North Carolina P, 1991.

Wegener, Frederick. "'Enthusiasm Guided by Acumen': Edith Wharton as a Critical Writer." *Edith Wharton: The Uncollected Critical Writings*. Princeton: Princeton UP, 1996. 3–52.

———. "Form, 'Selection,' and Ideology in Edith Wharton's Anti-Modernist Aesthetic." *A Forward Glance: New Essays on Edith Wharton*. Ed. Clare Colquitt, Susan Goodman, and Candace Waid. Newark: U of Delaware P, 1999. 116–38.

———. "'Rabid Imperialist': Edith Wharton and the Obligations of Empire in Modern American Fiction." *American Literature* 72.4 (2000): 783–812.

Wharton, Edith. *The Age of Innocence*. 1920. New York: Collier, 1993.

———. "The Architecture of Humanism." *The Uncollected Critical Writings of Edith Wharton*. Princeton: Princeton UP, 1996. 130–34.

———. *Artemis and Acteon*. London: MacMillan, 1909.

———. *A Backward Glance*. New York: Appleton-Century, 1934.

———. "The Criticism of Fiction." *The Uncollected Critical Writings of Edith Wharton*. Princeton: Princeton UP, 1996. 120–33.

———. *The Custom of the Country*. 1913. New York: Simon, 1997.

———. "A Cycle of Reviewing." *The Uncollected Critical Writings of Edith Wharton*. Princeton: Princeton UP, 1996. 159–63.

———. *The Decoration of Houses*. With Ogden Codman, Jr. 1897. New York: Norton, 1997.

———. "The Descent of Man." 1904. *The Collected Short Stories of Edith Wharton, Vol. 1*. Ed. R. W. B. Lewis. New York: Scribner's, 1968. 347–63.

———. "Donnée Book 1902." YCAL ms. 42. Yale Collection of American Literature, Beinecke Rare Book and Manuscript Lib. Yale U, New Haven.

———. *French Ways and Their Meaning.* New York: Appleton, 1919.

———. *The Fruit of the Tree.* New York: Scribner's, 1907.

———. "George Eliot." *The Uncollected Critical Writings of Edith Wharton.* Princeton: Princeton UP, 1996. 71–78.

———. "The Great American Novel." *The Uncollected Critical Writings of Edith Wharton.* Princeton: Princeton UP, 1996. 151–59.

———. *The House of Mirth.* 1905. New York: Penguin, 1985.

———. *In Morocco.* New York: Scribner's, 1920.

———. "Introduction to *The House of Mirth.*" *The Uncollected Critical Writings of Edith Wharton.* Princeton: Princeton UP, 1996. 264–70.

———. *Italian Backgrounds.* London: Cape, 1928.

———. *The Letters of Edith Wharton.* Ed. R. W. B. Lewis and Nancy Lewis. New York: Collier, 1988.

———. "Life and I." YCAL ms. 42. Yale Collection of American Literature, Beinecke Rare Book and Manuscript Lib. Yale U, New Haven.

———. "Memories of Bourget Overseas." *The Uncollected Critical Writings of Edith Wharton.* Princeton: Princeton UP, 1996. 221–26.

———. "Mr. Sturgis's Belchamber." *The Uncollected Critical Writings of Edith Wharton.* Princeton: Princeton UP, 1996. 106–110.

———. "Permanent Values in Fiction." *The Uncollected Critical Writings of Edith Wharton.* Princeton: Princeton UP, 1996. 175–179.

———. *Summer.* 1917. New York: Simon, 1998.

———. "Tendencies in Modern Fiction." *The Uncollected Critical Writings of Edith Wharton.* Princeton: Princeton UP, 1996. 170–74.

———. "The Vice of Reading." *The Uncollected Critical Writings of Edith Wharton.* Princeton: Princeton UP, 1996. 99–106.

———. "William C. Brownell." *The Uncollected Critical Writings of Edith Wharton.* Princeton: Princeton UP, 1996. 205–11.

———. *The Writing of Fiction.* London: Scribner's, 1925.

White, Michael, and John Gribbin. *Darwin: A Life in Science.* New York: Simon, 1995.

Williams, Raymond. *Keywords.* Oxford: Oxford UP, 1976.

Wilson, Edward O. *Consilience: The Unity of Knowledge.* New York: Knopf, 1998.

Wolff, Cynthia Griffin. *A Feast of Words: The Triumph of Edith Wharton.* New York: Oxford UP, 1977.

Wordsworth, William. "Preface to Lyrical Ballads." Rpt. in *The Norton Anthology of English Literature.* 5th ed. Ed. M. H. Abrams. New York: Norton, 1986.

Young, Robert M. "Darwin and the Genre of Biography." *One Culture.* Ed. George Levine. Madison: U of Wisconsin P, 1987. 203–24.

———. "The Development of Herbert Spencer's Concept of Evolution." *Actes du XIe Congrès International d'Histoire des Sciences.* Warsaw: Ossolineum, 1967. 273–78.

Index